Best of General Science
from
Science Teacher's Workshop

Best of

General Science

from

Compiled and Edited by
The Board of Editors of the

Parker Publishing Company

SCIENCE TEACHER'S WORKSHOP

Science Teacher's Workshop

West Nyack, New York

BEST OF GENERAL SCIENCE
FROM SCIENCE TEACHER'S WORKSHOP

COMPILED AND EDITED BY

THE BOARD OF EDITORS OF THE
SCIENCE TEACHER'S WORKSHOP

© 1972 BY

PARKER PUBLISHING COMPANY, INC.
WEST NYACK, NEW YORK

LIBRARY OF CONGRESS
CATALOG CARD NUMBER: 79–181390

PRINTED IN THE UNITED STATES OF AMERICA
ISBN–0–13–794479–9
B & P

About This Book

This book presents a broad selection of innovative yet highly practical activities and demonstrations for teaching general science. It includes materials for teaching all areas of the diverse general science curriculum—basic chemistry, life science, introductory physics, and earth and space science. In addition, it offers a variety of special exercises for introducing basic techniques, mathematics and measurement, electricity, and meteorology.

Each selection has been carefully chosen from articles submitted by outstanding science teachers to *Science Teacher's Workshop,* a monthly teaching service for secondary school science teachers across the country. It represents a successful and workable technique for involving students more meaningfully in the basic concepts and processes of science.

Practicability as well as effectiveness has been an important criterion in the selection of activities. Few of them require expensive or elaborate apparatus. Most are the product of the science teacher's efforts to make the best use possible of the resources at hand in devising new and better ways of teaching and learning science.

As an aid in using activities, each includes all of the details and directions you will need for its immediate use or adaption in your own classroom or laboratory.

- Objectives are clearly stated to pinpoint the specific purposes of the activity.
- Materials for carrying out procedures and constructing any needed apparatus are presented in convenient checklist fashion.
- Source notes are provided for obtaining items not normally found in the general science classroom or laboratory.
- Procedures are complete and organized in a clear, step-by-step manner.
- Caution notes are included where appropriate to protect the teacher and his students in working with materials requiring special handling.

5

- Analyses of results are provided in many cases to serve as guidelines to working out exercises.
- Examples of student work are included where useful to furnish a concrete idea of what to expect.
- Illustrations of apparatus and procedures are abundant and functional.
- Follow-up ideas are presented to help the teacher stimulate and guide students to further investigation.

This book offers you dozens of practical and tested ways to enrich, reinforce, or replace different parts of your regular teaching program. Each one represents a further opportunity to give students a richer, more rewarding science experience and, at the same time, a means to save valuable preparation and teaching time.

We hope it will help to make general science a more challenging and enjoyable experience for both you and your students.

The Board of Editors
Science Teacher's Workshop

Contents

About This Book 5

1   Basic Techniques for General Science 11

"Discovering" the Laws of Science
    by Charles L. Roberts 12
Provocations to Thought: Open-Ended Experiments
    by George E. Pitluga 14
Demonstrations for General Science
    by Irene Bireline 17
Models and Motivation
    by John R. Altizer 19
A Laboratory Exercise in Description
    by Vernon DeWitt 22
Simplicity in Lab Procedures—Investigating Evaporation
    by David D. Porter and Robert F. Dixon 24
Activities for Slow Learners in Junior High Science
    by Richard L. Upchurch 30
Visual-Auditory Testing for Science Teachers
    by Laurence W. Aronstein 33

2   Mathematics and Measurement 39

Demonstrating the Role of Mathematics in Science
    by D. W. Tomer 40
Number Pairing to Teach Relations and Functions
    by Merrill Sanders 43
A Laboratory Approach to the Metric System
    by Mary-China Corrie 47
A Unit on Measurement
    by Alan Mandell 50
Measurements in the Physics Laboratory
    by David Kutliroff 58

3   Chemistry Investigations 63

Some Techniques of Investigating Matter
    by Julian C. Clark 64

Junior High School Chemistry Experiments
    by Ernest A. Dunning 69
Chemistry Experiments That Interest the Student
    by Ernest A. Dunning. 71
Chemical Changes by Heating
    by Ralph S. Vrana 75
"Micro" Chemistry Experiments on a Limited Budget
    by Betty Jo Montag 78
Quantitative Isolation of Calcium
    by Nelle B. Norman 80
E.S.T.P.—Structured Unstructured
    by Francis E. Cote and Charles E. Horner 84
Oxidation-Reduction Made Interesting
    by Robert Pearce 91
Demonstrating Air Pollution from Automobiles
    by Ernest Starkman 94

4 **Life Science Activities** **101**
An Approach to Seventh Grade Life Science Units
    by Ronald F. Romig 102
Free Aquaria
    by Ralph S. Vrana 104
Teaching the Sense of Sight
    by Bernadette Beres Stundick 107
Demonstrations in Respiration
    by George C. Clark 112
A Frog on the Moon
    by George H. Ratzlaff 117
Life Science for the Underachiever
    by C. R. Cronin and L. J. Paulk 120
Bottle Caps, Pop Beads, and Genetics
    by Mary Jane Myers 124
High School Study of Air Pollution
    by William E. Porter 127
An Inductive Approach to the Compound Light Microscope
    by Donald C. Orlich 132
Plant Activities with Lemnaceae, or Duckweed
    by Richard Allan Digon 134
Observation: A Key to Outdoor Science
    by Ray Deur 139
The Dandelion—A Gold Mine for Outdoor Science
    by Ray Deur 142
Testing for Water Pollution
    by Richard Carnes 145

5 Physics Activities for General Science **151**

Basic Physics Activities for General Science Teaching
  by Betty Jo Montag 152
Ripple Tanks for Classroom Demonstrations
  by C. Howard Johnson 154
Photographing the Pendulum
  by Peter F. Steele 158
Student-Constructed Demonstration of Newton's Third Law
  by Paul A. Wilkinson 162
The Considerate Coke Bottle
  by Michael A. Iarrapino 163
Making a Hydrometer
  by Edward A. Terry 164
Attention, Archimedes!
  by Terrence P. Toepker 166
A Student Exercise in Molecular Movement and Energy
  by Leslie Howell 167
The Problem of the Backward Rotating Radiometer
  by James E. Creighton 170
A Parabolic Mirror – Real Image Demonstration
  by Donna Parsons 172

6 Demonstrations in Electricity **175**

Homemade Equipment for Static Electricity
  by J. R. Stevenson 176
Demonstrating Static Electricity
  by William J. Muha 179
Teacher Demonstrations in Electricity, Electrons,
  and Gaseous Ions
  by Dudley W. Davis 180
Production of Motion from Electricity
  by Ralph S. Vrana 186
Making an Electric Motor—A Class Exercise
  by C. Howard Johnson 190

7 Earth Science Activities **195**

Water Problems and Investigations
  by Marjorie Elliott 196
Demonstrating Sedimentation
  by George R. Wells 203
A Model for Studying Topographic Maps
  by William T. Jackson 205
"Gonna Build a Mountain"—An Earth Science Project
  by Ole C. Davis 206

Student-Centered Earth Science
  by Merrick A. Owen 209
A Useful Model to Illustrate Earth Phenomena
  by Donald F. Brandewie 211
Earthquakes: A Long-Term Lab Exercise
  by Nicholas K. Yost 214
The Use of Gravel Pits in Field Investigations
  by Jerry W. Vincent 217
A Field Trip for Earth Science
  by Harry F. Pomeroy, Jr. 221
Staking a Mining Claim
  by C. E. Riddell and W. G. Casper, Jr. 225
Creating an Economic Mineral Display
  by Harry F. Pomeroy, Jr. 228

8 Meteorology 233

Barometers for Determining Atmospheric
Highs and Lows
  by Raymond F. Gray 234
A Simple Weather Indicator
  by Edward A. Terry 237
Cloud Study and Weather Forecasting
  by Alice Weschgel 238

9 Astronomy and Space Science Exercises 243

The Coriolis Effect—An Inductive Approach
  by Harrie E. Caldwell 244
Build a "Stellorama"
  by Donald B. Peck 252
Some Astronomical Calculations Made Easy
  by William R. Minardi 259
Observations of the Moon
  by Verne A. Troxel 263
Lunar Mirrors—One Dollar Each
  by Robert E. Kyrlach 265
The Planetarium as a Laboratory
  by Merrick A. Owen 271
A Celestial Sphere for Teaching Astronomy Concepts
  by William R. Minardi 274

Index 279

1 Basic Techniques for General Science

"Discovering" the Laws of Science   12

Provocations to Thought: Open-Ended
    Experiments   14

Demonstrations for General Science   17

Models and Motivation   19

A Laboratory Exercise in Description   22

Simplicity in Lab Procedures—Investigating
    Evaporation   24

Activities for Slow Learners in Junior High
    Science   30

Visual-Auditory Testing for Science
    Teachers   33

"Discovering" the Laws of Science

by Charles L. Roberts

State University of New York at Morrisville

It is true that most basic laws of science can be "told" to the student, reinforced by some examples, and the task of "teaching" is done. The student will remember these laws—but! He experiences no practice in problem-solving, no opportunity to test conclusions, and no satisfaction of accomplishment or development of determination. In short, "telling" the student enables him to clear the first hurdle—learning the law—but fails to give him the skills needed to solve the more complex problems that may follow.

> Note: To acquire these skills and a working understanding of the basic laws of science, the student cannot simply be told. He must be given the opportunity to become more actively involved with what he is learning.

One method of accomplishing this involvement is to challenge students to "discover" these laws themselves. The "discovery method" of learning has been shown to be very effective in science teaching, and even in classes of 30 or more, using simple household items to overcome cost factors, it is possible to give each student the chance to "discover" many of the basic laws of science.

DISCOVERING A "LAW OF LEVERS"

In the following example of the discovery method, paper clips, common pins, and soda straws are used to allow each student to develop his own "law of levers." Throughout the whole experience, the student is *not told* what he should find. He is only encouraged to look for some relationship in his data.

Procedure

To begin, have students construct the simple apparatus shown in Fig. 1, as follows:

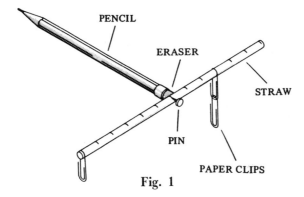

Fig. 1

1. Group students in pairs and provide each station with a straw, ruler, common pin, and a handful of paper clips. Instruct students to locate and mark the center of the straw, then mark even units in both directions from the center. Next, have them punch the pin through the straw's center and into an eraser on the end of a pencil. The straw should be turned on the pin several times so that it is loose.

2. When the straws have been fastened, have students make several balancings by placing paper clips in single chains on both sides until the straw stays horizontal. Each balancing should be a different combination of forces (F—paper clips) and distances from the center (L—length). Instruct students to keep a chart of their trials.

Some possibilities are shown in the accompanying sample charts (any choice of letters will do):

F_l (clips)	F_r (clips)	L_l (units)	L_r (units)
2	4	4	2
6	4	2	3
6	6	2	2
3	1	2	6
3	6	2	1

C_l (clips)	U_l (units)	C_r (clips)	U_r (units)
2	4	4	2
6	2	4	3
6	2	6	2
3	2	1	6
3	2	6	1

3. After students have made and recorded data for five or six trials, instruct them to find some "rule" to their data. Several examples of students' work are:

$$\frac{F_1}{F_r} = \frac{L_r}{L_1} \qquad \frac{C_1 U_1}{C_r U_r} = \text{one}$$

$$F_1 L_1 = F_r L_r \qquad \frac{F_1 L_1}{F_r} = L_r$$

Such a variety of insights clearly indicates that students are doing their own work.

The teacher then plays his role by showing that all versions are actually varieties of the same "rule." Then the importance of this law and its usual version may be explained.

Law of Levers: $F_1 L_1 = F_r L_r$

NOTE: Through experiences such as this, the student is given more than facts. He will also become more interested in his work and perhaps even have "fun" in science class.

Provocations to Thought: Open-Ended Experiments

by George E. Pitluga
State University College at Oswego, Oswego, New York

Today's science teacher is frequently torn between two philosophies of science education. The traditional philosophy suggests that science must be primarily concerned with giving students basic facts and concepts of the discipline under study. Until these facts are mastered, it maintains, the learner is not ready for investigations on his own. This approach tends to develop lab exercises—or "experiments"—which smack of mother's cookbook, except that "add the whites of two eggs" may read "add 10cc. HCl, and shake well."

The second approach, now on the uprise, suggests that science is a method of investigating the world. It sees the so-called facts of science—while useful and important—as merely the by-product of this method of investigation. In essence, it maintains, science education is concerned with guiding the learner in the *process of practicing science*. Supporters of this approach place much emphasis on the "open-ended" experiment. The learner is presented with a problem, assisted in proposing one or more hypotheses, and guided in designing strategies for testing his hypotheses and drawing conclusions.

> COMPROMISE: Fortunately, or unfortunately, many texts and laboratory manuals, local and state syllabi, and standardized examinations strongly encourage the first approach. However, among teachers forced into the traditional pattern by these factors, there are many who recognize the merit of the open-ended experiment. Here they will find suggestions for giving at least some students some of the time, experience in practicing the investigatory method of science.

Using Investigations

These suggestions for open-ended experiments may be used with individual students or small groups who have completed the assigned laboratory exercises, or possibly as a substitute for a not-too-critical assigned exercise. They might also be used for extra credit activities.

Two potential advantages from using these experiments seem evident:

- For a teacher who is unsure of "newer" methods, they represent a chance to try his hand without a radical departure from "tried and true" procedures.
- For the teacher who may be forced to continue using the traditional approach, they offer a means of stimulating and encouraging the many—not all—students who really do enjoy the challenge of the open-ended experiment and the satisfaction of its solution.

PROBLEMS FOR OPEN-ENDED INVESTIGATION

The accompanying list of problems for open-ended student investigation is of course only suggestive. To this list, each teacher might add literally dozens of investigation ideas probably more pertinent to his students and the content they are studying. However, these problems do serve as useful illustrations, bearing in mind that the facts their solutions produce are not nearly so important as the methodology they require.

Experiment 1: What determines how long it takes a candle to burn out? Is it the kind of wax? Is it the length of the candle? Is it the size of the wick? Can you make one or more hypotheses? Can you devise a strategy for testing each one? Should we deal with just one variable at a time?

> MATERIALS: Some string, waxes, cylinders, molds, and a time-keeper and beam balance may be all the equipment needed.

Experiment 2: What determines how long it takes a pendulum to swing through one complete arc? How far out you pull it? The length of the string? The weight of the bob? or....? (The essential equipment is simple.)

> **NOTE: Even beginners can design good strategy for investigating this problem, but they must be warned to watch for one variable at a time.**

Experiment 3: Which freezes quicker—hot or cold water? (Some people insist that hot water pipes always freeze more quickly than cold water pipes.)

Experiment 4: Present students with a glass brimful of water in which an ice cube is floating. What will happen when the ice melts? Will the water overflow? or....?

> **NOTE: This problem gives students excellent practice on a very elementary level in hypothesis making.**

Experiment 5: If you live along the sea coast and teach earth science, you, yourself, may get some surprises together with the students by posing this problem: Where is the moon in reference to our meridian when it is high tide here? (Several hypotheses suggest themselves. The strategy requires careful thought, and even after the answer has been found, you may discover that, like most true experiments, this one raises more questions than it answers.)

Experiment 6: Where does the sun rise and where does it set? (This is a particularly good investigation problem for it teaches students that nature rarely gives the answer quickly—not even in a 60-minute lab period. It will help students to understand why scientists often carry on the same experiment for months, or years.)

Experiment 7: What's in the box? To acquaint students with the dilemma often faced by the true scientist, use the black box problem. Present students with a series of sealed boxes, in turn. One box may contain a piece of chalk, another a glass marble, and a third a block of wood. Challenge them to propose what is within the boxes without opening the boxes and revealing the contents. Students may be allowed to manipulate the boxes in any way they wish; however, they may not open them.

> **NOTE: Students can gain valuable insights into the nature of science with these black boxes. The teacher can supply parallel problems from the history of science itself. (I regret to say that astronomy is essentially still in the "black box" stage.)**

Experiment 8: More carefully made black boxes, such as those shown in Fig. 1, will delight and exasperate physics students. Each is sealed and has only two external binding posts. Note that electrical symbols are shown. The teacher can determine values. Of course, A.C. and D.C. current sources are essential.

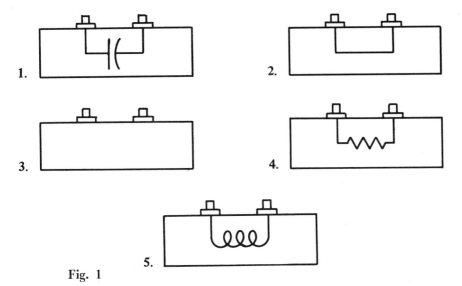

Fig. 1

CAUTION: Since meters are involved, the teacher must be certain to approve any strategies the student plans before he begins work.

Provocations to Thought

The preceding examples don't begin to scratch the surface of the simple yet effective open-ended investigations students can undertake. You can surely think of many more situations in which your students can practice science—situations simple enough so that the strategy need not be overwhelmingly complicated. Certainly no one investigation makes a full-fledged scientist out of the student. But it is interesting to speculate as to the understanding and attitude toward science a student might have who had enjoyed 50 or 100 such provocations to thought.

Demonstrations for General Science

by Irene Bireline
Edison School, St. Joseph, Missouri

Demonstrations are no substitute for laboratory exercises or for learning proper techniques of handling lab equipment, but they can be an effective means of supplementing and clarifying the material being taught. Some demonstrations may be best used by the teacher to illustrate a lecture point; others may meet a specific need which originates in a discussion. Many can be used to help students "discover" facts for themselves.

INVOLVEMENT: In all cases, the students should participate as much as possible through asking and answering questions, observing and recording results, and manipulating demonstration materials.

Experience shows that some concepts are difficult for students to understand because they tend to be abstract, or because students lack the necessary background. Following are several suggestions for overcoming such difficulties using demonstrations.

UNDERSTANDING DENSITY

Though many students can readily define density and buoyancy, when they perform standard buoyancy experiments they often have trouble drawing correct conclusions. This difficulty may be alleviated by giving students a better grasp of density through handling objects of the same shape and volume but of different weights.

- Use paper drinking cups with covers to provide identical volume and appearance. Fill the cups with various substances to give each cup of material a different density. (Sand, water, and bits of cork or foam rubber are only a few of the materials that will fill and take the shape of the container.)

  NOTE: By handling the various cupfuls of material, the students will observe that the weight per unit volume of each cupful is different. Once they understand density, the principle of buoyancy in water or air should become clearer to them.

BALANCING EQUATIONS

Balancing chemical equations often seems particularly difficult for general science students. To help them better understand this process, a visible representation using marbles and plastic bags can be effective. Following is an example, balancing $CO_2 + H_2O \rightarrow C_6H_{12}O_6 + O_2$.

- Place three different colored marbles representing the three elements involved in the right proportion in two plastic sandwich bags, each bag representing one molecule of the compounds.
- Have students observe that six molecules each of carbon dioxide and water must be used to obtain sufficient carbon and hydrogen for the glucose molecule.

- To finish balancing the equation, place the remaining marbles—representing the oxygen atoms—in the bags.

FINDING DEPTH AND TOPOGRAPHY

In the study of oceanography, the indirect methods used in determining depth and topography may be presented by having students do some indirect measuring of their own, as in the following procedure:

- Obtain a long, narrow rectangular box or tank about 15 to 20 inches long and 5 or 6 inches deep.
- Place a few fairly large rocks in a line on the bottom of the box along the front edge.
- Fill the box with fine dirt or sand until level with the top.
- Supply each student with a piece of graph paper.
- Thrust a stiff piece of wire into the sand or dirt until it strikes the rock below.
- Remove the wire and have students measure and record the distance the wire penetrated on their graph paper.
- Repeat the preceding two steps at regular intervals across the surface of the sand or dirt.

If care is taken in making graphs, the students will soon observe the forms of the invisible rocks, and a few simple questions about the size and number of rocks will help them interpret their graphs. When the graphs are completed, the rocks should be removed from the box to give students the opportunity to compare their results with the actual rocks.

Models and Motivation

by John R. Altizer
Turkey Creek Junior Senior High School, Plant City, Florida

Following is a technique that I have found to be very successful in helping the student become motivated. Many teachers have used it, but if you have not, try making models.

NOTE: Do not force the idea on the students. Let the actual plan for making models come from them.

ROUSING CURIOSITY

Here is an experience that I had last year. I was teaching photosynthesis and needed a model of the leaf in cross-section to explain leaf structure. I took the lid of a styrofoam ice chest and began to cut out the various cells: epidermal cells, guard cells, etc.

During the day, I planned the lessons so that they were finished about five minutes before the bell each period, and used this five minutes to work on the leaf model. No explanation of my activity was given to the students.

After a day or so, students began to ask me what I was doing. Some who had not asked me a question all year stopped by my desk on their way out of the room and asked what I was making. I finally told them that I was making a model of the leaf showing the different layers of cells. They were not very impressed.

At the end of about a week, I took the parts home, painted them, and assembled the model. I brought the finished product back to the classroom and set it on my desk. The students now asked if this is what I had been making, and I told them again that it represented the structure of a leaf. They began to ask about the different colors and shapes of the cells, and I started to explain the structure to them.

> NOTE: Finally, many students were asking if they could make something. This is what I had been waiting for, and we began to make our plans. We made several models from the lids of styrofoam ice chests.

MODEL-MAKING

This year I used the same approach—guiding students until they *want* to make something—and we again made several models. In this model-making activity, students are allowed to work in pairs and to make anything they desire as long as it is related to biology. The are given freedom of movement and permitted to talk in the classroom. Naturally they want to see each other's models and discuss their own.

Of course, they do a great deal of general talking also; but sooner or later they talk about their model. They begin to use such terms as "sporozoite," "merezoite," etc., without memorization, and they not only learn the parts of their model but also learn those of other models.

> NOTE: Some students did not want to make models and I did not require them to do so. I observed these students with interest. They cut out parts, sanded wood, and painted for other students. Eventually they became so involved that all but one turned in a model of his own.

Frequently, students came in during the lunch period to work on their models. They would bring their friends to see their work. I noted that these friends would ask them questions about their model just as students had asked me questions about the leaf model.

Building a Styrofoam Cutter

This year the school provides styrofoam, and I built a cutter (Fig. 1). The cutter is easily made and requires only a few materials: an electric train transformer, a piece of galvanized pipe bent at a right angle, insulated wire, and a nichrome wire. Some of the students were so impressed with the cutter that they built their own at home.

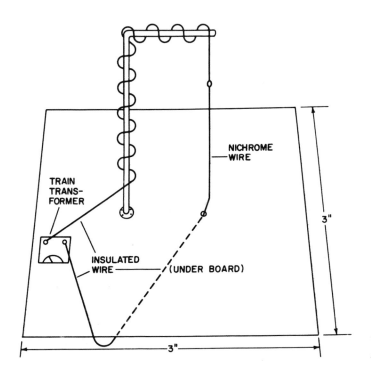

Fig. 1: Styrofoam Cutter

Organizing Aids

One problem we had was with materials. Since some of the students could not find the particular parts they needed, we set up a *share box.* Any surplus material (old jewelry, pipe cleaners, toothpicks, bb's, marbles, paint, fine wire, beads, hair netting, etc.) that a student did not need for his particular model, was placed in the share box for any student's use. The students cooperated so well that we had an excess of materials.

PAINTING STATIONS: To handle the process of painting the models, we set up four painting stations, each consisting of a cardboard box, newspaper, brushes, and paint.

Another problem was finding storage space for about 70 models. This was solved by having each pair of students bring in a small cardboard box with their names and period labeled on it. Each class stacked their boxes containing materials in a certain area.

Results

I find that any problems which arise on our model-making activity are minor compared to the end results. Students gain confidence in themselves and become active. Their terminology and spelling improve. They conduct research without being asked. Most important, they admire each other's work and help each other.

A Laboratory Exercise in Description

by Vernon DeWitt

McCluer High School, Florissant, Missouri

Most of us would rather tell what an object is—name it—than describe it. In biology and other sciences, we seem to rely too heavily on the naming of objects; often the best grades are given to the students who name the most objects. Usually students receive little experience in observing objects and making accurate and useful descriptions of their various properties.

> **OBJECTIVE:** This student exercise involves the description of the taste, sound, feel, texture, and odor of six white powders, and is designed to help both the teacher and students become more proficient in describing objects.

MATERIALS AND PREPARATION

To perform the exercise, it is recommended that students work in groups of four. Each group will require these materials:

6 Petri dishes or small, flat containers
6 small beakers, glasses or baby food jars
stirring rod
tap water
½ teaspoon each of:
    baking powder
    baking soda (bicarbonate of soda)
    quinine

cornstarch
powdered sugar
powdered salt

SOURCES: Quinine can be procured from a drugstore. The other white powders should be available in supermarkets.

Prior to the exercise, the teacher should number the bottoms of the six Petri dishes for each group from one to six, then place about ½ teaspoonful of each powder to be tested in its own container. For interesting results, the materials should be arranged differently for each group. Group A might be given (1) baking powder, (2) quinine, (3) baking soda, etc., while group B might have (1) quinine, (2) baking powder, (3) baking soda, etc. (Make certain to keep a list of the numbering for each group.)

NOTE: Caution students not to contaminate or mix the powders or they will confuse their descriptions.

PROCEDURE

When materials have been distributed, instruct students to make a chart similar to the following one in which to record their data during the lab session:

Material	Taste	Sound	Feel	Texture	Odor
1					
2					
3					
etc.					

Emphasize use of the senses in testing each of the materials, and instruct students not to name the material; for instance, not to say "It is sugar," but rather to use comparisons, such as "It is sweet, like sugar." Encourage them to use words such as fragrant, soft, hard, sour, sweet, bitter, smooth, coarse, no detectable sound—or odor, taste, etc.

CAUTION: While all of these powders can be tasted in small amounts, warn students that _MANY_ white powders are poisonous and should _NEVER_ be tasted.

After students have completed the first part of the exercise, instruct them to fill the six small beakers about half full of water, then pour each of the white powders into a beaker—one at a time—and stir for 30 seconds. (Students might detect a slight "fizzing" sound in this part of the exercise.)

Ask them to describe what happens to each material during the stirring and at the end of 30 seconds in a second chart.

Material	While Stirring	After 30 Seconds
1		
2		
etc.		

FOLLOW-UP

Have students try to identify each of the materials tested according to their own descriptive terms. (Students will probably not know baking powder, baking soda, or quinine.) At the end of the exercise, place the materials in labeled containers so that students can identify powders they did not know.

Simplicity in Lab Procedures— Investigating Evaporation

by David D. Porter and Robert F. Dixon
Portland Community College, Portland, Oregon

Have you ever interrupted a lab 10 to 15 minutes after students have begun work by saying, "Stop. What is the purpose of all this? Why are you carrying out *that* procedure?" Students' most common answer is, "Because you told us to." A few laughs always result—a good thing—but when you continue, "Yes, but what is the purpose of this particular experimental procedure?" you will sometimes get only silence.

> NOTE: It is entirely possible—and may happen more often than we think—for a lab group to work through a complete lab procedure, earnestly following directions, and "miss the point."

One major cause of students' failure to grasp the purpose of labs is that equipment and procedures are sometimes unnecessarily complex for the job of teaching basic science. To avoid this pitfall of overcomplexity, we have developed and used successfully the following simple procedure with students in the first weeks of a non-majors' physical science course.

NOTE: This procedure can be adapted for use from seventh grade through college, whenever the student is confronting fundamentals.

OBJECTIVES

The *experimental* purpose of the procedure is to measure the evaporation rate of different liquids and to investigate the effect of air movement on this rate. Its *pedagogical* purposes are to give students experience with:

- The concept of evaporation as an example of the movement of molecular particles.
- The operation of the laboratory balance, metric units, and fundamental measurement procedures.
- Graphing techniques, especially the use and value of slopes.
- The exchanging of data and the importance of accuracy when other students must depend upon the student's results.
- Conversion of units.

PREPARATION

Prior to doing this exercise, students should have some understanding of kinetic molecular theory acquired through either individual reading and research or class discussion. They should be familiar with the behavior of molecules in the everyday phenomena of boiling, freezing, and evaporation. (The teacher may also ask students to prepare a data table similar to that in Fig. 1 before coming to the lab.)

Fig. 1

Time (min.)	Methanol Mass (gm.)	Ethanol Mass (gm.)	Water Mass (gm.)
0			
2			
4			
6			
(Leave room for at least 20 lines of data)			

MATERIALS

The following materials are necessary for each group of six students. (Students can work in pairs, then "pool" their data for graphing and calculations.)

3 graduates
Droppers
3 Petri dishes

DISH TYPE: The Petri dish is chosen for its vertical sides. If a large watch glass or evaporating dish is used, the surface area would constantly change.

20 ml. methanol
20 ml. ethanol
20 ml. tap water
3 triple beam balances

PROCEDURE

About 2 hours is required to complete the procedure. With each pair of students working on a different liquid, the data for the three liquids is available to each person in about one hour. Within the second hour graphing is finished, and calculations are begun, with some discussion.

1. Place the triple beam balance on the table before you. A Petri dish should already be standing upon the pan of the balance.
2. Measure out approximately 20 ml. of one of the liquids—water, methanol, or ethanol—using your graduate. Pour the liquid into the Petri dish and immediately measure the total mass of the dish and liquid.
3. After 2 minutes, remeasure. Continue taking mass measurements for 7 to 9 intervals.

   NOTE: Care should be taken during the intervals not to disturb the air about the Petri dish by any unnecessary movement.

4. Without interrupting the procedure, using some broad-surfaced object, such as your textbook, notebook paper, etc., begin fanning the liquid. Complete 7 to 9 more measurements at intervals of 2 minutes. (A 15-second pause in the fanning is usually enough to complete the weighing.)
5. Now exchange data with the two other pairs of students on your team. Graph and calculate results from all three liquids, being sure to indicate which data you and your partner gathered.

GRAPHING AND MAKING CALCULATIONS

Students will probably report their data in the four-figure form shown in Fig. 2. (Data in Fig. 2 is fictitious. It is meant to show the pattern that results in each liquid, but represents none in particular.) The fourth figure is *certainly not* significant when taken during evaporation, although it usually is on a triple beam balance. This is an excellent example to build on for a discussion of significant figures.

At our school we teach graphing at about the same time this procedure is performed, thus the students are able to plot their data (Fig. 3) and to measure the slopes of the resulting line. This activity offers an interesting illustration of a slope with a "message." The slope here is the rate of loss of the liquid. We so often use only the positive values examples for slopes that this easily understood negative is especially useful.

Time (min.)	Mass of Dish and Liquid # 1 (gm.)	
0	58.23	
2	57.01	
4	56.37	
6	56.03	
8	55.52	
10	55.41	
12	54.84	
14	54.28	
16	53.27	fanning
18	52.22	begins
20	51.41	
22	50.64	
24	49.85	
26	48.99	
28	48.31	
30	47.64	
32	46.88[2]	

Fig. 2

Fig. 3

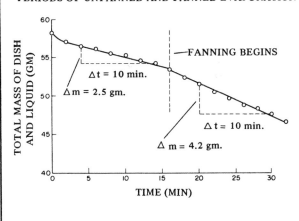

MASS OF LIQUID #1 VERSUS TIME DURING PERIODS OF UNFANNED AND FANNED EVAPORATION

Loss of Liquid from Entire Surface

S_u = unfanned loss rate
S_u = 2.5 gm./10 min.
S_u = 0.25 gm./min.

S_f = fanned loss rate
S_f = 4.2 gm./10 min.
S_f = 0.42 gm./min.

We ask the student to produce results in gm./min. from the entire surface of the liquid in the dish, then to calculate gm./min./cm.^{2}, the loss rate from a small segment of the surface, and finally, to estimate the loss in molecules/sec./cm.^{2}. He may not fully understand the last step, but we believe it will be worth his time to attempt this. We furnish the student with approximate number of molecules/gm., since he does not have any background knowledge of Avogadro's number, etc.

Rate of Loss from a Unit Surface Area

Diameter of Petri dish = 12.0 cm. radius = 6.0 cm.

Area = πr^2 = 3.14 × 36.0 cm.^{2} A = 113 cm.^{2}

$S_u = \dfrac{0.25 \text{ gm./min.}}{113 \text{ cm.}^2}$ $S_f = \dfrac{0.42 \text{ gm./min.}}{113 \text{ cm.}^2}$

$S_u = 0.22$ gm./min.$^{-cm.^2}$ $S_f = 0.37$ gm./min.$^{-cm.^2}$

Rate of Loss in Molecules per Unit Surface Area

To change to loss in gm./sec.$^{-cm.^2}$, divide by 6.0. Then to change from grams to molecules, multiply by the number of molecules per gram. For example, suppose Liquid #1 contains $1.3 \times 60^{22} \dfrac{\text{molecules}}{\text{gram}}$ (the approximate value for ethanol, which is furnished to students):

$$S_u = 0.22 \frac{\text{gm.}}{\text{min.}}\text{-cm.}^2 \times \frac{1 \text{ min.}}{60 \text{ sec.}} \times 1.3 \times 10^{22} \frac{\text{mol.}}{\text{gm.}}$$

$$S_u = 4.9 \times 10^{19} \frac{\text{mol.}}{\text{sec.}}\text{-cm.}^2$$

Similarly,

$$S_f = 8.0 \times 19^{19} \frac{\text{mol.}}{\text{sec.}}\text{-cm.}^2$$

NOTE: If the student can grasp the concept of 8.0×10^{19} molecules per second passing through every square centimeter of surface—all unseen—he has quite an impressive idea.

Having exchanged data, the students can now plot all three liquids on one graph. The form of this will be similar to that shown in Fig. 4. Each line yields two slopes, and each slope is expressed in three forms. This gives students considerable practice in dealing with slopes.

FOLLOW-UP AND VARIATIONS

Many pertinent questions arise in relation to this work, some of which follow.

1. Does a graph always have to go to zero? (If the student tries to

MASS VS. TIME FOR THREE LIQUIDS,

DURING PERIODS OF UNFANNED AND

FANNED EVAPORATION

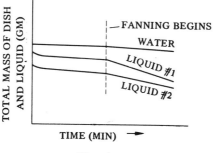

Fig. 4

plot these graphs to zero, he quickly learns the advantage of *not* doing so.)

2. Why do the graph lines seem to drop steeply in the first time intervals? This occurs so often that we think it is a real phenomenon and not caused by irregularities in measurement. What is the explanation? Maybe the initial evaporation cools the surface layer, thereby slowing the rate. Or, could it be that during the first few seconds the layer of air just above the liquid is in process of becoming saturated?

3. Is the rate of evaporation dependent on molecular weight? Density?

4. By what factor does fanning increase the rate? Do all the liquids increase by the same rate?

5. Would the depth of the liquid make any difference?

6. Could the slope of the water line on the second graph be seen and used more effectively if it were plotted separately and on a different scale?

7. What about other liquids? Kerosene? Gasoline? Oil? Salt water?

8. Would a mixture of methanol and ethanol have an evaporation rate in between the other two? Water and alcohol?

9. Would mercury evaporate fast enough to detect on this balance?

10. What about hot and cold liquids? How could one keep a sample of water at a hot and fixed temperature while doing this work?

11. What would happen if the air blown over the liquid was hot? (A hair dryer could be used to supply the air stream.)

12. Would more sensitive balances be of considerable advantage?

13. What effect does the rate of fanning have upon evaporation?

14. Should the six man teams have standardized the fanning rate used by each pair of students? If they did not, is the data then useless?

15. Is there some connection between m.p. or b.p. and the evaporation rate?

These questions should suggest some of the many extensions and variations of this procedure that you may wish to try.

EXAMPLE: After measuring the rates for ethanol and water, have the students predict the behavior of a 50% water—50% ethanol mixture. The prediction should then be tested by experimentation.

If it is desirable to stress graphing techniques, the data can be plotted in several ways with slightly different meanings, as indicated in Fig. 5. (The loss per interval is difficult to see as a constant due to measurement difficulties.)

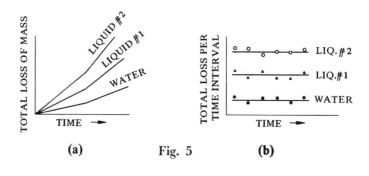

(a)   Fig. 5   (b)

Activities for Slow Learners in Junior High Science

by Richard L. Upchurch
Formerly Fitzgerald Junior High School, Warren, Michigan

It's not uncommon for a science teacher to reveal disappointment when he hears his assignment is a low-ability group. His complaint against these classes may be students' poor reading ability, lack of interest, and the fact that they are often disciplinary problems. There is little he can do to alleviate the reading problem, but he can take significant steps to create interest. If this is accomplished, the discipline should take care of itself.

Here are a few suggested activities for slow learners which require no elaborate preparation by the teacher, no requirement of grade-level reading ability, and yet, provide meaningful science experiences.

TEAM DEBATE

Young people enjoy an argument regardless of their ability level. A little guidance in their thinking plus some basic organization in the form of a team debate can lead to enthusiasm and excitement.[1] At the same time, skills in communication and elementary research may be developed. When a controversial topic such as "flying saucers" is introduced, the teacher may ask for volunteers to take sides and debate the question in front of the class.

A reasonable time for preparation is then set for the debate. Teams are provided with rules, evaluation criteria and instructions for gathering their material on their own time. However, the teacher may wish to give them class time for library work.

The remaining classmates will act as judges, choosing the winning team by such points as amount and source of evidence, individual participation and organization.

SCIENCE CHARADES

When working with low-ability pupils, teachers find that concept reinforcement is not an easy task. An activity that requires much student involvement and which has been successful at the junior high level is "science charades." When a student must act out a written concept such as "Green plants produce oxygen," he and his classmates are less likely to forget it as quickly as when they merely hear it spoken or read it from a chalkboard. A competitive atmosphere is provided by dividing the class into two groups and comparing the time taken to correctly identify the phrase. Some of the most passive students cannot resist the urge to participate in this form of activity.

> **NOTE: Through science charades, the teacher not only capitalizes on the opportunity to reinforce concepts, but also gives the slow learner a chance to improve his social development and possibly become a better student.**

CONCEPT IDENTIFICATION

Something less exhilarating, but effective, is "concept identification." Two methods may be employed.

1. The concepts may be reinforced by showing slides of situations on

---

[1] Richard L. Upchurch, "Debating in Junior High Science," *The Science Teacher,* XXXII, April, 1965, p. 46.

a screen. The students study the picture and attempt to recognize the concept suggested. Examples would be pictures of:

(a) An automobile wreck (inertia).

(b) A rocket in flight (action-reaction).

(c) Plants growing toward sunlight (tropism).

(d) Two magnets joined (opposites attract).

NOTE: Magazine pictures or posters placed on a screen with an opaque projector could also be utilized for this purpose.

2. Students may take turns telling short stories or anecdotes. Classmates attempt to give the *concept* rather than the *moral* of the story. An example would be: "My mother placed a can of beans on the stove to heat, but forgot to open the can. It blew up and beans were all over the kitchen." (Gases expand when heated.)

"BLACK BOX"

One activity which was primarily created for high school science classes but has proved very beneficial in the junior high area is the "black box."[2] The activity does require some initial construction, but once the box is completed, the science teacher has an excellent tool for the development of problem-solving skills in current electricity.

Materials necessary for the construction of a black box are:

1. A piece of ½ inch plywood 2½ × 3½ feet.

2. Twelve feet of 3-inch furring strips (2 pieces each of 2½ and 3½ feet).

3. Bell wire (amount varies).

4. One or two 1½ volt dry cells.

5. Three or four 2½ volt lamps with base.

6. Six to ten knife switches (assorted double throw and single throw).

7. Nails, screws, paint and carrying handle.

Once the sides and handle are attached and the box is painted, the wires, switches and lamps can be placed in a maze or puzzle arrangement suitable for exercises in problem-solving. Fig. 1 shows a suggested electrical layout.

The finished product may be utilized in several ways. Students may pick a lamp and attempt to light it by tracing the current flow, or the box may stimulate them to ask questions such as: "Why does the lamp light with the switches thrown in one pattern, but not light when the switches are thrown in another?"

They may also draw out a pattern on paper and then test their hypoth-

---

2 Peter Dean, "Problem-Solving Techniques in Teaching Secondary School Physics," *Science Education,* XLV, Dec. 1961, p. 401.

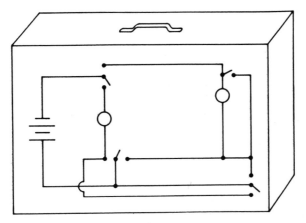

Fig. 1

eses. Students of all ability levels show high motivation in figuring the path of current, understanding simple concepts in current electricity and solving a problem in a logical manner. The author constructed two of these boxes with gratifying results. Individuals have also taken the initiative to build smaller or even larger models for experimentation at home.

Science is too intriguing to reserve only for the "better" students. The slower pupils deserve a chance to experience it also. The above activities are not elaborate or paper and pencil centered, and they do not place a heavy load on the teacher. However, they do allow the youngster an opportunity to learn the ways of a scientist and to participate in a practical science program. A teacher can be just as proud of his accomplishments with slow students as with those who are more gifted, if he finds the means to reach them.

Visual-Auditory Testing for Science Teachers

by Laurence W. Aronstein

State University College at Buffalo, Buffalo, New York

Science teachers face a problem of evaluating student learning in the absence of adequate testing devices. The problem is most critical when the learner is a poor reader who is incapable of expressing himself on paper. This student finds himself doubly penalized every time he is tested. He is graded lower for his inability to cope with the abstracts involved, and even more discouraging, he is victimized for his inability to read and interpret a question.

ALTERNATIVE: I believe a more accurate measurement of the achievement and growth of *all* learners can be obtained using the visual-auditory testing technique described here. The central idea behind this technique is to test general concepts in lab-demonstration settings substituting "live" lab demonstrations for written descriptions.

INADEQUACIES IN TESTING

Today, many science curricula provide learning experiences centered around a laboratory-demonstration setting where "learning by doing" and "discovering" are the objectives. However, when a learner is tested, he finds himself working in an artificial "paper and pencil world" in which mastery of a technical vocabulary and reading ability have a major emphasis. Why must the test setting be separated from the laboratory-demonstration setting in which learning originally occurred?

Probably most contemporary science teachers recognize the inadequacies of the present testing technique used in science classrooms, namely, the "multiple-guess" objective question. Principally, the real aim of the objective-type exam is to facilitate the time factor of paper grading rather than to function as a sensitive feedback device for student and teacher.

NOTE: The objective-type exam is downright destructive in its discrimination against the poor reader who finds himself failing not in science, but in reading!

How often has the teacher been confronted by the type of student who "knows his work" in class yet when it comes to an exam, is marked as a failure? Wouldn't we all feel a lot more honest and objective in our ratings if we could measure what each student learned more accurately?

USING VISUAL-AUDITORY TESTING

Testing students in an actual lab-demonstration setting offers a fairer and more accurate evaluation than present testing techniques. Though it may be impossible to duplicate a lab or demonstration in every case, an attempt should be made to simulate the "live" setting as closely as possible.

EXAMPLES: The following two examples illustrate the visual-auditory testing and provide the teacher with models for adapting this technique in his own evaluations.

Example 1: Almost all science teachers have used the "Ball in Ring Demonstration" (Fig. 1) which illustrates the elementary concept that heat causes materials to expand. Typically this concept is tested through an

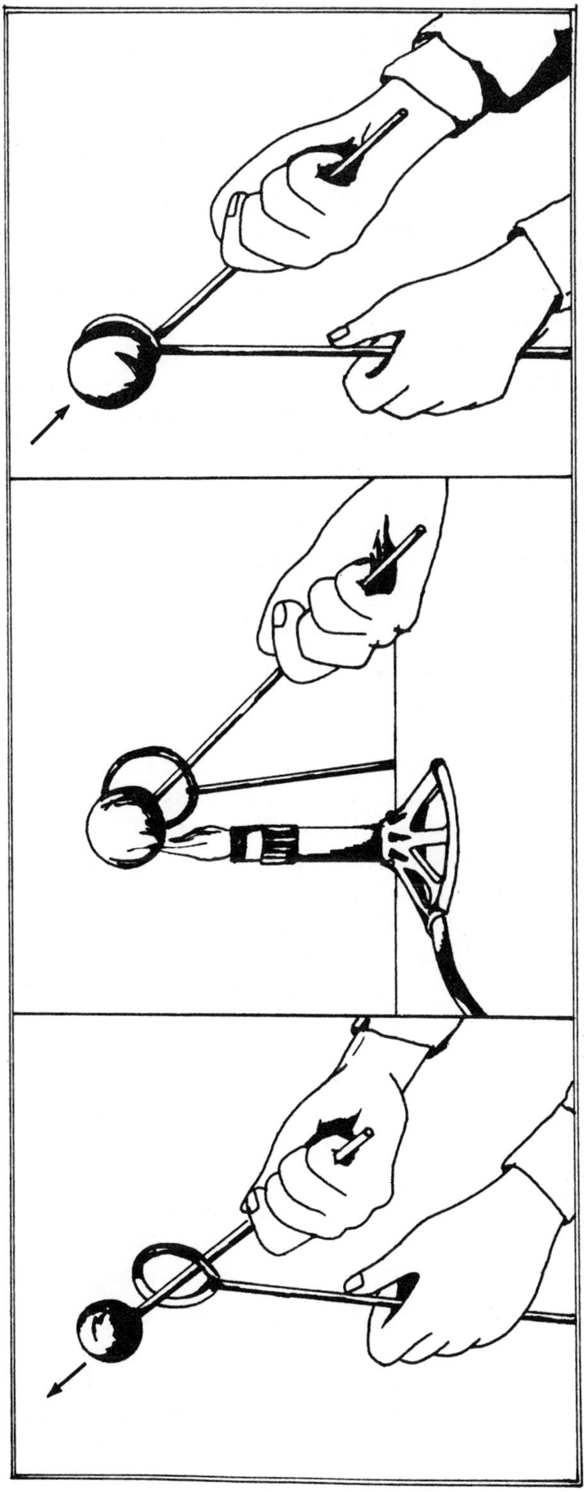

Fig. 1: Ball in Ring Demonstration

35

objective-type question reading something like this: *"When a metal ball is heated, we find it can no longer pass through a ring through which it had previously passed. This is because the diameter of the ball has: (a) expanded, (b) contracted, (c) remained constant."* In some cases, a science teacher who is willing to spend a few hours reading essays will phrase the following kind of essay question: *"Explain the principle behind the ball in ring demonstration."*

Both of these typical questions test the basic concept, yet both depend on verbal cues presented in written form. What if the reader does not associate the name "ball in ring" with a mental image of the demonstration? What if the learner cannot recognize symbols such as "diameter," "constant," "expand," "contract," "principle"? Analogously, how often have you been asked whether you know Mr. So and So and you respond, "Well, if I saw him, I'd probably know who you mean"?

> **NOTE: It would be most preferable if the teacher would repeat the same demonstration during the exam and simply ask:** *"Why doesn't the ball fit through the ring now?"*

Less preferable, but still preferable to the short-answer or essay question is showing the student a well-drawn transparency on an overhead projector, visually describing the demonstration. In addition, the teacher would ask the question orally.

Example 2: Let us assume that a science teacher wants to evaluate student learning from the demonstration of carbon monoxide emission from automobile exhaust as presented in "Demonstrating Air Pollution from Automobiles," by Ernest Starkman (page 94).

Ideally, the teacher and students would return to the car for visual-auditory testing where the demonstration is restaged. However, reasonable substitutions might be made if moving each class back to the street with paper and pens and squeeze bulb apparatus proves too cumbersome. The teacher might provide a video tape or a short movie sequence of the original demonstration, or he could show a transparency to illustrate his point. A diagram and model question designed for such a transparency are shown in Fig. 2.

In either case, the student would briefly state his answer in a few simple words (see answer components in Fig. 2) or by diagram, or even on a tape recorder. The use of a time limit so that the learner does not get bogged down on one question is optional but preferable. When the teacher evaluates the students' responses, he could use previously written model answers and appropriately weigh the value of each concept included within the answer.

ADVANTAGES OF VISUAL-AUDITORY TESTING

Using the visual-auditory testing technique provides a means of working around the reading problem to afford greater communication between the

Fig. 2

teacher and student. The technique can be seen as merely an extension of good teaching methodology into the realm of evaluation. In thinking through the development of specific questions for this type of exam, the teacher will more readily identify the most important general concepts of the unit.

The greatest advantage of this technique, however, is the feeling of success it gives to the poor reader, who in many cases for the first time will be able to fully comprehend exactly what is being asked of him. Now he will be able to earn full credit for the quality of his response, rather than quantity, penmanship, spelling, or grammar.

> **PROGRESS: If science teachers think in terms of better communication through providing relevant visual and auditory cues, we may begin to break through the problem of evaluating student learning.**

REFERENCES

Abramowitz, Jack, "How Much Subject Matter for the Slow Learner?" *Social Education,* 47, Oct. 1963, 11–13.

Aronstein, Laurence W., "Two Strikes, Then You're Out!" *The Science Teacher,* Vol. 36, Oct. 1969, 76–80.

Goehring, Harvey J., Jr., "A Film Slide Test to Measure Ability to Apply Scientific Method in the Area of Mechanics in High School Physics," *Science Education,* 46, Oct. 1962, 347–357.

Hoffman, Banesh, "Tyranny of Multiple-Choice Testing," *Harper's Magazine,* March 1961.

Hutto, Thomas A., "The Use of Objective Tests in Teaching Science," *Science Education,* 47, Oct. 1963, 386–388.

Link, Frances R., "An Approach to a More Adequate System of Evaluation in Science," *The Science Teacher,* 34, Feb. 1967, 20–22.

Lisonbee, Lorenzo, "Testing, What For?" *The Science Teacher,* 33, May 1966, 27–29.

Norton, Jerry I., "The Need for an Activity Centered Science Program," *Science Education,* 47, April 1963, 235–291.

Starkman, Ernest, "Demonstrating Air Pollution from Automobiles," *Science Teacher's Workshop,* Vol. 4, No. 2, Oct. 1969.

2 Mathematics and Measurement

Demonstrating the Role of Mathematics in
    Science   40

Number Pairing to Teach Relations and
    Functions   43

A Laboratory Approach to the Metric
    System   47

A Unit on Measurement   50

Measurements in the Physics Laboratory   58

Demonstrating the Role of Mathematics in Science

by D. W. Tomer

Hanford Joint Union High School, Hanford, California

To the scientist, mathematics is an analytic tool applied to experimental data with the hope of cranking out a formula that describes, at least approximately, some basic tendency of nature. I have devised an exercise that illuminates the role of math in discovering and describing the physical world.

> NOTE: The method described here has been successfully used at the 11th and 12th grade levels, and may successfully be used in classes as low as the 7th grade.

MATERIALS AND PREPARATION

For the particular exercise described here, you will need:

One meter of heavy, bare, solid metal wire
Wire cutters
Weighing scale
Centimeter scales for each student
Graph paper for each student

Before class, carefully balance the scales. Cut a piece of wire and fasten it to the bottom of the weighing pan with a minimum of cellophane tape. This piece of wire must be concealed from the class; it represents an unsuspected fact in nature.

> NOTE: Some may think that this deception is not sound at this level. I believe it illustrates how unknown and unsuspected facts upset experimental results, and the deception has an essential role in science education.

When the class is assembled, pass out the centimeter scales and graph paper, explaining that this is an exercise illustrating the problems of scientists in applying mathematics to research. Show the length of wire whose properties are to be investigated, then cut off at random five or six pieces of widely differing lengths. Hand one piece of wire to the first student in each row, asking him to measure it carefully and pass to the second student, and so on, until all students in the row have measured it and come to an agreement as to the most probable value of its length. As soon as the students are in agreement, collect the pieces and weigh each *except the last*. Tabulate the results on the board.

This might result in the following set of data:

Wire	1	2	3	4	5
Centimeters	4.00	6.50	5.48	1.50	3.12
Grams	1.23	1.72	1.51	.79	

THE PROBLEM

The problem is now obvious to the students: Predict the missing weight. You may wish to let class members suggest ways of doing this, but it may ultimately be necessary for you to suggest graphing. For some classes, it is necessary to spend a previous class period on graphing so that the problem at hand does not become lost in the technicalities of making a graph.

If everything has been carefully done, the plotted points will fall in a nearly straight line (See graph, Fig. 1). The following questions may come up.

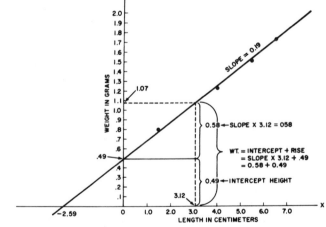

Fig. 1

1. Some students will want to plot straight-line segments between each pair of adjacent points. Explain that broken lines are very difficult to handle mathematically, and just as scientists often start by simplifying a complicated problem, the student is wise to plot a straight line of best fit. (The line should be extended to the left across both axes, as shown at Fig. 1.)

2. Occasionally, a student, reasoning that a wire of zero length would

have a zero weight, will want to curve the line down through the origin. Congratulate the good thinking, but explain that it contradicts the equally plausible assumption that uniform wire should exhibit a uniform change in weight for each change in length (constant slope → straight line), and since zero length and weight are not part of the data, it is better to stick to the assumption that keeps the problem simple. Tell the student to go along with the straight line and the difficulty will soon be resolved.

When the graphs are complete, most students will be able to predict quickly the required weight by interpolation. Let them compare results and come to an agreement on the most probable value. Immediately thereafter weigh the wire (on the same loaded balance, of course). While *exact* agreement between the predicted and measured values will be attained only by accident, the agreement will usually be close enough to convince even the most skeptical student. Faith in the graph will then permit you to derive from it a more general result, namely, a formula.

DERIVING THE FORMULA

Point out that, on the graph, a vertical distance represents a weight whose magnitude can be determined by comparison with the scale along the Y-axis. Thus, in the example under consideration, the students located the length of the unknown (3.12) on the X-axis and found the vertical distance up to the straight line was equivalent to 1.07 on the weight scale on the Y-axis. Therefore, 1.07 grams may be represented as the sum of two parts:

1. The height of the intercept on the Y-axis, or 0.49 grams in this case.
2. The amount the line rises in going from zero to 3.12 cm, or 0.58 grams.

   In general terms: Weight = Intercept + Rise

The value of the intercept may be read directly from the graph. The rise may be computed by multiplying the length by the rise per unit run (slope) of the line. Thus:

$$\text{Weight} = b + m \times \text{Length} \quad (b = \text{intercept}; \ m = \text{slope})$$

To find the slope, the simplest method is to pick two extreme points, construct and measure Δ X (weight) and Δ Y (length) and divide. In the illustration used, you will find that the line rises close to 0.19 grams per unit on the centimeter scale. Thus:

$$\text{Slope} = 0.19 \text{ grams/cm.}$$

The specific formula for the example used here then becomes:

$$\text{Grams} = 0.49 + 0.19 \times \text{centimeters.}$$

At this point, let the students practice with the formula. Cut a different length of wire, measure it, and let the students predict its weight by both graph and formula, and check it on the scales. Emphasize that the formula is found from the graph and says the same thing as the graph. Argue that the formula is more useful than the graph, since it is more compact, easier to remember, and extends beyond the range of the graph.

Finally, focus attention on the constants, 0.49 and 0.19. Since these are derived from physical measurements, they may have physical meaning; i.e., they may describe something real. What do they describe? For a clue, look at their labels.

The 0.19 was obtained by dividing weight by length ($\Delta W / \Delta L$), so its proper label is grams/centimeters. It is the linear density of the wire, or the amount the weight increases for each additional centimeter of length.

The 0.49 appears as a point on the Y-axis or weight scale. It must be the weight of something. The line also crosses the X-axis at -2.59 centimeters. Could this be the length of something? Where is there something that is 2.59 centimeters long and weighs 0.49 grams?

It is well to provide a little time for the students to form hypotheses. Do not evaluate any of these; just encourage them to propose as many as possible. When the ideas run out, reveal that although you balanced the scales initially, you next unbalanced them with a small piece of wire that has a length of—guess how much? (The weight of the cellophane tape usually does not matter.)

Summarizing, the mathematical analysis produced a description of one of the wire's properties. It also found the length and weight of an unsuspected piece of wire.

> **NOTE: Identifying the last relation is quite difficult; it is a rare student who will suspect this form of deception. Point out, however, that nature is often deceptive, and when the experimentalist, Boyle, discovered the gas law $PV = K$, it was a rare theoretican, Bernoulli, who suspected the nature of its cause.**

Number Pairing to Teach Relations and Functions

by Merrill Sanders

Northwest Community College, Powell, Wyoming

Since many of the laws of physical science are most usefully expressed by mathematical relations, it is important that students understand how to arrive at these relations starting with data derived from experimentation.

An effective means of helping students to this understanding is through the basic idea of number pairing. This procedure of number pairing was part of my approach to teaching IPS students how to draw and interpret graphs.

PRESENTING THE PROBLEM

The teacher may begin by observing that in science, experiments are performed so that various quantities can be paired and the relations between them found. Then students can be asked to consider, for instance, an exercise in density in which they will find the relationship between mass and volume of a substance.

To start the investigation, have students find the mass of a number of different sized objects, all of the same material. These may be granular or solid. Next, ask them to determine the volume of the same objects by liquid displacement. When the volume of each object is paired with its corresponding volume, a set of ordered pairs results:

$$\{(V_1M_1)(V_2M_2)(V_3M_3)\ldots\}$$

Finding a Rule

It should be explained that the problem now is to find a rule whereby a value of volume (V) can be found which corresponds to any value of mass (M). When this rule is found, it—together with the set of ordered pairs—constitutes what is known mathematically as a relation. A relation in which no two ordered pairs have the same first element is called a function; students should be aware that the relations in science are of this type.

To find the rule relating mass to volume, ask students to calculate the ratio between mass and volume for each ordered pair. They will find it to be nearly constant for all ordered pairs:

$$\{R = (V_1M_1)(V_2M_2)(V_3M_3)\ldots\}$$

$$\frac{M_1}{V_1} = K; \quad \frac{M_2}{V_2} = K; \quad \frac{M_3}{V_3} = K$$

This means that the ratio of any ordered pair is equal to the ratio of any other ordered pair:

$$\frac{M_1}{V_1} = \frac{M_2}{V_2} = \frac{M_3}{V_3} \cdots$$

From the data, a value of K can be found; knowing that,

$$\frac{M}{V} = K \quad \text{or} \quad M = KV,$$

the mass of any given volume can be found. Consider as an example the following relation which pairs the weight of iron with its volume:

$$\{(1 \text{ ft.}^3, 440 \text{ lbs.})(2,880)(3,1320) \ldots\}$$

$$K = \frac{440}{1} = \frac{880}{2} = \frac{1320}{3} = 440$$

The rule to find the volume of any given weight would be:

$$W = 440V$$

Calculating Values

Students should then be shown that knowing the ratio of any ordered pair equals the ratio of any other ordered pair in a relation also provides a way to calculate values for volume corresponding to any given weight:

$$\frac{W_1}{V_1} = \frac{W_n}{V_n}$$

If W_n equals 2,200 lbs., then

$$\frac{400}{1} = \frac{2200}{V_n} \quad \text{or} \quad V_n = \frac{2200}{440} = 5$$

Graphing Relations

A model of any relation can be obtained by putting the ordered pairs on a graph, and should help students understand the relation. Students can prepare their own graphs, plotting the first element of each ordered pair on the horizontal (*abscissa*) of a coordinate system and the corresponding second element on the vertical axis (*ordinate*). A smooth line is then passed as close as possible to all points as experimental determined ordered pairs tend to scatter somewhat due to uncertainty.

It should be explained that the first element of each ordered pair is called the *independent variable* and the second, the *dependent variable*. However, in many experiments it is difficult to determine which quantity is independent and which is dependent. In such cases, the one changed by the experimenter is the independent quantity and the effect of this change is the dependent quantity.

> **VALUE OF K: Students can also find the value of K from the graph. This can be done by noting that the slope—the ratio of over to up—is numerically equal to the ratio between ordered pairs.**

FURTHER DEVELOPMENT

The preceding exercise can be used as a step-off point to further development of students' understanding of relations and graphing. This should cover the following points.

In evaluating a relation experimentally, only a limited number of ordered pairs can be taken. These can be used to establish a graph. The graph can then be used to find other points. The process of finding points between the measured points is called *interpolation*. Finding points beyond the range of the data is termed *extrapolation*.

Relations which give constant ratios between ordered pairs also give a straight-line graph. Such relations are the simplest of all and are called *direct relations* or *direct proportions*.

NOTE: Students must understand how to establish that two quantities are directly related if they are to succeed in physical sciences.

If two quantities are directly proportional, such as mass and volume, we say that the mass of an object is "proportional to" its volume, or that its mass "varies directly" with its volume. In symbols: $M \propto V$ where M is the mass of the object, V its volume; the symbol $\propto$ means "is proportional to." Direct proportions can also be expressed using the constant value of the ratios, which is called the *constant of proportionality*.

Many relations do not give constant ratios or straight-line graphs, for example, the relation between pressure of a gas and its volume. In an experiment students can try to find the relation by varying pressure and noting the effect on the volume. From this they will get a set of ordered pairs:

$$\{(P_1V_1)(P_2V_2)(P_3V_3)\ldots\}$$

When they apply the tests for a direct proportion, they discover that it is not such a relation. Instead, they will find that as the pressure increases the volume decreases. The graph produces a curved line, which depicts a relation termed an inverse relation. For instance, if one has the relation

$$\{(P_1V_1)(P_2V_2)(P_3V_3)\ldots\}$$

This relation is inverse if

$$P_1V_1 = P_2V_2 = P_3V_3 = K_1$$

Replacing one element by its inverse and then plotting the new set of ordered pairs produces a straight line.

NOTE: Other relations can be handled using the same basic approach, an approach that has the advantage of more closely connecting this modern math idea to the physical sciences. It also makes it possible for the student to see more clearly "why."

A Laboratory Approach
to the Metric System

by Mary-China Corrie

Florence High School, Florence, South Carolina

In teaching science, I believe the metric system is a must. Among my classes is a "basic," or below-average, group, so I start out the year by teaching the metric system to them.

Two points about a basic group: (1) A basic student is one who has to have every idea put to work so that it will mean something to him. (2) In the fall of the year they have some ambition and are willing to meet you halfway.

Before getting into my laboratory approach to the metric system, I give them some simple, introductory things they know: Ten pennies make a dime and one hundred pennies make a dollar. I ask them simple questions such as asking them to give two ways to show 30 cents (three dimes or thirty pennies). To lead into a short explanation of the development of the metric system, I ask them to make comparisons with their neighbors on (a) the span of the hand; (b) the length of the foot, and (c) the length of the arm from the nose to the tip of the fingers. From these comparisons, it is easy for them to see how unfair it was for a "foot" to be the length of the king's foot in any country, or a "yard" the length of the arm.

After this, I tell them a bit about the development of the metric system; the standardization of weights and measurements in this country; and the adoption of the metric system by scientists.

NOTE: My lead-in toward measurement is a simple one. My first "lab sheet" for the semester is to have the student print the alphabet, in capital letters, on a single sheet of paper (Fig. 1). It must, however, cover the entire sheet,

Fig. 1

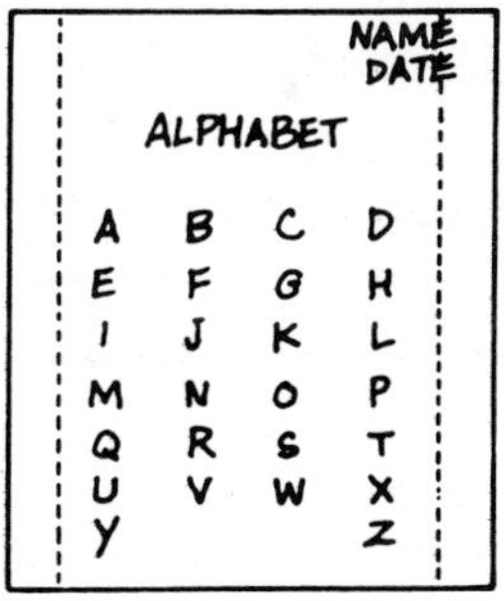

NAME
DATE

ALPHABET

A	B	C	D
E	F	G	H
I	J	K	L
M	N	O	P
Q	R	S	T
U	V	W	X
Y			Z

> from top to bottom, and from left- and right-hand margins. To do this properly, the students find that they must measure the spaces carefully; this leads naturally into measurements.

Here is how I approach the metric system against the background given:

1. I have each student bring in a piece of light or white ribbon 40 inches long. (They may bring a long strip of white paper or non-bias tape. To be on the safe side, I keep a supply of adding machine tape handy, cut into strips.)

2. I pass out meter sticks. Some of the students will see that it is longer than a yard. Make sure all know this. Then, using the yard side (they are all familiar with these measurements) have them make their own yardsticks on the ribbon or paper. It should be marked to quarter-inches. This "yardstick" is then put to use. I have the students measure the lab sheet, the desk, and the textbook; these measurements are drawn on the lab sheet under the heading "Apparatus."

> NOTE: Every demonstration performed has to be written up on lab sheets under the headings "Apparatus," "Procedure," and "Conclusion." Thus, we start out right away. The drawings in this demonstration are in proportion, and the dimensions put on the drawing. (See Fig. 2.)

Fig. 2

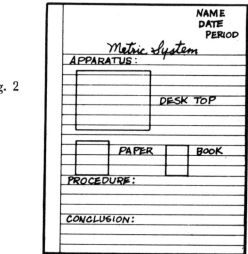

3. The next step is to translate these measurements into the metric system. I use red, green and blue construction paper. With red construction paper I have the students make strips $2\frac{1}{2}'' \times 1''$; these are divided into $\frac{1}{2}''$ blocks and put "1 mm." in each. (See Fig. 3.) Before they cut up these

strips, point out that they have 1 cm., like our dime. Then have them cut up ten of these strips, counting to make sure they are conscious of the fact that they have 100 mm.

Fig. 3

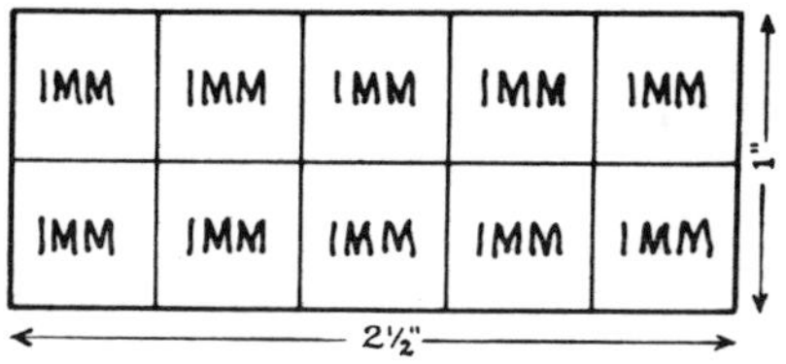

IMM	IMM	IMM	IMM	IMM
IMM	IMM	IMM	IMM	IMM

← 2½" →

4. Then use green paper and have them measure a 5″ × 5″ square, and divide this into ½″ squares, putting 1 cm. in each. Put the following chart on the board:

$$10 \text{ mm} = 1 \text{ cm}$$
$$100 \text{ cm} = 1 \text{ meter}$$
$$1000 \text{ m} = 1 \text{ K.M.}$$

5. Make up combinations to use trying to illustrate the chart. Use the pieces of paper to make "change" like money; i.e., give me 10 cm in two ways (10 cm, green, or 100 mm, red).

6. Using a sharp point on a pencil, use the opposite edge of the cloth or paper to make a meter stick. Start with the ends, the 50 cm. mark, and each 10 cm. in between. Then mark the mm. in each cm. As they work, emphasize that they are going to need 39.37 inches for the meter stick.

7. Have the students measure the sheet, desk and book with the meter stick they have made. Then have them convert the inch measurements to cm by multiplying by 2.54. The measured material should be about the same answer as they obtained by multiplication.

> **NOTE: On his lab sheet, the student will write under "Procedure" everything that was done during the experiment, and under "Conclusion" what he has learned about the metric system.**

If time permits, you can add the following things:

- Weigh the students on the infirmary scales and find heights and convert to grams and centimeters.
- If you don't have a liter measurer, you can demonstrate the liter with an ordinary measuring cup and a two-quart jar. In a two-quart jar put one quart and two ounces of water. This is your demonstration liter. By multiplication they will find out that four liters equals four quarts and one cup. From a container in which you have previously measured four liters, use a quart measure to get out four quarts. The remaining cup of water demonstrates the difference.

If, through these demonstrations, you have shown them that 10 millis make a centi, and 100 centis make a whole, and 1000 centis make a kil, you have achieved your aim. The prefixes can then be used easily with any of the metric forms.

A Unit on Measurement

by Alan Mandell
School of Education, Old Dominion College, Norfolk, Virginia

Much of the science we teach has a quantitative aspect, and our general experience with students conditions us to expect that they will not understand, like, or succeed as well in those areas of instruction which have a mathematical basis. Recognizing this we either leave out the quantitative aspects of material and thus cheat students, or we devote time and effort to "teaching the math" and so feel we have reduced our coverage of science. One purpose here is to suggest a way in which we can "teach the math" and improve students' understanding of some science concepts as well.

From the elementary grades on into high school physics, the concepts related to scientific measurement, the Metric-English system conversions, and the desired attitudes with respect to accuracy, are taught and stressed. Yet each time measurement is mentioned in a new class, the teacher gets the feeling that the students either don't know or don't remember anything but a few scattered facts. They seem to have no understanding of the basic interrelationships in measurement systems or the reasons for "multiplying by 2.54 cm." Thus a second major purpose of the following material is to strengthen students' weakness in this area.

> **USE: The basic form of this unit has been used (modified appropriately) for General Science 8 and 9 and for high school Physics. At present it is used in a college methods course for prospective teachers of science. The unit involves a minimum of materials, is student-activity oriented, and employs the "problem-solving" approach to learning.**

OBJECTIVES

Basic objectives of this unit are:

1. To develop understandings related to: (a) measurement devices, (b) measurement systems, (c) interrelationships of units, (d) interrelationships of units.

2. To develop skill in making and interpreting measurements.
3. To develop skill in arithmetical operations and conversions.
4. To develop attitudes favoring accuracy in measurement and computation.
5. To develop appreciations related to the scientific approach to problem-solving situations.

ORGANIZATION

Tables 1 through 5 are student activity sheets for each of the unit investigations. The body of the description of these investigations is based upon the student activity forms and includes comments, explanations, and directions for the teacher.

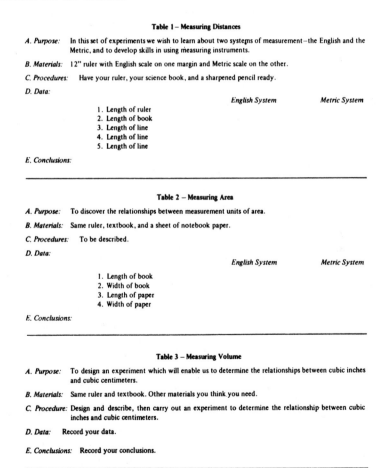

Table 1 – Measuring Distances

A. Purpose: In this set of experiments we wish to learn about two systems of measurement – the English and the Metric, and to develop skills in using measuring instruments.

B. Materials: 12" ruler with English scale on one margin and Metric scale on the other.

C. Procedures: Have your ruler, your science book, and a sharpened pencil ready.

D. Data:

	English System	Metric System
1. Length of ruler		
2. Length of book		
3. Length of line		
4. Length of line		
5. Length of line		

E. Conclusions:

Table 2 – Measuring Area

A. Purpose: To discover the relationships between measurement units of area.

B. Materials: Same ruler, textbook, and a sheet of notebook paper.

C. Procedures: To be described.

D. Data:

	English System	Metric System
1. Length of book		
2. Width of book		
3. Length of paper		
4. Width of paper		

E. Conclusions:

Table 3 – Measuring Volume

A. Purpose: To design an experiment which will enable us to determine the relationships between cubic inches and cubic centimeters.

B. Materials: Same ruler and textbook. Other materials you think you need.

C. Procedure: Design and describe, then carry out an experiment to determine the relationship between cubic inches and cubic centimeters.

D. Data: Record your data.

E. Conclusions: Record your conclusions.

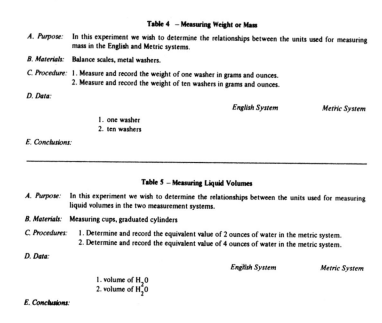

Table 4 — Measuring Weight or Mass

A. Purpose: In this experiment we wish to determine the relationships between the units used for measuring mass in the English and Metric systems.

B. Materials: Balance scales, metal washers.

C. Procedure: 1. Measure and record the weight of one washer in grams and ounces.
2. Measure and record the weight of ten washers in grams and ounces.

D. Data:

	English System	Metric System
1. one washer		
2. ten washers		

E. Conclusions:

Table 5 – Measuring Liquid Volumes

A. Purpose: In this experiment we wish to determine the relationships between the units used for measuring liquid volumes in the two measurement systems.

B. Materials: Measuring cups, graduated cylinders

C. Procedures: 1. Determine and record the equivalent value of 2 ounces of water in the metric system.
2. Determine and record the equivalent value of 4 ounces of water in the metric system.

D. Data:

	English System	Metric System
1. volume of H_2O		
2. volume of H_2O		

E. Conclusions:

EXPERIMENT 1—MEASURING DISTANCES (TABLE 1)

Purposes

In this first unit exercise the teacher plans to introduce the concept of measurement, the varieties of measurement man uses, and the instruments involved. Another goal is to help the student realize that if he applies two different systems of measurement to the same concrete object, he can make an equivalence statement about his two sets of measurements.

Materials

Most students will already have a ruler such as the one described, and they should be asked to bring them to class. (The experienced teacher knows that he had better have several on hand for forgetful students.)

Procedures

To introduce the unit, you may wish to begin a discussion about the many kinds of measurements man makes, e.g., distances like height, length, width; mass or weight; volumes; time; temperature. Consider and demonstrate (if appropriate) the various types of devices used to make these measurements, for example, the ruler, the caliper, the micrometer, various types of scales, and chronometers. In addition, you will probably want to emphasize the need and desirability for accuracy in measurement. (A bridge span which is 1/4 of an inch short will fall into the river.)

Following the introduction:

1. Have the students measure the length of the textbook in inches to the nearest eighth of an inch. (It may be necessary to discuss the actual markings of the rulers being used with the class before they begin. *Suggested Questions:* How long is the ruler in inches? In feet? In half-inches? What is the shortest distance between any two marks on this side of the ruler? How long is the ruler in centimeters? In millimeters? In meters? What is the shortest distance between any two marks on the other side of the ruler? How many millimeters in one centimeter's length?)

2. Have students measure the length of the textbook in millimeters to the nearest millimeter. Both measurements should be recorded in the data table.

3. Have students draw a line 1 inch long (accuracy) and measure its length in millimeters, and record the data.

4. Have students draw a line 2 inches long and measure and record its length in millimeters.

5. Have students draw a line 3 inches long and measure and record its length in millimeters.

Data

(The measurements used throughout are typically obtained values.)

	English System	Metric System
1. length of ruler	12″ (1′)	30.5 cm (305 mm)
2. length of book	10.5″	267. mm
3. length of line	1″	25.5 mm
4. length of line	2″	51.0 mm
5. length of line	3″	76.0 mm

Conclusions

Students should be asked this question: Using our table of data, how can we accurately determine how many millimeters equal one inch? Discuss the fact that because both systems were used to measure the same concrete thing, i.e. the book, we can find the relationship between the two systems. We can even write an equation: 10.5″ = length of book = 267. mm.

> **NOTE: This is one of the most important concepts to be learned in all of these experiments.**

To explain the mathematics involved, try this approach. Our equation says that 10.5″ = 267. mm. We wish to know how many mm.'s equal 1 inch. To change 10.5 inches to 1 inch we must divide it by 10.5. If we do this to one side of the statement, we must do the same thing to the other side to keep our statement a true one. Thus, 267. mm. divided by 10.5 equals

25.4. Our equation now says that 1 inch = 25.4 mm. Is this correct? How can we check?

Let's apply the same reasoning to our measurements of the lines. Here we find slight disagreements (i.e., 25.5 and 25.3). Which is correct and why the disagreements? A discussion of measurement accuracy should develop with a consensus that errors are a constant measurement threat; that care and repetition are essential for accuracy. To find a definitive check on our class results we might refer to reference books or tables.

Formal conclusions may be stated as follows:

1. One inch equals 25.4 millimeters or 2.54 centimeters.
2. Two measurement systems can be compared if they are used to measure the same concrete object.

EXPERIMENT 2—MEASURING AREA (TABLE 2)

Purposes

Here we are concerned with applying the concepts learned in the first experiment to a new situation. The resulting relationship (1 square inch equals 645.16 square millimeters) is not the essential outcome; it is the application of the processes learned in Experiment 1 that is our major objective.

Materials

By having students use the same textbook and standard notebook paper for their area determinations, all will have comparable data.

Procedures

Have students measure and record the length and width of the textbook and paper in inches and in millimeters.

Data

	English System	Metric System
1. length of book	10.5″	267. mm
2. width of book	7″	178. mm
3. length of paper	11″	279. mm
4. width of paper	8.5″	216. mm

Conclusions

You may wish to review area determination formulas. *Suggested Questions* include:

- What is the area of the book in the English system? (73.5 sq. in.)

What is the area of the book in the Metric system? (47526 sq. mm.)
- Can we make an equivalence statement of our two findings? (Yes.) Why? (Both systems have measured the same concrete object, the book cover.) Can we determine how many square millimeters equal one square inch? (Yes.) How? (By dividing both sides of the statement by 73.5.) How many square millimeters equal one square inch? (47526/73.5 equals 646.6 sq. mm.)
- How can we check the accuracy of our answer? (By a reference book.) But, can't we figure out another way to check an answer? (Compare the area of the paper measured by the two systems.) What do we find this time? (1 square inch equals 644.5 sq. mm.) Which is correct? Can we check another way?

Let's think a minute. One square inch equals one inch times one inch. If 25.4 mm. equals one inch, then one square inch should equal 25.4 mm. times 25.4 mm., or 645.16 sq. mm. (Problem-solving approach or scientific reasoning in action.)

The formal conclusion might be stated as follows: One square inch equals 645.16 square mm. As a follow-up, ask students to convert 645.16 sq. mm. to sq. cm. The same type of reasoning is involved. If one cm. equals 10 mm., then 1 sq. cm. equals 1/100th of a square mm.

EXPERIMENT 3—MEASURING VOLUME (TABLE 3)

Notice that this experiment is entirely in the hands of the students. They are asked to design and carry out an experiment to determine the relationship between cubic inches and cubic millimeters. Generally they will measure the thickness of the book, determine its volume in the two systems, and develop the conversion figure. Since the books may vary in thickness (use and abuse) some slight disagreement in answers may occur. The scientific check involving the relationship—one cubic inch equals $(25.4 \text{ mm.})^3$ should give the right answer.

EXPERIMENT 4—MEASURING WEIGHT OR MASS (TABLE 4)

Purposes

This experiment is a continuation of the others, except that our variable is mass rather than length. Students should see that our basic idea of comparing two systems of measurement against a concrete object (number of washers) applies in other situations besides measuring with a ruler.

Materials

Most likely there will be fewer balance scales than students and so the team approach may be used. The classroom teacher, knowing his groups best, will have to decide the mechanism of grouping (e.g. homogeneous or heterogeneous).

Procedures

Have the students determine the weight of one washer in ounces and grams, and record the data. Then have them determine the weight of ten washers in ounces and grams, and record their data.

Data

	English System	*Metric System*
1. one washer	2.5 oz.	71.0 gm.
2. ten washers	25.0 oz.	709.0 gm.

Conclusions

Based on what we have learned in the previous experiments, can we make an equivalence statement about our data? (Yes, although a bright student might say we don't know that we can do this. He is correct and what we are really doing is testing our idea in a new situation. If we make this assumption and check our results against a reference book, we have again proved the usefulness of our idea for comparing two systems of measurement.)

The formal conclusion might appear: Ounce (av.) equals 28.35 grams or 1 pound equals 453.6 grams. (Use "scientific reasoning" to deduce this latter conclusion.)

EXPERIMENT 5—MEASURING LIQUID VOLUMES (TABLE 5)

Purposes

Here again is an extension of the applications of the ideas we have gathered from the preceding experiments, this time to liquid volume measurement.

Materials

Once more, the lack of materials may require the team approach to experimentations.

Procedures

Have the students measure out 4 ounces of water in the measuring cup and pour it into the graduated cylinder. The volume is read and data computed. Repeat this procedure, measuring out 2 ounces of water.

Data

	English System	Metric System
1. Vol. of H_2O	4 oz.	236.0 cc.
2. Vol. of H_2O	2 oz.	118.0 cc.

Conclusions

The students should be ahead of you by this time and proceed to set up their equivalence statements and determine conversion factors. You may wish to discuss and demonstrate the relationship between cubic centimeters and millimeters as a follow-up to the experiment.

> **VARIATION: This experiment gives the most variable results, especially if ten-cent store measuring cups are used for ounce measurements. Also, the "last-drop" problem and meniscus reading lend variance to the measurements obtained. Variation can be put to advantage by the teacher as he emphasizes the need for accurate instruments, measurements, and calculations.**

SUMMARY

This series of experiments has been designed to teach some science—measurement systems; some skills—measuring, and some scientific approaches. It incidentally teaches some mathematics and some desirable attitudes. Many teachers seem to like to follow this series with another involving the measurement of various temperatures (e.g., ice, water, steam) with Fahrenheit and Celsius thermometers. This applies the same skills, principles, and rationale as the preceding experiments.

Addendum

A useful item to put on the test which attempts to evaluate the learnings that occurred through these experiences is the following:

> As the scientist-astronaut who first visits a new planet, you are concerned about the manner in which the natives measure height. They use a metal rod with many equal-spaced notches in it. How would you find out the relationship between their measuring device and a measuring device used on earth?

If the student's response suggests that he will measure some concrete object with both devices and set up an equivalence statement, the unit work has not been in vain.

Measurements in the Physics Laboratory

by David Kutliroff

New Brunswick Senior High School, New Brunswick, N.J.

It is important to emphasize at the start of the physics course that it is a quantitative science. The physics laboratory is a place to make measurements. The necessity to base much of our understanding of the physical sciences on indirect measurements justifies spending some time at the beginning of an introductory course in physics familiarizing students with some of the techniques.

Here are some simple laboratory exercises in different areas of measurements:

TRIANGULATIONS

Take students out to the school parking lot or athletic field and ask them to measure the distance between two distant objects without actually laying out a tape. You may select two trees, a car and a telephone pole, and so on.

> NOTE: Going outside for an early lab emphasizes the idea that a laboratory is not necessarily a room filled with stainless steel instruments. It can be any place where measurements are made.

A base line will be selected and measurements made by triangulation. Materials needed:

Cork board (or soft wood board which can hold straight pins)
Paper and pencil
Straight pins
Meter stick

> NOTE: Some laboratory exercises use simple range finders, parallax viewers, and so on. At an early stage, it is well to emphasize that these are just methods of triangulation; the student should understand what he is doing rather than rely on working with what to him, at that point, is a "black box" instrument.

Two students can work on this problem. Their cork board with a paper tacked onto it must always have one side parallel to the base line and a corresponding base line drawn on the paper parallel to that side. One

58

student then stands on a spot on the base line which he marks and calls "A." He marks a similar point on the base line on the paper and marks it "A¹." He then sights with straight pins to the two distant objects, thus constructing the viewing angles at one end of his base line between the base line and the lines of sight to the two distant objects. (See Fig. 1.)

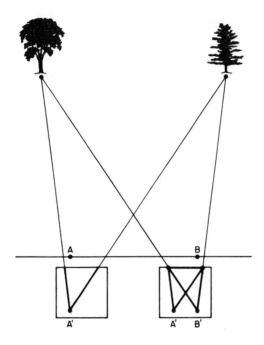

Fig. 1

The partner's function at this point is to make sure that the base line on the sighting tablet is always parallel to the actual base line while the first student is constructing the angles. They then walk over to the other end of their selected base line which can be called "B" and mark point "B¹" on the corresponding base line on the sighting pad. The sight lines are drawn and the sighting angles are constructed similarly to the way the sight lines were found from point A.

The sight line from both ends of the base line are then extended until they intersect. The intersection of the sight lines on the paper give the positions of the two objects sighted in real space.

Since simple geometry can indicate that all the figures on the paper are similar to the geometry of the actual spaces measured, and corresponding parts of similar figures have the same ratio, the student can, by measuring base lines A¹—B¹ on the paper and the actual base line A—B from whose ends he made the sightings, determine the distance between the two distant

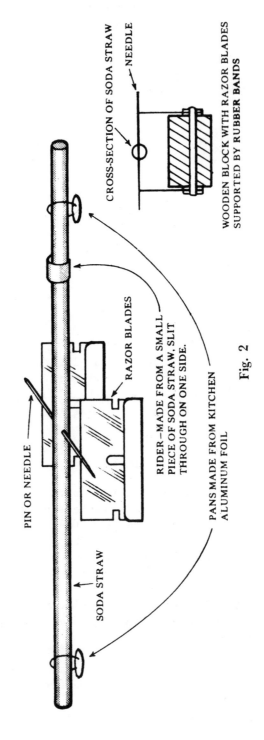

CROSS-SECTION OF SODA STRAW

NEEDLE

WOODEN BLOCK WITH RAZOR BLADES
SUPPORTED BY RUBBER BANDS

PIN OR NEEDLE

RAZOR BLADES

RIDER—MADE FROM A SMALL
PIECE OF SODA STRAW, SLIT
THROUGH ON ONE SIDE.

PANS MADE FROM KITCHEN
ALUMINUM FOIL

SODA STRAW

Fig. 2

objects to which he sighted, or the distance from either of these objects to any point on the base line.

NOTE: After completing his figure, the student ought to be encouraged to make the direct measurement to check himself and calculate the percent of error.

IRREGULAR AREAS

You can ask your students, for example, to find the area of the county in which they live and to use two different methods of computing the area.

NOTE: This could be assigned as a homework lab. This is a good practice once in a while as it again emphasizes that the location of a laboratory is unimportant so long as it is a convenient place to make measurements.

- Method 1: Obtain a road map and cut out the county whose area is being determined. Trace the outline of the county on a piece of graph paper, and determine the area represented by each square by the scale given on the map. The area of the county can then be determined by counting squares and estimating partial sequences.
- Method 2: You can also determine the area by *weighing* it. The first step is the construction of a simple, sensitive equal arm balance with a soda straw, straight pin, razor blades and a little aluminum foil. (See Fig. 2.)

NOTE: The balance once recommended in the very early versions of PSSC laboratory manual would be quite satisfactory.

In this method, we assume, of course, that the road map is made of a fairly homogeneous paper of common thickness and density. The cut-out section of the map is placed on a pan of the balance, and cut-out squares of graph paper are then placed on the other pan until they balance. Then a square of road map paper, whose area is known because of the marked scale on the map, is placed on the scale and balanced similarly with cut-out squares of graph paper. The area can be determined because the ratio of their areas is equal to the ratio of their weights.

3   Chemistry
Investigations

Some Techniques of Investigating
    Matter   64
Junior High School Chemistry
    Experiments   69
Chemistry Experiments That Interest the
    Student   71
Chemical Changes by Heating   75
"Micro" Chemistry Experiments on a Limited
    Budget   78
Quantitative Isolation of Calcium   80
E.S.T.P.—Structured Unstructured   84
Oxidation-Reduction Made Interesting   91
Demonstrating Air Pollution from
    Automobiles   94

Some Techniques of Investigating Matter

by Julian C. Clark
Kunsmiller Junior High School, Denver, Colorado

In our school we spend one semester in the eighth grade studying matter and energy. Since we are able to use the laboratory to complement class discussion, we have developed some laboratory procedures using these criteria:

1. The chemicals used must be common and inexpensive.
2. The glassware must be inexpensive.
3. Instruments must be homemade but accurate.
4. The experiments can be done at home as well as at school.

MATERIALS

The chemicals we use are table salt, baking soda, baking powder, vinegar, and water. The glassware consists primarily of test tubes. However, if these are not available, baby food jars can be used for most of the investigations. In the later experiments presented here, a source of heat is needed (a hot plate will do) and, in addition, a heat resistant container is needed that will withstand heating to at least 270°C.

INVESTIGATIONS

An outline of the investigations is given below:

1. Physical properties of substances
   a. Appearance (color, state, etc.)
   b. Mass
   c. Volume
   d. Density
   e. Solubility
2. Chemical properties
   a. Changes due to heat

b. Identification of compounds
c. Identification of radicals

1. PHYSICAL PROPERTIES OF SUBSTANCES

Appearance

The chemicals are distributed in coded containers for the students to identify. At this point students do not think of too many characteristics except color and taste, and tasting unknown substances should be discouraged. With some prompting, they will check the odor of the various chemicals; vinegar is strong enough that the students will remember the demonstration of how to smell a substance correctly. Any and all tests that are contributed by students and can be performed should be done, but this is not yet the time for identification.

Mass

Students will say that one substance weighs more, less, or the same as another. They are challenged to prove their statements. To weigh the substances, a simple balance can be made from a plastic clothes hanger and paper cups as shown in Fig. 1. The balance can either be suspended

Fig. 1

from a string held by hand from above, or pivoted on a nail in a wooden support. (Some very ingenious and sensitive balances have been made with Popsickle sticks.) As a practical suggestion, the balances should be limited in size so that they will fit into a shoebox for easy storage.

Setting up a massing system poses some problems. Any set of objects can be used but they must be standard for the class. I decided to have the masses calibrated against a gram weight, and made some standard weights using iron filings to calibrate paper clips and small beads. One student who wanted his own standard weight used heavy solid solder to make weights comparable to my standard gram weight.

> NOTE: The calibration leads to a good exercise on graphing. An understanding of the principles involved will solve many problems that could arise during other investigations.

Volume

A graduated cylinder for each student is made by marking plastic pill bottles. Most students can find one at home; but, since the sizes will vary, it is best to calibrate them against a standard glass cylinder. Students can mark their bottles directly by placing a piece of paper on the outside of the container and making marks on the paper at the desired intervals before taping over the strip with cellophane tape. A more accurate technique is to rub a pencil over the raised millimeter gradations on the ruler, then stick a cellophane tape over these marks before placing it on the container. Once this is done the marks can be calibrated against the standard graduated cylinder.

Density

If calibrations have been made against the metric system, calculating the density of each of the unknown objects will provide a check as to how well each of the two previous exercises have been performed. If arbitrary values have been used, the check will be in agreement within the class. Either technique should lead to a lively discussion about the variation in the results and how much of it is acceptable.

Solubility

Now that a system for weighing and making volume measurements has been created, it is possible to compare the solubility of the three solids, the table salt, baking soda, and baking powder. The biggest problem encountered by the students in this procedure is telling when the substances have been dissolved. The students are not entirely sure when they have a saturated solution which is the best end point. Moreover, the baking soda has a tendency to disintegrate, and the baking powder contains cornstarch, which does not dissolve.

Many possible avenues for discussion and experimentation are now open:

- The type of container best suited to observing the solution of the materials.
- The effect of temperature on solubility.
- The difference between a mixture and a solid.
- Filtration as a way of separating a mixture.
- Measurement of the dissolved and undissolved portions of baking powder.
- Fractional crystalization of the dissolved portion of baking powder to complete the separation of the mixture.

NOTE: By this time the procedure need no longer be written out for the students. They are now confronted with the problem and working out a technique to solve the problem. Classroom discussion should lead to better procedures.

2. CHEMICAL PROPERTIES

Heating a Substance

This phase of the investigation is best done in two steps. The first is a fairly simple procedure involving weighing of the baking soda before and after heating, with observations made during the process. Students should notice the water droplets at the top of the container and the bubbles of gas escaping through the dry powder. The reaction is:

$$2NaHCO_3 \xrightarrow[270°C]{\Delta} Na_2CO_3 + CO_2 \uparrow + H_2O$$

A second and more detailed investigation may be performed to obtain a quantitative estimate of each substance. It can be carried out either at this point or after the next investigation. The necessary equipment is shown in Fig. 2.

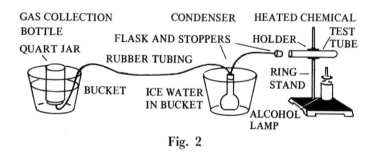

Fig. 2

NOTE: Since this exercise is fairly complicated, you may decide that it is best done as a demonstration.

Because the weight of water is small, the entire container should be weighed before and after the procedure. If a small amount of baking soda is used, the gas displacing the water will be a mixture of air and CO_2. The volume can be measured by marking the amount of gas in the jar with a glass marking pencil, and filling the jar with a measured amount of water. To be certain that the pressure on the gas is the same as the atmospheric pressure, the level of the water inside and outside the jar should be the same when the mark is made on the jar.

Identification of Compounds

CO_2 can be identified with limewater. Enough should be produced for a definite test even though it is mixed with water.

Water is somewhat difficult to identify because the dissolved CO_2 will give an acid reaction to pH paper. Density is the best property to use.

Identification of the substance left in the test tube is a challenge. Tests of density and solubility will not give positive identification, so additional tests must be used. A flame test of the original baking soda and the residue will show that both contain sodium, but pH paper will show that they are not the same. When samples of each compound are compared under a microscope, there is a definite difference in the way that light is transmitted by the two substances.

Identification of Radicals

The previous tests show that the substances are different and yet sodium is present in each. At this time the teacher can demonstrate the use of a strong acid to identify anions with particular emphasis on the carbonate radical. Vinegar can be used to show that salt and baking soda are not the same even though they both contain sodium. Vinegar can also be used to show a difference between heated and non-heated baking soda by titration.

For purposes of titration the same amount of baking soda and residue are put in separate containers and dissolved in enough water to make weak solutions. Vinegar is added a drop at a time from the graduated cylinder until some end point is reached. The end point can be the first appearance of bubbles, the end of bubbling, or the color change of an indicator such as litmus or phenolphthalein. In any event, the solutions must be stirred constantly while the vinegar is being added or the results are confusing. The amount of vinegar used gives an estimate of the amount of carbonate present in each substance.

At this point, enough information should have been gathered to discuss the law of conservation of matter in some detail. The possibilities of other household reagents such as ammonia water, rubbing alcohol, lyes, chlorine bleaches, boric acid, Epsom salts, and others, have not been explored. If nothing else, the techniques described here can be repeated using some of these untested substances.

HOME EXPERIMENTS: Credit for the creation of the simple balance and the pill bottle graduated cylinder must be given to the writers of the Princeton Project materials.[1] These two things eliminate the biggest problem in performing experiments at home. Nothing gives me greater pleasure than to have the students bring in carefully collected data that will confirm or refute data collected in the classroom. The techniques described here have produced this result.

---

[1] These ideas were demonstrated to me at a summer institute by the writers of the course *Time, Space, and Matter*, McGraw-Hill (Secondary School Science Project, Princeton Project), copyright 1967.

Junior High School Chemistry Experiments

by Ernest A. Dunning

North Kirkwood Junior High School, Kirkwood, Missouri

At the junior high level, I have found that laboratory experiments, using relatively unsophisticated materials, are effective in developing and maintaining the interest of the students.

Here are a few chemistry experiments which I have found to be effective.

PRODUCTION OF CHARCOAL AND WOOD DISTILLATION

A simple experiment can show the production of charcoal; an expanded version shows wood distillation. For the production of charcoal, the following materials are needed:

1. Several small wood splints.
2. Large test tube.
3. One hole stopper with 10 cm glass tubing.
4. Bunsen burner.
5. Vertical stand and clamp.

Procedure

Place several wood splints in the test tube, and clamp to the stand (see Fig. 1). Insert stopper with glass tubing attached. Apply heat. Charcoal

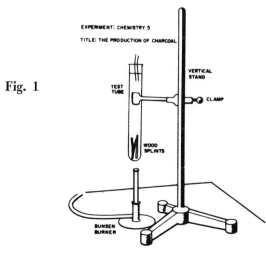

Fig. 1

EXPERIMENT: CHEMISTRY 5
TITLE: THE PRODUCTION OF CHARCOAL

VERTICAL STAND

TEST TUBE

CLAMP

WOOD SPLINTS

BUNSEN BURNER

is produced in the test tube. The combustible gas which is also formed in the tube can be set afire at the mouth of the tubing.

Using the same materials, plus a beaker with water, a test tube with a two hole stopper, rubber tubing, a jar for collecting gas, and a tray or dish of water, the experiment can be expanded to show the distillation of a liquid from the wood. (See Fig 2.) When heat is applied to the test tube, a liquid will condense in the test tube immersed in water, which is a product of the wood. The gas is collected by water displacement.

NOTE: By measuring all of the materials both before and after the experiment, the density of the gas is obtained.

Fig. 2

Fig. 3

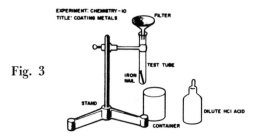

COATING METALS

Here's a simple demonstration to show the chemical coating of metals. Materials needed:

1. Copper ore (malachite).
2. Open end glass container.
3. Dilute hydrochloric acid.
4. Funnel and filter paper.
5. Large test tube.
6. Iron nail.
7. Stand and clamp.

Procedure

Place the ore sample in the glass container, and pour a little of the dilute HCl solution over it. Filter the solution and pour into the test tube. Insert the iron nail and set aside. The nail will become coated with copper. (See Fig. 3.)

QUICK CLOUD CHAMBER

For a quick cloud chamber, use the following materials:

1. Glass container (1,000 ml).
2. Felt pad, cut to fit bottom of the container.
3. 20 ml denatured alcohol.
4. Dry ice.
5. Asbestos plate.
6. Flashlight.

Procedure

Place the dry ice on the asbestos plate. Plate the felt pad in the glass container, and add the alcohol; then place the container over the dry ice. Darken the room and flash the flashlight through the glass chamber.

The dry ice causes the alcohol to become supercooled, and vapors form; the light of the flashlight will show the tracks of subatomic particles. These particles travel through the vapors and ionize a few molecules. The temperature, therefore, drops below the dew point and the students can see the reflection of light.

Chemistry Experiments That Interest the Student

by Ernest A. Dunning
North Kirkwood Junior High School, Kirkwood, Missouri

At the junior high school level, science demonstrations and experiments that use relatively simple materials, or which are related to things which are a part of the students' everyday lives, are effective in attracting and keeping the interest of the students.

In the simple experiments that follow (which can be done either in the lab or at the classroom demonstration table), the students will be working with results that bear a relationship to things they know about or which are visually interesting.

MAKING SOAP

Not a day goes by that the student doesn't use soap. This simple experiment shows how it can be made. The materials needed are:

1. Lye (NaOH), 10 grams.
2. Metal can (coffee can, large fruit can, etc.).
3. Grain alcohol, 26 ml.
4. Lard, 30 grams.
5. Safety glasses.
6. Bunsen burner.
7. Vertical stand, tripod.
8. Salt (NaCl), 28 grams.

Procedure

Carefully dissolve the lye in 65 ml. of water, and add the alcohol and lard. Place the can on the stand, and heat for 25 minutes, stirring constantly. *Safety glasses should be worn by anyone doing the heating and stirring.* Care should be taken not to boil the mixture. Remove from heat and add 180 ml. of water, and heat again, but do not boil. Remove from heat and cool for 6 minutes. Slowly stir in the salt, and allow the mixture to cool. (Fig. 1.)

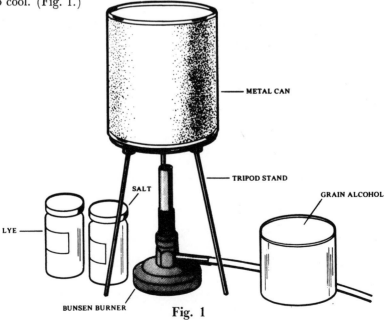

METAL CAN

TRIPOD STAND

GRAIN ALCOHOL

SALT

LYE

BUNSEN BURNER   Fig. 1

The substance on top of the mixture after cooling is soap. Be sure to warn the class that this soap is unpurified, and under no circumstances should be used on the skin, and may be used to wash apparatus only if rubber gloves are worn.

TESTING THE BUOYANCY OF LIQUIDS

Everyone knows, of course, that a piece of wood floats on water, but that an iron bolt, for example, will sink. Here is a visual demonstration that various liquids have different buoyancies. The materials needed are:

1. Mercury, 15 ml.
2. Graduated cylinder, 100 ml.
3. Iron bolt.
4. Small piece of wood.
5. Moth ball.
6. Piece of cork.
7. Carbon tetrachloride, 15 ml.
8. Kerosene, 15 ml.
9. Vertical stand.
10. Tripod stand.

Procedure

Place the mercury in the graduated cylinder, and add the iron bolt. The students will notice that it floats on the mercury. Slowly add the carbon tetrachloride, and place the moth ball on the carbon tetrachloride. Then slowly add 15 ml. of water, pouring carefully so the students will see that

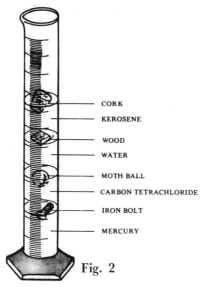

CORK
KEROSENE
WOOD
WATER
MOTH BALL
CARBON TETRACHLORIDE
IRON BOLT
MERCURY

Fig. 2

it does not mix with the carbon tetrachloride. Place the wood on the water, and again slowly add the kerosene, and place the cork on the kerosene. (Fig. 2.)

The result illustrates the buoyancy of the different liquids. You can also have the students check the density of each of the liquids, and the figures will show the relationship to the sequence in the cylinder.

THE PRODUCTION OF RAYON

With synthetic fabrics the order of the day, a demonstration to produce rayon is very topical.

> NOTE: I prefer this as a demonstration, rather than a student experiment, for two reasons. One, there are safety factors involved, as will be seen in the procedure. Two, I frankly find that my students are not too successful with it.

1. Wood or cotton cellulose, cotton preferred, 250 ml.
2. Lye (NaOH), 20 grams.

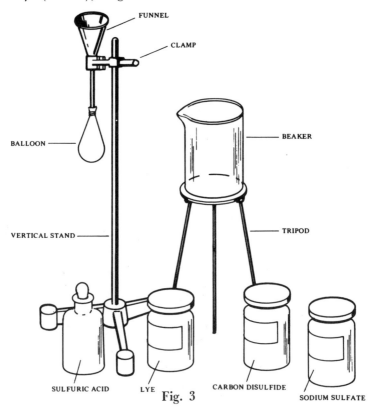

Fig. 3

3. Beaker, 500 ml.
4. Carbon disulfide.
5. Sodium sulfate.
6. Sulfuric acid, 50 ml.
7. Funnel.
8. Rubber balloon.
9. Straight pin.

Procedure

Place cellulose in beaker and add lye. *Caution:* NaOH is a very caustic substance, and should be handled with care; hands should be washed after using. Set aside the beaker for two or three days. At the end of this time, pour the solution from the beaker into a temporary glass receptacle and dispose of any remaining lye.

Add carbon disulfide slowly until a jelly-like substance appears. Set this aside. *Caution:* This compound is very combustible; make sure there are no flames or sparks nearby. Prepare 250 ml. of saturated sodium sulfate, and add the sulfuric acid, and stir gently.

With the funnel, pour the jelly-like substance into the rubber balloon, and tie the end of the balloon and attach to the vertical stand. Puncture the balloon with the pin, and slowly force the mixture through the tiny opening into the acid solution. (Fig. 3.) A rayon thread is formed.

Chemical Changes by Heating

by Ralph S. Vrana

California State Polytechnic College, San Luis Obispo

Here are a few experiments and demonstrations showing the chemical changes made by heating which have proved effective at the junior high school level.

MICA GRIDDLES

One of the simplest ways of heating a very small quantity of a solid is to place the material on a very thin piece of mica (you can get it from an old toaster). The mica should be held with a forceps or tongs to keep the hand a reasonable distance from the Bunsen flame, candle, or alcohol burner. (The clamp can be made from a packing-box iron band.)

NOTE: The mica can be discarded after use, thus avoiding the cleaning necessary if a more expensive holder is used.

Sugar can be cooked on such a miniature griddle to determine the percentage of carbon. Care must be taken to keep the sugar from dripping off the griddle or burning, since this would prevent an accurate measure of such a percentage.

NOTE: You can avoid oxidation by making a sandwich of mica sheets with the material inside clamped together in tongs and heated.

BORAX BEAD TESTS

Make a tight loop at the end of a short nichrome wire and dip it into borax powder. If the loop is heated in a Bunsen flame, the powder will turn into a glassy bead. The presence of metallic impurities in the borax, and the metal wire itself, will tend to color the bead.

It is possible to obtain a clear white bead in many cases, and this bead can be used to test for other metals by dipping it into a compound of the metal such as copper sulfate. The color change is sometimes quite pronounced.

NOTE: This is not, of course, a rigorous test for the presence of metals, since the wire tends to discolor the bead. However, some correlation between color and metal will be observed if many tests are made.

Observed Colors

The Bunsen flame will seem to change to red when a compound containing lithium is heated with the borax. It will turn violet when potassium is heated. These colors give additional verification of the presence of metals and are called "flame tests."

NOTE: The yellow color which comes to a Bunsen flame when glass tubing gets hot in it is from the sodium in the glass.

COMPLETE BURNING OF SUGAR

Glass tubing is a good means of showing the complete burning of sugar. A *few* grains of sugar are placed in the end of the tubing and that end of the tubing is heated in the Bunsen flame. The process which goes on as the tubing heats has several steps:

- First the sugar turns brown and liquid.
- Then it blackens and dies.
- Finally the black material (carbon) disappears, leaving the tubing much as it was.

NOTE: If too much sugar is placed in the tubing, it will not have sufficient oxygen to go through the full cycle, and the black carbon material cannot be driven off.

Care should be taken to see that the end of the glass tubing is not melted shut during the process; free circulation of air along the length of the glass tubing is necessary for the success of the experiment.

BURNING OF A SEED

Compare the burning of the sugar by burning a small seed in the end of the tubing. Roasting the seed on a spit by wrapping a turn or two of nichrome wire will do the job more quickly, although there is some carry-off of the minerals by the pressure of the gases in the flame. The mineral content of the seed tends to remain behind, in this experiment, whereas there seems to be little or nothing left of the sugar.

EXPERIMENTS WITH CANDLES

There are some experiments with candles that are worth while to perform.

1. Hold a square of asbestos or mica over a lighted candle until it has a thin layer of carbon deposited on it. This can then be blown off by using a blowpipe in the candle flame. The blowpipe serves to supply oxygen providing for a more complete burning of the fuel.

NOTE: Care must be taken in the location of the blowpipe or the flame will be blown out.

2. If care is taken, a portion of the inner flame of the candle can be drawn off through a short piece of glass tubing, and burned by applying a lighted match to the upper end of the tubing. The tubing should be held as nearly vertical as possible in the flame in order that the hot gases may pass through unrestricted.

NOTE: The same result can be attained by putting a piece of glass tubing in the Bunsen flame.

"Micro" Chemistry Experiments on a Limited Budget

by Betty Jo Montag

Cupertino High School, Sunnyvale, California

In our four years of developing a lab-oriented textbook for use in grades 8–9, many inexpensive substitutes have been found for the more expensive equipment listed in the catalogues. Teachers on a limited budget may find some ideas here that they can incorporate in their own situations.

HEAT SOURCE

Since many general science classes meet in rooms not really equipped for science, the first prerequisite is to have a heat source. Obviously, Bunsen burners are not practical without gas outlets, but alcohol burners work admirably in a conventional classroom and furnish more than enough heat for most experiments.

NOTE: Desks can be protected by 2′ x 2′ pieces of asbestos purchased in a roll.

After the original expenditures for burners (approximately 75¢ each), they can be used indefinitely with the addition of an occasional wick. The asbestos can be reused many times, too. Instead of using alcohol from the supply houses, that purchased for use in boat motors or ditto fluid works most adequately for a fifth of the price of laboratory alcohol.

RINGSTAND

Next one needs a ringstand of some sort. A number 2½ food or coffee can (furnished by the students) with nail holes punched in the top and sides does nicely. If you wish a slightly more sophisticated system, both ends may be cut out of the can and an asbestos wire square used on one end. The can is then put over the alcohol burner and the material to be heated on the top of the can.

ELEMENTS

Since an understanding of chemistry is essential to an understanding of matter's behavior in *all* science, we start with this discipline. Our first lab combines a lesson in observation with the physical characteristics of some common elements. If you can't "borrow" the elements from the chemistry department, very small quantities are adequate. Thus, after the initial expenditure, they may be used year after year.

WEIGHING SCALES

One way elements may be compared is by weight. Because most schools cannot afford enough scales for general science, some dowling, plywood and aluminum party cups from the dime store can become a reasonable scale. The knife edge is a small piece of sheet copper glued into a slit in the upright dowling which in turn is secured in a hole in a piece of $\frac{1}{2}''$ plywood $3'' \times 2''$. Another piece of dowling is notched in the middle and on the top of both ends (be careful that the notches on the top are equal distance from the center notch). With three strings attached to the aluminum cups and slipped over the notches on the ends of the balanced dowling, an adequate scale is available.

WEIGHT SETS: Since weight sets are expensive, too, either split shot (used by fishermen) or fish weights can be used. If you wish to get across the idea that "weight" is a man-made unit adopted for convenience, students can begin by using the fish weights or split shot as units. You may make this system more sophisticated by calibrating the shot or weights in grams. It's amazing how slight the variance is.

SIMPLE EXPERIMENTS

From here you may wish to do some simple chemical experiments. Most of these can be done on a glass slide. For instance, a drop of dilute HCl and a drop of dilute NaOH can be evaporated on a microscope slide being held by a wooden clothes pin over the alcohol burner. Explaining the correct way to evaporate prior to the experiment keeps the slide mortality to a minimum. We have used this technique to demonstrate the reaction of sodium in water. With a drop of water on a slide and the teacher giving a piece of sodium about the size of a pinhead to each student, they can then test before and after with litmus and see the change.

IMPORTANT: It is *extremely* important that only the teacher handle the sodium and that the "chips" be *very* small.

This type of "micro" chemistry has several advantages: it demands very little material, limits the possibility of accidents and allows every student to actually see what happens in a chemical reaction. There are many other similar experiments that can be done with a minimum of equipment if the teacher has some imagination and initiative. Also, it's amazing how cooperative other departments (such as industrial arts) can be—cutting and drilling the plywood bases for scales, for instance.

Quantitative Isolation of Calcium

by Nelle B. Norman
William Raines Senior High School, Jacksonville, Florida

One of the procedures we frequently use for individual investigations and lab demonstrations is the quantitative isolation of calcium. We have found that eighth grade students can handle the techniques involved, and often proceed to other investigations which grow out of the original problem. Some of the applications of this procedure we have used successfully over the past eight years include the isolation of:

- Calcium in sea shells or egg shells.
- Calcium in limestone, coquinas, or marble.
- Calcium in the ash of organic materials, such as leaves or foods.
- Calcium in the ocean, rivers, limestone springs, wells, or tap water.

The experiment is of particular value since it provides students with a wide range of experiences which are basic to the chemical laboratory. These include the opportunity to:

1. Secure a representative sample.
2. Determine and calculate the percent moisture.
3. Gain technique in weighing and filtering.
4. Become aware of the effect of hydronium ion concentration on solubility.
5. Learn to ash a precipitate.
6. Evaluate results mathematically.

OBTAINING REPRESENTATIVE SAMPLES

Following are procedures for securing representative samples of calcium from various solids, foods and leaves, and water.

Solids

For solids such as shells or limestone rock, grind the sample to a powder using a mortar and pestle. To obtain a representative sample, divide the ground portion into quarters, then select, combine, and re-quarter alternate quarters. Repeat the quartering method until little more than the final two samples of each of the original quarters remains in the quarters from which the weighing is to be done. Weigh out two samples of about 1.00 g. from alternate quarters. Simultaneous analyses are then run on these samples.

Foods and Leaves

With foods and leaves, weigh up to 1000 g. of the raw material and dry it to constant weight at 100°C. Calculate moisture content to add to the available data. Reduce the dried material to ash in a crucible, using a Meker burner for best results. The analysis is then run on the weighed ash, or up to 5 g., with duplicate samples for a check. The calculation is:

$$\% \ H_2O \text{ in sample} = \frac{\text{weight of dried sample}}{\text{weight of raw sample}} \times 100$$

(Foods with high calcium content are: ice cream, cheddar cheese, dried dates and raisins, green and ripe olives, wheat germ, puffed wheat, white and whole wheat bread, raisin bread, gingerbread, wheat pancakes, waffles, salmon, sardines, shrimp, clams, oysters, milk chocolate, broccoli, and spinach.[1])

Water

For a sampling from water, evaporate 1000 ml. of the water to about 50 ml. and proceed from there. Duplicate samples may be run simultaneously for a check.

> **BALANCES: We have consistently used an Ohaus Cent-o-gram balance with our beginning students. While its precision is limited, the error margin of 5 parts in 100 is no greater than the student's errors in technique. Junior high beginners are "instant" chemists and do not have the inclination to use our Voland analytical balance with its "creepy" rider.**

PERFORMING THE SAMPLE ANALYSIS

Procedure

To isolate the calcium in sample materials:
1. Dissolve the sample in 30–50 ml. of 1:1 HCl (one part concentrated HCl and one part distilled water). Bubbling, if noted, indicates that the calcium is present as the carbonate and may finally be calculated as such.

---

[1] William H. Sebrell, Jr., *et. al.*, *Food and Nutrition* (Life Science Library) New York: Time, Inc., 1967, pp. 194–95.

2. Bring the sample to a boil and simmer to insure solution of all soluble particles.

3. If only a calcium separation is desired, make up the sample to 50 ml. with distilled water and simmer it an additional 5 minutes.

4. Allow the liquid to cool, then add a strip of red litmus. Neutralize the acid to litmus by adding 1:2 ammonia solution (one part ammonium hydroxide and two parts distilled water).

5. Next, add a few additional milliliters of the ammonia solution. The metal oxides, iron, aluminum, and titanium, if present, will precipitate on boiling.

6. Filter off the insoluble material and the metal oxides. Wash the paper thoroughly with warm and cold distilled water using a polyethylene or lab-constructed jet spray wash bottle.

7. Make the filtrate acid to litmus with 1:1 HCl.

8. Now add 25–50 ml. of a 5% solution of ammonium oxalate. (This solution is prepared by dissolving 5 g. of ammonium oxalate in 95 ml. of distilled water. Heat it to complete solution of the salt.)

9. Stir the solution, then make it basic to litmus by adding 1:2 ammonia water.

10. Boil the solution 5 minutes, stirring it constantly. The calcium will come down as the white, finely grained calcium oxalate. Allow the materials to stand overnight.

11. Filter off the calcium through a low ash, close-textured paper, such as Whatman #40. Check the filtrate with some of the oxalate solution to be sure that all of the calcium has precipitated.

12. Wash the precipitate thoroughly and allow it to dry overnight.

13. Carefully fold the filter paper and transfer the precipitate to a weighed crucible. Using a Meker burner, if possible, ash the precipitate, slowly at first, then at maximum heat. *Ashing time:* about one hour.

> **CRUCIBLES: While a platinum crucible is desirable, good results can be obtained with a nickel one, which is much less expensive. We have also used a porcelain crucible, lengthening the ashing time to be sure that the calcium oxalate is completely decomposed to calcium oxide.**

14. Weigh the calcium oxide according to the equation:

$$CaC_2O_4 \xrightarrow{\Delta} CaCO_3 \xrightarrow{\Delta} CaO \qquad \Delta = heat$$

with CO being lost in the first change and CO_2 being lost in the final decomposition.

Calculations

A. To convert calcium oxide to calcium:

1. $\dfrac{Ca}{CaO} = \dfrac{40}{56} = .714$

(The weight of the CaO is multiplied by the factor .714, derived above, to convert the result to actual calcium.)

2. *Then:*

$\dfrac{\text{weight of Ca}}{\text{weight of sample}} \times 100 = \%$ Ca in original solid or ash

3. *In water:*

weight of Ca $\times$ 1000 = milligrams (mg) per liter

B. *To convert calcium oxide to calcium carbonate:*

1. If the analysis was run on a carbonate rock or shell, the results may be calculated and reported as carbonate content.

$\dfrac{CaCO_3}{CaO} = \dfrac{100}{56} = 1.79$

(Multiply the weight of CaO obtained by 1.79 to get the equivalent weight as $CaCO_3$.)

2. *Then:*

$\dfrac{\text{weight of CaCO}_3}{\text{weight of sample}} \times 100 = \%$ $CaCO_3$ in original solid or ash

NOTE: There are several stopping points in the procedure, which thus adapts itself well to the short lab or activity periods common in junior high school scheduling.

Further Investigations

Here are a number of suggestions for other possible student investigations using these procedures.

- In areas which are underlain by limestone aquifers, it is interesting to compare the Ca in water from artesian wells to the aquifer, with the Ca in a sample of the limestone which forms the aquifer. The limestone rock sample may be obtained from the recharge area for the aquifer, where the limestone will be outcropped at or near the surface.
- Calcium in ancient limestones of Mesozoic age may be compared with the Ca in Cenozoic deposits. Samples can be obtained from geological supply houses.
- Calcium in Pleistocene shells may be compared with the Ca in shells of the same present-day forms. The Ca-Sr ratio in the same shells may also be investigated as a possible means of age-dating.
- Shells from living crab or mollusk specimens may be examined for their Ca content and this information related to the Ca content of the sea water environment from which the specimens were taken. In

areas where estuaries penetrate the land from the sea, this same comparison might be run on specimens which live in both estuarine and marine environments. These processes could be used to acquaint the student with current research interest in invertebrate calcium metabolism.

- The thermogravimetric properties of the precipitated calcium may also be investigated. By weighing and controlled heating, a pyrolysis curve for the oxalate can be drawn, showing the loss of CO at 420°C., and the final loss of CO_2 above 850°C to CaO.[2]

- The preceding type of analysis can also be done in a single step, directly from limestone. (Heat a weighed sample slowly for 10 minutes and calculate the loss on ignition as water. Then increase the heat to 850°C. for one hour, using a Meker burner. Relate the % loss to % of CO_2 in the original sample.)

---

[2] C. Duval, *Inorganic Thermogravimetric Analysis*. Houston: Elsevier Press, 1953.

E.S.T.P.—
Structured Unstructured[1]

by Francis E. Cote and Charles E. Horner
West Springfield Junior High School, West Springfield, Massachusetts

We believe that the purpose of junior high school science teaching, and science teaching at any level, should be to provide experiences through which children can acquire understandings, attitudes, and skills applicable to any field of endeavor in our society. In accord with this viewpoint and in response to the peculiar needs of beginning junior high school students, we have developed our own laboratory-enriched program which we call the Eclectic Science Teaching Program, or E.S.T.P.

E.S.T.P.

This program stresses the repetition of important concepts through a variety of experiences which possess common characteristics. It seeks to provide the student with the tools and knowledge he will need for the more formalized science of high school without being locked into either a rigid subject-oriented approach or a wholly unguided free inquiry approach.

---

[1] This article is based on a student manual, *Stepping Stones to Scientific Exploration**, now being developed by the authors.
* © by Francis E. Cote and Charles E. Horner.

An Example

While a complete understanding of the E.S.T.P. method cannot be obtained from a description of one experiment, the following example, "Nature of Particles in Solution," will at least provide a glimpse of the Program in action. This experiment is part of the series of events included in the outline of Classroom Curriculum ("II. Discussion"). Concept repetition is achieved through overlapping objectives in various experiments and stressing key concepts at each step of the presentation sequence:

1. Clear-cut statement of objectives (primary and secondary).
2. Discussion of the ideas to be demonstrated.
3. Pre-lab session to demonstrate use of apparatus (or to perform similar experiments).
4. Lab period to give student firsthand experience with the concept.
5. Post-lab session to conduct similar experiments, re-emphasize ideas, and bring out practical applications.

   NOTE: In the E.S.T.P. manual, each experiment includes a student worksheet section and a corresponding Teacher Notes and Answer Sheet section. For purposes here, student-directed and teacher-directed materials are dealt with together.

NATURE OF PARTICLES IN SOLUTION

I. Objectives

The student worksheet for this experiment states the purpose of the exercise as: To determine from a series of electrical tests some of the differences between solutions containing ions and those containing molecules.

In the corresponding Teacher Notes section for the experiment, these learning objectives are cited:

a. Determining the two general types of solute particles in a solution.
b. Introducing the idea that solutions have saturation points.
c. Understanding that atoms, ions, and molecules are involved in chemical changes.
d. Introducing the idea of concentration of solutions.
e. Introducing the idea of a chemical change.

II. Discussion

A discussion for each experiment is intended to give students those definitions which will be demonstrated in the experiment. In this case, definitions are provided for ion, molecule, ionic compound, *molecular compound, ionic solution,* and *molecular solution.* In addition, a section is devoted to an explanation of the nature of the conductivity of solutions. Included in the Teacher Notes is a section titled "Student Background Information Needed for This Experiment," which gives the teacher the pertinent classroom curriculum. For this experiment, the information is as follows:

A. A basic understanding of atomic structure is necessary to understand the difference between ions and molecules.
B. Classroom Curriculum:
   1. Definition of a solution.
   2. Parts of a solution.
   3. Characteristics of a solution.
   4. What is dissolving?
   5. Structure of matter.
   6. Ions, molecules, and polar molecules.
   7. Actual dissolving process explained.
      (a) Organic matter
      (b) Inorganic matter
      (c) Polar vs. non-polar molecules
   8. What is a conductivity apparatus, and how does it work? (Tool of Science)

III. Materials and Equipment

This section is included with each experiment so that the student can check to see whether everything is ready. Materials and apparatus for this experiment include:

For Parts A and B:

Beaker of salt	Conductivity apparatus (Fig. 1)
Beaker of sugar	Spatula
Beaker of water	Stirring rod
Wash bottle	2—250 ml. beakers
Disposal can	

For Part C:
A tray containing:

Alcohol	Copper sulfate
Cobalt chloride	Nickel sulfate
Ammonia	Vinegar

The corresponding Teacher Notes for the experiment are intended to give the teacher the necessary information to successfully carry out the experiment.

A. The conductivity apparatus in this experiment can be made from a block of wood with a hole drilled at one end to take a #8 and #9 stopper or cork (2-hole). Assemble the wire in series with a lamp socket. The bulb should be of clear glass so that faint illumina-

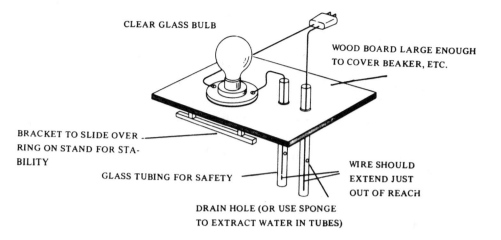

CLEAR GLASS BULB

WOOD BOARD LARGE ENOUGH TO COVER BEAKER, ETC.

BRACKET TO SLIDE OVER RING ON STAND FOR STABILITY

GLASS TUBING FOR SAFETY

WIRE SHOULD EXTEND JUST OUT OF REACH

DRAIN HOLE (OR USE SPONGE TO EXTRACT WATER IN TUBES)

Fig. 1: Conductivity Apparatus

WARNING: The teacher must warn students on their worksheets and orally not to touch any of the wires on this apparatus.

tions can be noticed. The wire electrodes should be covered with glass tubing to prevent accidents. A metal base or support bracket can be put on the bottom of the board so that it can be attached to a ring stand or other support. (See Fig. 2.)

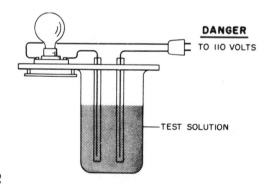

DANGER
TO 110 VOLTS

TEST SOLUTION

Fig. 2

B. Mix the solutions for Part C in covered gallon jugs.
C. Chemicals can be set up to serve groups of 4 students.
D. Quantity: 1 lb. each of sugar and salt (per class), normal laboratory supply of other electrolytes. Replace as needed.

IV. Procedure and Observations (Student)

The student procedure for the three-part experiment is as follows:

Part A: Nature of Salt, Sugar, and
Water Particles (Conductivity)

(1) Take the beaker of salt, and carefully place it into the electrodes of the conductivity apparatus. Note results on Chart 1.

CAUTION: Do not touch any wires in this experiment. If something is not right, call the instructor.

Next, remove the beaker of salt, and dip the electrodes in the rinse water beaker. (It is very important to dip the electrodes in the beaker of rinse water each time they are used. Handle all equipment with great care.)

(2) Using the same procedure outlined in (1), take the beaker of sugar and place it into the electrodes of the conductivity apparatus. Note the results on the chart, then dip the electrodes again.

Chart 1

Material Tested	Bulb Lights Up? (Yes–No)
1. Salt	
2. Sugar	
3. Water	

(3) Using the same procedure, take the beaker of water and place it into the electrodes of the conductivity apparatus. Note the results on the chart, and dip the electrodes.

Part B: Nature of the Solute Particles
of a Sugar and a Salt Solution

Section 1: Salt Solution

(1) Take the 150 ml. beaker and fill it about 1/2 full of water from the wash bottle.

(2) Add 1/2 spatula full of salt and stir. Test this with the conductivity apparatus. Note the results on Chart 2, and rinse the electrodes as before.

(3) Add 1 more spatula (level) full of salt to this saltwater solution. Test with the conductivity apparatus. Note the results on Chart 2 and rinse the electrodes.

(4) Add 1 spatula (level) full of salt to this saltwater solution and test the solution. Again, note the results and dip the electrodes.

(5) Pour the saltwater solution from the beaker into the disposal can, and rinse out the beaker thoroughly with water from the wash bottle.

Section 2: Sugar Solution

(1) Refill the beaker about 1/2 full of water from the wash bottle.

(2) Add a level spatula full of sugar and stir. Test the solution with the

conductivity apparatus and note the results of Chart 2. Dip the electrodes.

(3) Add 1 more level spatula full of sugar to the sugarwater solution and stir. Test the solution and record the results. Rinse the electrodes.

(4) Pour the contents of the beaker of sugarwater solution into the disposal can. Rinse the beaker thoroughly with water from the wash bottle, and place the beaker back on the tote tray.

(5) Be sure to fill in Chart 2 with the observations made in this part of the experiment.

Substance Tested with Apparatus	Bulb Lights Up? (Yes–No) (Dim–Bright)	Solute Particles (Ions) or (Molecules)
Saltwater—½ spat.		
Saltwater—1 spat.		
Saltwater—2 spat.		
Sugarwater—1 spat.		
Sugarwater—2 spat.		

Chart 2

Part C: Testing for Kind of Solute Particles in Other Solutions

(1) In the tray on the laboratory table are 7 beakers containing common water solutions. Test each with the apparatus to find out whether they conduct electricity. Dip the electrodes *each* time as noted in the previous parts of the experiment.

(2) Note the results of the 7 tests on Chart 3.

Water Solution of Substance Tested	Bulb Lights Up? (Yes–No)	Bulb Lights Up (Dim–Bright)	Solute Parts Are— (Ions–Molecules)
Copper Sulfate			
Nickel Sulfate			
Cobalt Chloride			
Ammonia			
Alcohol			
Food Coloring			
Vinegar			

Chart 3

Conclusions: (1) Solutions that conduct electricity are made up mostly of solute particles called _____. (2) Solutions that do not conduct electricity are made up mostly of solute particles called_____.

Thought Question: When adding salt to water, the light continued to brighten; after awhile the light remained at a constant brightness, even when more salt was added. WHY?_____.

IV: Procedure (Teacher)

The Teacher Notes corresponding to the experimental procedure are intended to give the instructor a detailed analysis of what to do. This analysis is divided into three parts: the preliminary period, the laboratory period, and the post-laboratory period.

A. Pre-lab Period:

1. Review what ionic and molecular materials are.
2. Demonstrate the operation of the conductivity apparatus.
3. For a homework assignment, have students outline this experiment.

B. Laboratory Period:

1. Stress safety and re-emphasize the use of goggles.
   (a) Spillage
   (b) Goggles
   (c) High voltage in conductivity apparatus (normal 110 volts is acceptable but hazardous if the proper safety precautions are not taken).

   WARNING: 110 volts can produce fatal accidents. The apparatus design (Fig. 2) must be carefully followed and checked for broken glass tubes, loose or exposed wires, and improperly fitted parts.

2. Stress the need to keep chemicals pure so that the results can be reliable. This also includes keeping the electrodes clean.
3. Have the students connect the conductivity apparatus.
4. Do Part A with the students and emphasize that solid ionic compounds do not conduct an electrical current.
5. Do the sugar part (section 1) of Part B with the students, and let the students do section 2. When the light does not change intensity, have the students answer the Thought Question.
6. Let the students do Part C themselves, but emphasize the rinsing of the electrodes between each test.

C. Post-lab Period:

1. Emphasize the nature of an electrolyte.
2. The following experiments can be done to stress the value of this experiment. All of these are solutions.
   (a) (no light)   (slightly ionized)
   $$CH_3COOH + NH_4OH \rightleftharpoons CH_3COO^-NH_4^+ \ H_2O$$
   (poor cond.)   (poor cond.)   (good cond.)

   This experiment stresses Objective e, "Introducing the idea of a chemical change." A new substance is formed.

   (b) (light)   (light)   (no light)
   $$Ba^{++}(OH^-)_2 + H_2^+SO_4^{--} \rightleftharpoons BaSO_4 \downarrow + H_2O$$
   (good cond.)   (good cond.)   (insol. ppt. forms)

(c) (light)   (bright light) (no light)

$$Ca^{++}(OH^-)_2 + H_2^+SO_4^{--} \rightleftarrows Ca^{++}SO_4 \downarrow + H_2O$$

(fair cond.)   (good cond.) (insol. ppt. forms)

Add blue litmus solution to show when the neutral point is reached. At this point you should have no ions.

3. Let the students add salt until the bulb will not get any brighter. Have them add one more spatula of salt after this, and ask them to explain why the intensity of light in the bulb gets *dimmer!*

"A STEPPING STONE TO SCIENTIFIC EXPLORATION"

The sample experiment, "Nature of Particles in Solution," shows how E.S.T.P. works to make theory discussed in the classroom become reality for the student. When he sees the light go on, he is convinced that different kinds of particles do exist. And the fact that the light goes on not only solves the immediate problem, but creates new questions in his mind about the nature of the particles of matter.

Oxidation-Reduction Made Interesting

by Robert Pearce

New Mexico Junior College, Hobbs, New Mexico

These student demonstrations will stimulate students and give them firsthand experience with the process of oxidation-reduction. Each demonstration is quite simple, and all may be conducted by students in any junior high school or senior high school science class, or even at home.

Prior to performing the demonstrations, students should be familiar with these rules relating to chemical oxidation-reduction:

- Oxidation is the adding of oxygen to a substance.
- Reduction is the removal of oxygen from a substance.

    NOTE: In a more generalized sense, of course, oxidation and reduction refer to the gain and loss of electrons in a chemical reaction and may involve elements other than oxygen, such as chlorine, sulfur, etc.

- A reducing agent is one that cause oxidation.
- An oxidizing agent is one that causes reduction.
- The reducing agent itself is oxidized.
- The oxidizing agent itself is reduced.

MATERIALS

Each student or team of students will need these materials to carry out the demonstrations:

Chemicals

Potassium permanganate solution (1%)
Saturated oxalic acid (ZUD)
Hydrogen peroxide solution (3%)
Sodium thiosulfate (hypo)
Sodium hypochlorite (bleach)
Copper oxide
Charcoal
Blood
Fountain pen ink
Iodine solution
Silver nitrate solution
Rust

Equipment

Mortar and pestle
4 test tubes
Bunsen burner
25-ml graduate cylinder
24 pieces of 3 cm-square (1-inch square) white cloth
Small beaker or tumbler (50 ml or 100 ml)

DEMONSTRATION TECHNIQUES

Following are student procedures for performing the demonstrations, together with brief explanations of the chemical reactions involved.

Reducing a Metal Oxide

This procedure demonstrates the process of oxidation-reduction in the reduction of a metal oxide :

1. Mix 0.1 gm of powdered copper oxide and 0.5 gm of charcoal thoroughly, using a mortar and pestle. Pour the mixture into a test tube.
2. Heat the test tube over a Bunsen burner until the mixture turns red.
3. When the mixture is red, remove it from the heat and allow it to cool.

4. Pour the cooled material onto a piece of paper and examine it. **NOTE: You should find that it contains small pieces of copper.**

The chemistry in this demonstration may be explained as follows:

copper oxide + charcoal $\xrightarrow{(heat)}$ copper + carbon dioxide

Copper oxide is reduced while carbon is oxidized. The charcoal is the reducing agent and is oxidized, while the copper oxide is the oxidizing agent and is reduced to copper.

Removing Stains

Stain removal offers a second illustration of oxidation-reduction. To demonstrate this:

1. Take 10 ml of 1% solution of potassium permanganate ($KMnO_4$) and immerse one of your fingers in it for 2 to 3 minutes. (The potassium permanganate should stain the finger brown; it has been reduced to MNO^{+2} ion:

$$KMnO_4 + finger \longrightarrow MnO_2^- + stained\ finger$$

The potassium permanganate is the oxidizing agent and the finger is the reducing agent. What is oxidized?

2. To remove the stain, place the stained finger into 10 ml of a saturated solution of oxalic acid or ZUD for 2 to 5 minutes.

3. Observe the results and write your answers to these questions: (a) What happened to your finger? (b) What happened to the oxalic acid? (c) What happened to the MNO_2^- ion stain? (d) What was the oxidizing agent? (e) What was the reducing agent? (f) What was oxidized? (g) What was reduced?

Further Demonstrations

Now that you have had some experience with the work of oxidation-reduction in stain removal:

1. Take 24 pieces of white cloth 3 cm-square (about 1-inch square) and stain four each with blood, fountain pen ink, iodine, silver nitrate, rust, and potassium permanganate.

2. Place one of each type of stained cloth into four test tubes containing these solutions: hydrogen peroxide solution (3%), sodium hypochlorite (bleach), sodium thiosulfate (hypo), and oxalic acid (ZUD).

3. Allow the cloth squares to soak for 5 to 10 minutes.

4. Remove each piece of cloth and examine it for any removal of the stain.

5. List the oxidizing agents and reducing agents in each instance, remembering that some chemicals are good oxidizing agents but poor reducing agents and vice versa.
6. Try other kinds of stained pieces of cloth and experiment to determine whether the stains can be removed with the four given solutions.

Demonstrating Air Pollution from Automobiles

by Ernest Starkman

Vice President-Executive, Environmental Affairs, General Motors Corporation, Warren, Michigan
formerly Executive-Director, Project Clean Air, University of California at Berkeley

Contamination of the atmosphere by motor vehicle engine exhaust is now universally recognized as a health hazard and in some urban communities, poses a critical problem. In developing students' awareness of this problem, however, the teacher is somewhat limited. For while smoke and haze are readily identified, we usually have no opportunity to observe the effects of the more dangerous colorless and transparent components of exhaust, such as carbon monoxide (CO).

NOTE: Following are background materials concerning vehicle exhaust and details for a simple, direct demonstration which can be used to show students how concentration of CO is related to the automobile.

Requiring only a relatively inexpensive test kit and an idling automobile, this demonstration should be easily understood by both junior and senior high school students. It should be particularly meaningful to chemistry students.

ELEMENTS OF ENGINE EXHAUST

Carbon Monoxide

Almost all internal combustion engines run on fuel of hydrocarbon composition (CnHm). When burned with air, the principal combustion products are: carbon dioxide, carbon monoxide, water vapor, hydrogen, and nitrogen. The concentration of each of these gases depends upon the amount of air available in the combustion process. As the quantity of air relative to the fuel is decreased, the concentration of carbon monoxide increases.

Typical of the hydrocarbons which constitute gasoline is octane, C_8H_{18}. When octane is burned with exactly the correct quantity of air, the theoretical chemical equation:

$$C_8H_{18} + 12.5O_2 + 47N_2 \longrightarrow 8CO_2 + 9H_2O + 47N_2$$

shows that only carbon dioxide, water vapor, and the original nitrogen should appear in the exhaust. However, the gasoline engine runs best when the fuel quantity exceeds the correct amount. This is particularly true when the engine is idling or when it is fully loaded, as during acceleration. Under such circumstances there may be 20 percent or more excess of fuel over air. At such a "rich" mixture, the chemical reactions of combustion then produce exhaust products according to the following equation:

$$1.2C_8H_{18} + 12.5O_2 + 47N_2 \longrightarrow$$
$$6.1CO_2 + 3.5CO + 1.5H_2 + 9.3H_2O + 47N_2$$

NOTE: It is apparent that the products of combustion thus contain 3.5 parts of carbon monoxide, by volume, out of a total of 67.4 or 5.2 percent. Similar equations can be written for other fuel-air mixtures.

Unburned Hydrocarbons and Oxides of Nitrogen

The other two principal pollutants in engine exhaust are not so easily accounted for by simple balancing of chemical equations. This is a consequence of the mechanisms by which they are produced.

- In the case of unburned hydrocarbons, it is a quenching of the flame within the combustion chamber, near the relatively cold surfaces of the cylinder head and piston, which causes these fuel molecules not to burn.
- The oxides of nitrogen (*nitric oxide,* NO, to be exact) are formed at the high temperatures of combustion, out of the oxygen and nitrogen in the same air as was intended to burn the fuel.

Generally, the quantities of unburned fuel and oxides of nitrogen found in the exhaust are much less than that of carbon monoxide. Their concentration is measured in parts per million of exhaust, rather than percent. For reference, the quantities of unburned hydrocarbon usually found in the exhaust range from 100 to 1000 parts per million, or .01 to 0.1 percent. The oxides of nitrogen are measured in quantities from 500 to 5000 parts per million (.05 to 0.5 percent).

NOTE: Fig. 1 illustrates how the concentrations of all three of the principal pollutants—carbon monoxide, unburned carbons, and nitric oxide—depend upon the fuel to air ratio of the engine.

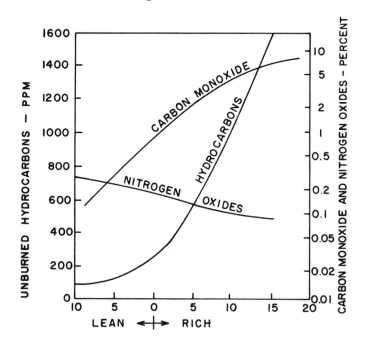

Fig. 1: Gasoline Engine Emissions

NOTE: The numbers indicated on the horizontal axis show the percentage of unburned hydrocarbons in fuel-air mixtures. For example, those to the right of "0" would indicate 5% rich, 10% rich, 15% rich, etc. By the same token the numbers to the left of "0" indicate the percent of leanness.

MEASURING EXHAUST EMISSIONS

Necessary Apparatus

As might be expected, the accurate, continuous determination of hydrocarbon and nitric oxide content of vehicle exhaust requires relatively sophisticated instruments. Even carbon monoxide, which is ten times as plentiful, cannot be measured accurately on a continuous basis using inexpensive equipment. However, there is one simple batch sample method which is reasonably accurate and relatively inexpensive to perform.

USE: This method can be used to identify the presence and approximate concentration of any of a number of selected gases, and most particularly carbon monoxide and nitric oxide.

Fig. 2 shows the most simple type of apparatus needed to conduct the batch test. The apparatus depends upon the ability of the specified gas, in this case carbon monoxide, to change the color of an absorbing chemical gel in proportion to the amount of carbon monoxide to which the indicating medium is exposed. The indicating media are supplied in glass vials, with a breakable tip at each end. These vials are fitted tightly to an assembly incorporating a squeeze bulb. The sample to be tested is aspirated through the glass vial, both ends having been broken off to allow the free flow of that sample through the vial.

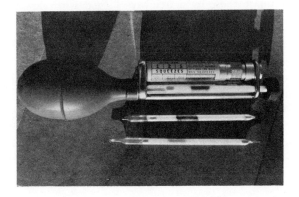

Fig. 2: Apparatus for Measuring Carbon Monoxide

One or more squeezes of the bulb may be used, depending upon the concentration which is to be measured. Carbon monoxide content is determined by comparison of the resulting color of the sensitized gel to a chart, which is an integral part of the device. The illustration in Fig. 2 shows the instrument with three glass vials. One is in place in the apparatus. (It has just been used to measure a concentration of 0.02 percent carbon monoxide in the area at the rear of a passenger car, with engine idling.) The other two vials are, respectively, used (with tips broken) and unused.

NOTE: Another available instrument of the same kind indicates the concentration of gas as a length of the stain in the indicator crystals rather than the color of that stain. Both types of instruments are designed to detect 10 to 2000 parts per million of carbon monoxide in air (.001 to 0.2 percent).

The approximate price for either tester is $55, complete with 12 glass tubes. The tubes are $6.60 per dozen. Purchase may be made through most scientific equipment supply houses, or directly from: MSA (Mine Safety Appliance Company) 201 North Braddock Avenue, Pittsburgh, Pennsylvania 15208.

Demonstration Procedure

Either of the instruments described can be used to show students how the motor vehicle pollutes the atmosphere and under what circumstances that pollution might be hazardous. In addition, any parked automobile with engine idling is required.

> **PURPOSE: Specifically, this demonstration illustrates how the carbon monoxide concentration behind a vehicle may exceed recommended human exposure. The conditions approximate those on a freeway clogged with slow traffic or in an equally congested metropolitan area.**

Fig. 3 shows how this demonstration takes place. Directions are follows:

- Select a calm day so that the exhaust will not be dissipated easily by the wind, and an open site for conducting the demonstration.
- Break off the tips of the vial at either end and insert it in the apparatus.
- Start the engine of the vehicle and allow it to idle. (A cold engine will produce even more carbon monoxide than one which is hot.)
- After the engine has idled for two or three minutes, hold the apparatus about 1 foot from the exhaust pipe (Fig. 3) and squeeze the bulb.

Fig. 3: Method of Sampling Exhaust Gases from Rear of Automobiles

For multiple samples, the distance should be varied to show the effect of distance on atmospheric dilution. (The distance behind the exhaust pipe can be as great as 15 or 20 feet on a calm day and the carbon monoxide will still be detected in significant quantities.)

POTENTIAL EFFECTS OF CARBON MONOXIDE ON HUMAN BEINGS

Interpreting Results

Fig. 4 illustrates what might be the effects of prolonged exposure to levels of carbon monoxide as measured in this demonstration. Caution should be used in explicit interpretation of the information shown in this graph since many factors enter into individual susceptibility. However, the potential consequences are apparent.

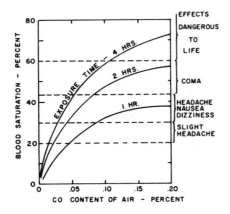

Fig. 4: Health Effects of Carbon Monoxide

NOTE: Health authorities presently recommend that concentrations of no more than 20 to 30 parts per million (.002 to .003 percent) be allowed in the atmosphere for periods of up to eight hours.

Controlling Vehicle Emissions

The accompanying table, "Passenger Car Exhaust Emissions," may be used as evidence of our society's real concern with pollution from vehicle exhaust. This shows how the principal pollutants from exhaust are being and will continue to be controlled in newly manufactured motor vehicles registered in the state of California. Most of this control of carbon monoxide and unburned hydrocarbon to date has been through better carburetor adjustment to leaner fuel mixtures, as illustrated in Fig. 1. Oxides of nitrogen remain a separate problem, but research is continuing and solutions are becoming available.

PASSENGER CAR EXHAUST EMISSIONS

POLLUTANT	PRIOR TO CONTROL (1965)	AFTER CONTROL					
		CALIFORNIA 1966 AND U.S. 1968	U.S. 1970	1970	CALIFORNIA 1971	1972	1974
Carbon Monoxide, Per cent	4.5	1.5	1.5	1.0	1.0	1.0	1.0
Hydrocarbons PPM	1000	275	275	180	180	125	125
Oxides of Nitrogen PPM	1500	1500	1500	1500	1075	800	350

4 Life Science Activities

An Approach to Seventh Grade
    Life Science Units   102

Free Aquaria   104

Teaching the Sense of Sight   107

Demonstrations in Respiration   112

A Frog on the Moon   117

Life Science for the Underachiever   120

Bottle Caps, Pop Beads, and Genetics   124

High School Study of Air Pollution   127

An Inductive Approach to the Compound
    Light Microscope   132

Plant Activities with Lemnaceae, or
    Duckweed   134

Observation: A Key to Outdoor Science   139

The Dandelion—A Gold Mine for
    Outdoor Science   142

Testing for Water Pollution   145

An Approach to Seventh Grade
Life Science Units

by Ronald F. Romig

West Chester State College, West Chester, Pennsylvania

Any approach to teaching life science in the seventh grade is dependent to a certain extent on the way science has been treated in the lower grades. It could be, in some cases, that the student's first real exposure to science will come in the seventh grade. If, on the other hand, the treatment has been broad and deep, then the content of the course requires much thought, because the students may well be ready for having the greater portion of the school year spent in a more specialized scientific study.

An effective method of handling the units in a seventh grade life science course is explained here. It treats the *process* of science as having equal status with the subject matter, permits increased student activities and decreased teacher lectures and demonstrations, and is practical from the point of view of materials at this particular level.

> NOTE: The assumption here is that the students have already been taught such things as observation, measuring, identifying pertinent data, record keeping, and the application of findings. To this, the treatment of our units is assumed to aim at teaching grouping by characteristics, problem recognition, and the evolution of new problems.

Units in such a life science course, taught in six blocks of six weeks each, cover such things as worms, an aquarium, fruit flies, "us," and the out-of-doors. To illustrate, I am outlining here our handling of a unit on seeds, using seven labs as an example:

Lab I. Students are provided with a variety of soaked seeds (beans, corn, wheat, peas, pine, sunflower, and a number of others) to study. They are to note differences and similarities on a columned sheet. They may pull the seeds apart to study them better.

The class is asked to put similar seeds into separate paper cups. This leads, of course, to a new question for discussion: Can each cup of seeds be further broken down?

NOTE: The class may choose their own names to assign to the different seeds: two-parters, one-parters, browns, and so on. There is no need, at this stage, to insist on the proper names. Classification is the important thing.

Lab II. The similarities of the seeds are studied in the light of determining the answer to the question: Are there similarities of the features of seeds which would lead us to believe that those seeds which are similar come from similar parents?

NOTE: At this point, pictures or actual specimens of the parent plants should be shown for comparison purposes.

Lab III. In this lab, the students try to predict the appearance of parent plants by merely seeing the seeds.

Unknown seeds are given to the students to study. They chart the characteristics of the unknown seeds and compare them to the chart they made in Lab I as the basis for their predictions.

Lab IV. The prediction exercise is extended to find out whether similar predictions can be made on the basis of other plant parts. The students are provided with leaves or stems or the reproductive parts of other plants. The students carry on their investigation much as they did in Lab III.

NOTE: As in the case of seed identification, at this point the students may make up their own names for plant parts: e.g.: the words "leaf stem," or "leaf attacher" are just as good as "petiole" at this point. The idea remains the same.

Lab V. By this time, the students have studied about the need of water for seeds to begin germination. It is not too early to bring this into the laboratory.

Weighed quantities of water are placed in small jars. Each team chooses a different type of seed and places a given number of these in a jar. They are left to soak for one day (with the jars lidded). One day later the seeds are taken out and the water weighed, and it will be seen that an unbelievably large amount of water has been taken out by the seeds. These questions can then be asked and answered:

- How much water is taken up per seed?
- What proportion of the seed's new weight is water?
- What would have been another good way of determining how much water is taken up per seed?

This kind of question, of course, leads to another one: At what time during the 24-hour period was the water uptake going on most rapidly? Students are then invited to hypothesize and suggest ways of finding out.

NOTE: Eventually, a test will be suggested which will be something like the following: Take some seeds out of the jars at time intervals and weigh them. Then, of course, they can do this several times to see if they arrive at similar data, and the data can be graphed, if desired.

And, from this test, of course, will come other questions: Do all seeds have the same peak period of uptake? Did the test seem to cover the appropriate amount of time for answering the questions?

Lab VI. This lab covers the effect of abiotic factors on the uptake of water, and would cover temperature, light, and soil chemicals. The students would be asked to suggest means of setting up the tests to do this, following the procedures already developed in Lab V.

Lab VII. This lab sets out to answer the question: What are some of the other things either used or given off by seeds during their germination? Two examples:

- After seeds have been germinating for a period of time, a lighted splint can be thrust into the jar to observe either the presence or absence of oxygen.
- Carbon dioxide can be tested by water displacing the jar's gases out through a tube which has its end submerged in a test tube of limewater.

As can be seen, the seeds themselves are merely a point of departure for a study which is designed to introduce some survey biology and a great deal of science process.

Free Aquaria

by Ralph S. Vrana
California State Polytechnic College, San Luis Obispo

If your budget does not permit you to buy aquaria for the classroom, you can make your own for almost nothing from one-gallon glass jugs (of the cider variety). If you can't get all you need from your students, the local soda fountain will probably be glad to oblige (they are used for Coke syrup and the like).

> NOTE: Since the process uses heat to crack the glass, the idea won't work with Pyrex.

It's a simple, two-step process if you take necessary pains to do it right. I've cut more than 100 jugs, and have broken just one. Here are some tips on doing the job:

SCORING THE GLASS

After washing off the label, place the jug sideways in a shallow drawer, such as the top drawer of your desk (Fig. 1). Close the drawer until the jug is wedged in, with the bottom against the side of the drawer. Hold a glass cutter (obtainable from the hardware store) against the front of the drawer with the pointed cutting wheel pressed against the bottle. With the other hand, hold the jug steady and turn it, resulting in scoring.

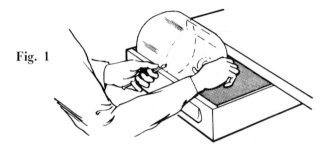

Fig. 1

NOTE: Although two people can do this, only apply enough pressure to score the jug. Keep the fingers holding the cutter against the outside of the drawer; if the jug should break, they will not move against broken glass.

Make sure the scoring goes all around the jug. The first few times, you may miss a spot; if so, go back over it until you have a complete scoring. To help guide the cutter, you can make a small notch in the desk drawer as a guide for the cutter; a large clamp, if you have one, will also serve. This will help make the start and finish of the scoring meet.

CRACKING THE GLASS

A simple device for cracking the glass with hot wire can be made with these materials:

Flat 8″ × 16″ board
Two porcelain light sockets
Switch (screw-down type)
Two binding posts (round-head brass screws will do, but the wood will char)
A few feet of plastic lamp-cord wire
Male plug
600-watt cone-type heating element
15 ampere fuse
24″ length of old toaster wire

NOTE: You can get unused wire of the latter type from the hardware store. It probably will come in tight coils, however, which have to be straightened out.

Mount the device on the board as shown in Fig. 2. If all connections are made properly, the wire will glow when the device is plugged in (use an extension cord) and the switch turned on.

IMPORTANT: Since the open wire carries electricity, it is not advisable to have students work the device themselves. They can help by turning the switch on and off while the teacher holds the jug.

Fig. 2

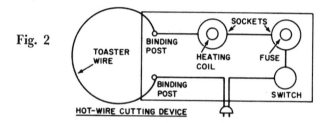

HOT-WIRE CUTTING DEVICE

Plug in device, turn on switch, and hold bottle until the glass cracks as shown in Fig. 3. Since the wire touches only half the glass, this is a two-step operation. The cracking of the glass can be seen and heard when it happens. Turn off switch, wait until wire cools sufficiently, turn jug around and adjust wire over other half of scoring, and repeat. When the glass cracks completely around, a dull thud is usually heard.

If you have scored the jug evenly, you should be able to lift the cut top off.

NOTE: Because of manufacture, the jug may vary in thickness. If it appears too thin at any one point, discard it; it could break easily.

Fig. 3

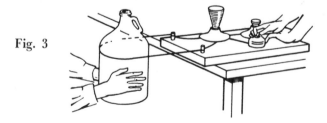

Put on the finishing touches by dulling the sharp edge of the aquaria. Use an emery cloth, a whetstone or file. Do not do this vigorously; just enough to take off the sharp edges.

IMPORTANT: This job should probably be done by the teacher, wearing goggles or glasses. No one should stand near unless they are wearing glasses.

After the edges are dulled, tape over with adhesive tape, and the job is done. Wind the tape around the jug once or twice so that it overlaps the edge and can be folded over onto the inside of the jug.

NOTE: You can make other pieces of equipment this way, using jugs of different sizes. For example, a half-gallon jug makes a good lung demonstrator, as shown in Fig. 4; in this case the scoring is done near the bottom of the jug. Small jars make satisfactory and sturdy Petri dishes; larger ones make suitable trays for photographic chemicals.

Fig. 4

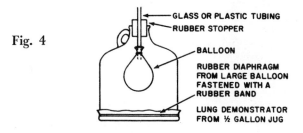

GLASS OR PLASTIC TUBING
RUBBER STOPPER
BALLOON
RUBBER DIAPHRAGM FROM LARGE BALLOON FASTENED WITH A RUBBER BAND
LUNG DEMONSTRATOR FROM ½ GALLON JUG

Teaching the Sense of Sight

by Bernadette Beres Stundick
Cherry Hill Junior High School, Baltimore, Maryland

Here are a number of exercises for making the study of the eye more stimulating and meaningful to your students. Each is designed to give the students an opportunity to learn actively through observation and analysis of their own reactions to tests and demonstrations related to sight. Each is simple to perform, yet effective, and can easily be worked into a unit on the eye.

LAB WORK: The descriptions of various exercises conclude with a detailed outline of a laboratory dissection of a cow eyeball, which can be used as the culminating activity in the unit. I have found that most students anxiously await this eye dissection lab.

INK BLOTS AND OPTICAL ILLUSIONS

Two good motivational devices for introducing the study of the eye to students are ink blots and optical illusions. Ink blots can be easily made, and a set of blots selected which has the greatest number of forms and figures for possible identification by students (Fig. 1). The opaque projector may be used to show these, or transparencies can be made and shown on the overhead projector.

Fig. 1: Ink Blot

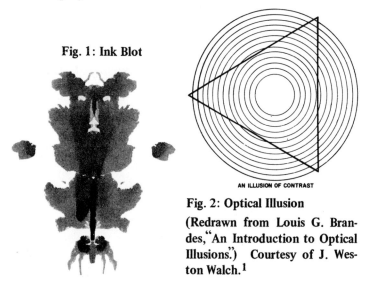

AN ILLUSION OF CONTRAST

Fig. 2: Optical Illusion (Redrawn from Louis G. Brandes,"An Introduction to Optical Illusions.") Courtesy of J. Weston Walch.[1]

Before showing the ink blots to the class, number them and give the numbers to the class, asking the students to number a sheet of paper accordingly. Then, as you present the blots on the projector, have the students individually record what they see without any discussion. They may record what they see in any portion of the ink blot, or observe the ink blot in its entirety.

Discussion of the ink blots may be followed by the presentation of a series of optical illusions (Fig. 2), and concluded by a written or oral summary of the similarities and differences between the ink blot test and the optical illusions. This summary might include some of the following points.

Ink Blots

- When standardized as the Rorschach test, ink blots may aid trained professionals in determining normal and abnormal personality.

---

[1] *An Introduction to Optical Illusions,* by Louis G. Brandes, contains 25 drawings of common optical illusions for bulletin board mounts, 50 pp. 8½ x 11, price $1.50. Orders under $2 must include cash. Order from: J. Weston Walch, Publisher, Box 658, Portland, Maine 04104.

- To each one of us, the ink blots depict figures and forms of those things which are present in our environment.
- We see that in which we are most interested, for which we have a liking, or with which we are most familiar.
- We may see that which we dislike intensely or for which we have a phobia.

Optical Illusions

- Optical illusions indicate that what we see depends on many factors, such as:
  Background
  Size, shape, and arrangement of nearby objects
  Shape of the observer's eyeballs
  Degree of color fatigue the retinal cells of the eye happen to have
  The distance of the object from the eye

DEMONSTRATING TRAITS OF THE EYE

Distance Judgment and Binocular Vision

After the introduction of the unit, many demonstrations can be worked into lesson plans to sustain a high level of student interest, and to illustrate in a concrete manner the various characteristics of the eye. One demonstration may be centered on the question, "Why are two eyes better than one?" To investigate this question, the following procedure may be used.

1. Have one student volunteer to come to the front of the room.
2. Give this volunteer a test tube and direct him to hold the tube half an arm's length directly in front of himself.
3. Give the student a straight pin to hold between the thumb and forefinger of his free hand.
4. Direct him to close one eye and by quickly swinging one arm, aim to drop the pin in the mouth of the test tube.
5. Then direct the student to reverse the procedure, closing the other eye and repeating the action.
6. Finally, have the student keep both eyes open and repeat the procedure.

Students will conclude from this demonstration that distance judgment is much better when we use both eyes. The reasons for this condition may be discussed.

Iris Light Reflex

The eyes' automatic adjustment to light and dark may be demonstrated by darkening the room and/or having the students cover their eyes with their hands. After they have kept their eyes covered for a short time, turn on the lights, or tell them to remove their hands and quickly observe the size of one another's pupils. The students will observe that in darkness or dim light, the pupils are dilated, while in bright light they diminish in size. The iris protects the sensitive nerve cells in the retina from damage by too much light. The brighter the light, the smaller the pupil; the dimmer the light, the larger the pupil.

The Eye's Blind Spot

To demonstrate the existence of the blind spot in the eye, cards marked as shown in Fig. 3 can be made and distributed to each student. The directions for using the cards are as follows:

1. Hold the cards 15 to 18 inches away from the eyes, with the cross (+) on the left and the spot (•) on the right.
2. Close the left eye and look at the cross with the right eye.
3. Observe that at a certain distance from the eye, the spot will suddenly disappear. (The spot is focused in line with the blind spot of the right eye, the point at which there are no rods or cones, where the end of the optic nerve joins the retina.)

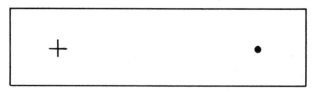

Fig. 3: Sample Card (The card should be about 1¼" x 5").

DISSECTING A COW'S EYEBALL

Background

By the end of the unit, the students should have acquired a knowledge of many terms used in connection with the eye. These provide them with some basis for performing an eye dissection lab. The lab, in turn, will provide the students with a concrete and working understanding of many of the terms they have learned.

Preparation of Materials

One day before the lab is scheduled, obtain cow eyeballs from a slaughter house in your vicinity. The eyeballs will cost about $.10 each. To make the eyeballs firm and comparatively easy to dissect, they should be placed in a solution of one part formaldehyde to five or six parts water, covered, and refrigerated until used.

Since it is very difficult to handle and cut fresh eyeballs, single edge razors should be purchased for the dissections. A new blade must be used for each dissection as they dull easily when cutting the tough sclerotic coat.

NOTE: Students should wear goggles to protect their eyes from the formalin.

Procedure

The following dissection procedure should be mimeographed and distributed to the students. It should include the illustration of the external structure of the eye shown in Fig. 4.

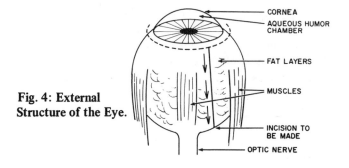

Fig. 4: External Structure of the Eye.

Part I

1. Hold the eye firmly in the position indicated in the illustration.
2. If the optic nerve, which looks like a thick white cord, is not visible, carefully cut away some of the fatty material and/or muscles to expose the nerve. *Handle the razor blade carefully.*
3. Cut down on one side of the eyeball as indicated in the illustration. Be certain to incise the side of the eyeball. Do not cut into the optic nerve.

NOTE: Do not squeeze the eyeball as the vitreous humor will ooze out.

4. Next, place the razor blade in the incision at the periphery of the cornea, following the dotted line shown in the illustration. Hold the blade on a slant to remove the *cornea* only. If more is cut, you may mutilate the *iris* and *lens*.
5. Cut around the iris and remove it.
6. Gently remove the lens and put it aside. Observe the ciliary body.
7. Remove the vitreous humor jelly.
8. Find the optic nerve in back and trace the nerve to the inside.

9. Peel the retinal layer to expose the choroid coat. Then attempt to separate the choroid layer and the sclerotic coat. Can you?
10. When you have finished the preceding dissection, wrap the eye in a paper towel and begin Part II.

Part II

1. Place the lens on a piece of printed material, then look through the lens at an object.
2. Complete the following exercises when you have finished with the lens.

   a. Describe the cornea.
   b. Describe the iris.
   c. Describe the appearance of the retina.
   d. What type of substance did you find in the vitreous humor chamber?
   e. What did you notice when you traced the optic nerve?
   f. What did the lens do to the printed material?
   g. Describe the image you saw upon looking through the lens.
   h. What was the shape of the cow's pupil? Does this have any effect on vision? What is the shape of a human being's pupil?
   i. What did you learn from this dissection?

Demonstrations in Respiration

by George C. Clark
Roton Middle School, Norwalk, Connecticut

During the many years that I have taught units on respiration, I frequently recalled the sophisticated equipment used to make my college Human Physiology course so interesting. The thought often came to mind of making some simple, inexpensive models of this equipment that could be used in secondary schools. I particularly wanted to make a spirometer.

> NOTE: I have seen various homemade models of spirometers described in science magazines, but all have seemed too messy to use or so bulky as to be impractical.

In the past year, I finally developed a simple design for a spirometer (Figs. 1 and 2). It has been used successfully with up to twenty-five students in a forty-five minute period. The effect on the students has been particularly rewarding. Many students have started running and exercising programs to improve their vital capacity; others have begun to explore the difference in vital capacity between smokers and nonsmokers.

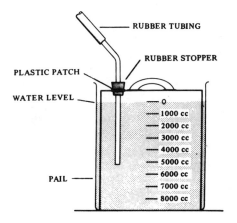

Fig. 1: Economy Spirometer

NOTE: If the pail is 18″ or more deep, the air space is not necessary. The first mark would then be 1000cc.

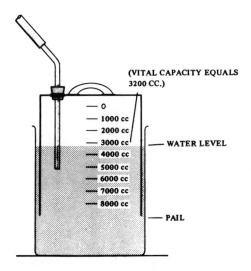

Fig. 2: Spirometer in Use

NOTE: Someone should steady the top, trying not to exert a downward pressure.

BUILDING A SIMPLE SPIROMETER

Materials

To build the spirometer, you will need:

Plastic bell jar

SOURCE: A very satisfactory plastic bell jar may be found in the Montgomery Ward Company's catalog (619 West Chicago Ave., Chicago, Ill. 60607). Advertised as a "rigid acetate bell jar," number 18 W 3120, the jar costs $5.50.

Epoxy glue
Plastic patches
Wood drill with regular bit stock
One-holed rubber stopper
Glass tube
Fine sandpaper
Marking pen and India ink
Rubber tubing

Construction Procedure

The directions are as follows:

1. Reinforce an area of about $2'' \times 2''$ on the top of the plastic bell jar by applying several plastic patches and coating them with a layer of epoxy glue.

   NOTE: I use about four layers of self-adhesive plastic and cover these with epoxy glue.

2. In the center of the reinforced area, drill a one-inch hole with a wood drill.
3. Coat the edges of the hole with epoxy glue to make certain that the layers of plastic are firmly bonded together.
4. After the epoxy is set up (allow 24 hours), to insure a tight fit of the rubber stopper, wrap the stopper in a piece of fine sandpaper, insert all into the hole, and twist it gently.
5. Insert a glass tube in the one-holed rubber stopper as shown in Fig. 1.
6. To calibrate the container, turn it upside down and pour in 1000 cc.'s of water, Mark the side at water level. Now pour in 1000 more cc.'s and mark again. Once the proper distance between marks has been determined, mark the rest of the container accordingly.

7. Then place the container in a bucket of water. If the bucket is not quite as tall as the spirometer, simply fill it to one of the upper marks and make the value of that mark zero, the next, one, then two, etc. The marks should go up to seven.

CAPACITY: Most of my seventh graders had a vital capacity of less than 3500 cc.'s. The adult teachers' capacity ranged from 3000 cc.'s to about 6500 cc.'s with the exception of one which was consistently recorded from 7000 cc.'s to 7300 cc's.

Preparing Mounthpieces

Rubber tubing such as that on Bunsen burners makes a very acceptable mouthpiece. The hose should be washed out well with water before use, or individual glass (flamed at both ends) can be inserted in the tubing. Fifteen hoses will suffice for thirty students, since both ends can be used.

Blowing into the Spirometer

For the greatest accuracy in measuring vital capacity, the student should use the following procedure while blowing into the spirometer (Fig. 2):

1. Take a deep inhalation.
2. Hold your nose.
3. Blow steadily but not hard into the rubber hose (or glass).
4. Pinch the hose when finished to prevent the escape of air from the container.

CAUTION: Since someone occasionally faints during the exercise, students should be sitting down while blowing.

(It is advisable to keep a record of the capacity of each student to provide a means of checking any future improvement.)

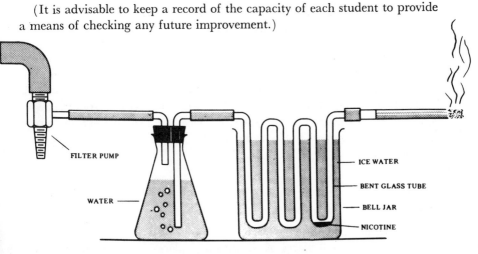

FILTER PUMP

WATER

ICE WATER

BENT GLASS TUBE

BELL JAR

NICOTINE

Fig. 3: "Smoking Machine"

MAKING A SMOKING MACHINE

A device that can be used in conjunction with the spirometer is a "smoking machine" which extracts the tars and nicotine from cigarettes (Fig. 3). Students are very impressed by the machine's work. The most talked about display I ever created in high school teaching was one showing many different brands of cigarettes in the form of empty packs stapled to a piece of poster paper. Mounted next to each brand was a small test tube containing the liquid distillate extracted from that pack by the smoking machine.

Materials and Construction

The cigarette machine that I used for many years is a glass tube with many bends which is immersed in a battery jar full of ice water. To one end a cigarette-holding device is attached. The other end leads to a flask which contains water to collect any tars not condensed in the test tube. The tube from the flask attaches to a source of reduced pressure.

SOURCE: A convenient type of suction device is sold by Welch Scientific Company (1515 Sedgwick St., Chicago, Ill. 60610). It is cataloged as number 5062.

After about six cigarettes have been smoked by the machine, there appears a small build-up of liquid at the bottom of the first bend in the glass tube. To remove this liquid, the rubber tubing is taken off both ends, the tube is tilted and blown into at one end, with the other end inserted in a test tube.

DEMONSTRATING THE EFFECT OF NICOTINE ON THE CILIA

An effective way to tie smoking in with respiration and to show in a dramatic fashion the effect of nicotine on the cilia, is a demonstration using a small section of the gills of a mollusk. Although any mussel or clam would probably work well, I use the Ribbed Mussel, *Modiolus demissus plicatulus*, which is easily collected on most Atlantic beaches. The cilia can be located by opening the mussel and looking for the two gills, found between the mantle and foot.

Procedure

The demonstration procedure is as follows:

- Remove the gills and place them on a wet towel.
- Cut off small pieces of the gills and place each piece in a drop of

salt water on a slide. (Under low power, one should be able to get a very good look at the cilia in action.)
- After each student has found and studied the action of the cilia, add a drop of the nicotine and have students observe the results.

NOTE: For a more quantitative study, the nicotine can be diluted to different strengths and the results recorded.

A Frog on the Moon

by George H. Ratzlaff

Central Junior High School, Hutchinson, Kansas

A student's question—"Would it be possible to grow plants on the moon and produce enough oxygen for people to survive?"—stimulated much discussion among my students, led them to extensive research in reference books, and, finally, to the planning and construction of the photosynthetic gas exchanger shown in Fig. 1.

APPLYING IMAGINATION

The ideas behind this gas exchanger were scientific in nature, but they also revealed the imaginative thoughts of students. In the fantasy of the student designers, the 500 ml. Florence flask was not a flask at all, but a space station on the moon. By the further use of their imaginations, the frog became a moon-based astronaut; the additional equipment, part of a massive lunar oxygen cycle research plant. The lamp, of course, represented the sun.

NOTE: Though a simpler apparatus than the one students designed could be devised to illustrate the oxygen cycle, this rather complicated apparatus may be more effective in rousing student interest.

SETTING UP THE GAS EXCHANGER

One of the first problems encountered in designing the photosynthetic gas exchanger was to decide what type of plant to use. The unicellular algae *Chlorella* was chosen for these reasons: it has a high photosynthetic rate, is easily grown in a liquid medium, and seems to have a tolerance for a wide range of temperatures.

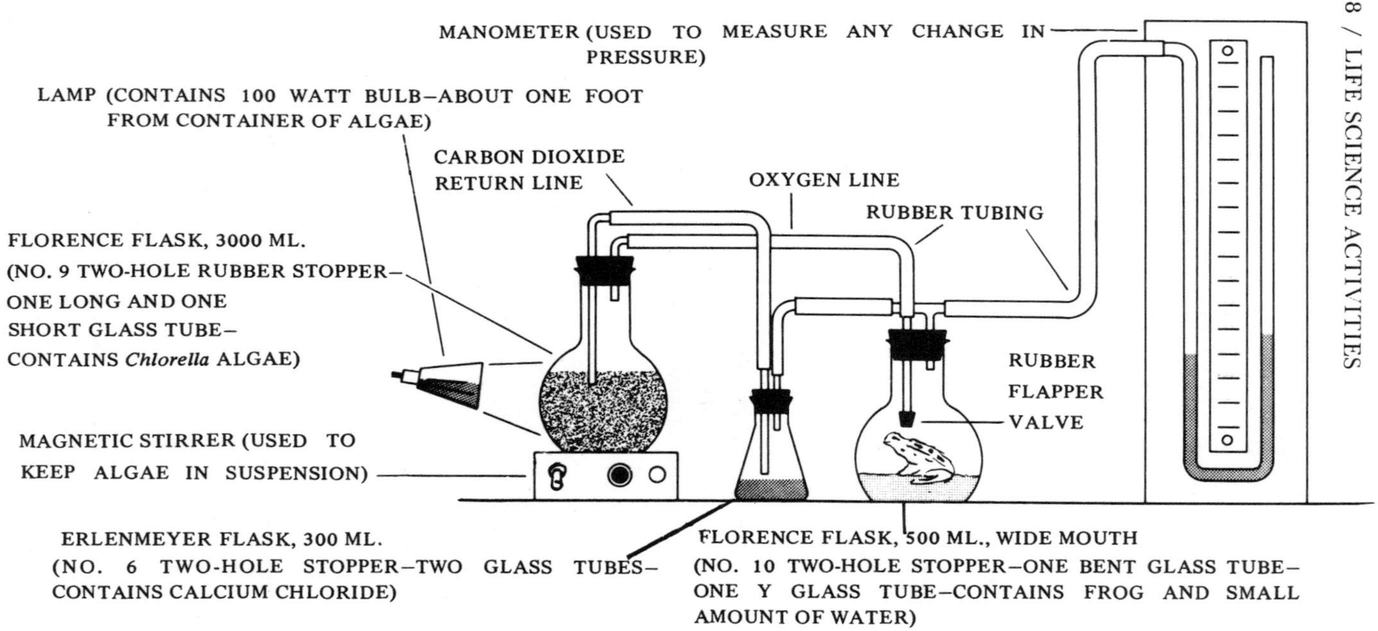

Fig. 1: Equipment Used to Construct the Photosynthetic Gas Exchanger

The steps in assembling the apparatus were as follows:

1. Boiled tap water (2,500 ml.) was put into the 3,000 ml. Florence flask. After the water had cooled and aged for 24 hours, enough *Chlorella* was added to turn the water a dark green.
2. Commercial plant fertilizer was then added to the flask of algae. A two-hole No. 9 rubber stopper, fitted with two glass tubes, was inserted into this flask. To insure one-way movement of air, the longer glass tube was positioned 1 cm. under the water level in the flask.

   STOPPER: If a three-hole rubber stopper were used in the algae container, a thermometer could be inserted into the liquid medium.

3. The short glass tube was connected by rubber tubing to the 500 ml. Florence flask which contained a frog. A rubber flapper valve was attached to the glass tube in the oxygen line to insure one-way air movement.
4. Next, a manometer was attached to the closed system to indicate any pressure increase. To remove any excess water vapor that might pass through the tubes, a 300 ml. Erlenmeyer flask, containing 30 grams of calcium chloride, was included in the return line. This line was then connected to the Florence flask containing the *Chlorella,* thus completing the cycle.
5. A magnetic stirrer was used to keep the *Chlorella* culture in suspension, and a lamp with a 100 watt bulb provided continuous artificial sunlight.

   LIGHT: The lamp should be positioned close to the algae culture, but not close enough to heat the water. A distance of about 50 cm. was found satisfactory.

USING THE APPARATUS

A small, well-fed amphibian or reptile is a good type of animal to enclose in the photosynthetic gas exchanger. The frog, for instance, is an excellent animal to use. Frogs are easy to obtain, can survive for several days without food, and can absorb water through their skin.

We have never attempted to leave a frog in the closed system as long as it could survive without additional food, but we have left them in the sealed gas exchanger for periods up to 12 days. This time seemed sufficient to prove that the apparatus was practical and functioning as theorized.

Life Science for the Underachiever[1]

by C. R. Cronin and L. J. Paulk

Coordinator; Biological Science Supervisor, DISCUS, Board of Public Instruction, Duval County, Jacksonville, Florida

A considerable segment of our school population has been conditioned to failure; many are doomed to eventually drop out of school. The problem of educating these students is primarily one of attitude rather than mental ability. Generally, the disadvantaged underachiever is seldom complimented for his achievement—which is often insignificant compared to that of other students. He expresses himself poorly; someone else always says what he is trying to say before he can say it—and usually better than he can say it.

NOTE: Unknowingly, the teacher in pursuit of academic excellence may force this student into such an intolerable situation that his only means of protecting what little ego he has left is to "turn off" the school and "sit out" his time until he can "drop out."

It was an interest in this underachieving student that motivated the initiation of Project DISCUS, A *D*emonstration of an *I*mproved *S*cience *C*urriculum for *U*nderachieving *S*tudents. Students were selected and randomly placed in experimental or control groups. Teachers were sensitized to the needs of the "underachiever" and introduced to guidelines to be used in directing classroom activities, such as the sample activity presented here. Typical of all activities used in the program, this exercise involves only simple equipment, objects which are familiar to students, and it is geared to lead students to meaningful, low-level abstractions.

SELECTING SUITABLE ACTIVITIES

Some of the guidelines for selecting this sample activity and the others used in the program are that the activity must:

- Lend itself to small groups of students.

1 This article is based on the ongoing project, DISCUS, created for the development of an improved science curriculum for underachieving students. The DISCUS program is currently being tested in 13 schools, where it is being taught by 32 teachers. Present funding for the program is under P.L. 89-10 Title I, and funding for a teacher training program was recently received from the National Science Foundation.

An article describing the pilot study which led into DISCUS appeared in *The Science Teacher*, 35, 8 (Nov. 1968), pp. 38–41.

- Be of measured difficulty so that each student may succeed.
- Relate to the students' common experience.
- Use "concrete objects" in controlled situations.
- Yield data that students can talk about.
- Yield data that can be used to formulate concepts as meaningful abstracts at a level which allows the students to express them successfully.

An Example

The sample activity is taken from the seventh-grade life science materials in the DISCUS program and is currently part of a unit on reproduction and development using the chick embryo. It is first presented as it appears in the teacher's manual, which contains Teacher Directions for all activities and, in some cases, resource sections giving the teacher background materials. Secondly, the activity is shown as it is written up on Student Activity sheets, which are distributed to the students at the teacher's discretion. (Italicized lines and notes have been inserted in both versions to clarify the original materials.)

TEACHER DIRECTION: TEMPERATURE CHANGES AND COLD-BLOODED ANIMALS

Materials for Groups of Three

1. Battery jar (widemouthed, gal. mayonnaise jar)
2. Live minnows or goldfish
3. Thermometer
4. Crushed ice
5. Warm water

As we wait for the development of the nine-day embryo, we will return to our discussion of temperature and the important part it plays in living organisms.

> NOTE: As previously stated, this activity is used during the study of reproduction and development using the chick embryo.

Suggested Statements to be Made to the Class

"We have discussed the importance of heat to a living organism. All animal life can be grouped on the basis of body temperature, one group called warm-blooded and the other, cold-blooded. What is a warm-blooded animal?" (An animal that maintains a constant body temperature.) "What are some examples?" (Man, dogs, cats, etc.) "All of these maintain constant body temperature regardless of their environment."

NOTE: The teacher may point out that man has a constant body temperature which in abnormal conditions, such as a heart operation (or hibernation in bears), can be dropped as much as 20 degrees. This cuts down on oxygen consumption during the operation. (Children may have seen a heart operation performed on television.)

"However, cold-blooded animals change body temperature in relation to their environment. For example, if the environment temperature drops, their body temperature also drops. Cold-blooded animals include: frogs, snakes, lizards, fish, and turtles. As the temperature drops, their body activities slow down. Among these activities is respiration rate. In fish, this rate can be measured by the number of times the gills open and close."

Directions for Conducting the Exercise

The students in each group are to place their goldfish in the jar, which should be half-filled with water, and continue to add ice *very slowly,* lowering the water temperature at the rate of 1 degree per minute until it is near freezing. Care should be taken not to excite the fish since excitement will upset its respiration rate.

Pass out B-47. (This reference is to the Student Activity sheet for the exercise.)

After all groups have collected their data, have them reassemble for a discussion of their results and compilation of the results for the entire class.

AUTHOR'S NOTE: By discussing a compilation of class results, fear of individual error is eliminated. (The discussion may center around a transparency (Fig. 1) which shows both group data and class averages for each temperature tested.)

STUDENT ACTIVITY: TEMPERATURE CHANGES AND COLD-BLOODED ANIMALS

Materials for Groups of Three

1. Battery jar
2. Live goldfish (or minnow)[2]
3. Thermometer
4. Crushed ice
5. Warm water

Procedure

Place the goldfish into a half-filled jar of water. Place a thermometer at

---

[2] If goldfish are not available and local fish are used in this experiment, the fish may die from temperature shock. The aquatic environment changes *very slowly* and animals in this environment are often not adaptable to swift changes in temperature.

CLASS RESULTS						
Degrees F	Fish 1	Fish 2	Fish 3	Fish 4	Fish 5	Average
32^0						
37^0						
42^0						
47^0						
52^0						
57^0						

Fig. 1: Transparency for Class Discussion

one side of the jar so that it can be read without disturbing the fish. What does the thermometer read? Record_____ .

NOTE: Students record their data on a chart like that shown in Fig. 2, which accompanies their activity work sheets.

RESULTS FOR OUR GROUP	Temp. in Degrees	Gill Beats per Min.
Temperature of the water at the start of the experiment		
Lowest temperature obtained after the ice was added		
Lowest temperature raised 5 degrees Fahrenheit		
+ 5 Degrees		
+ 5 Degrees		
+ 5 Degrees		
+ 5 Degrees		

Fig. 2: Student Data Chart

For one minute, count the gill beats and record the number. Add crushed ice very slowly to the water. The ice must be added slowly to reduce the shock factor and avoid exciting the fish. Continue to add ice until the water temperature is reduced to near freezing ($32°$ F).

Read and record the temperature of the water now.

Watch the movement of the gill covering. Count the number of times the covering moves during a one-minute interval. This figure represents the respiration rate. Record the number on your chart.

Slowly add warm water to the jar. Again, try not to excite the fish. Add enough water to raise the temperature of the water five degrees. Allow the fish to adjust to a new temperature at five-degree intervals, counting and recording the respiration rate each time the temperature is raised. Continue adding warm water until the temperature reaches $90°$ F.

Analysis and Interpretation of Data

1. What happens to the respiration rate as the temperature decreases?
2. What happens to the respiration rate as the temperature increases?

3. What do you think happens to the heartbeat as the temperature decreases?
4. Would fish need more food or less food in the winter?
5. Would you be more likely or less likely to be bitten by a snake in the winter? (Snakes are cold-blooded.) Why?
6. Would a frog become more active or less active in cold water?

FOLLOW-UP: This activity may serve as a beginning point for investigations with other animals, such as toads, frogs, or snakes. Students' data may also be used as a basis for additional work with graphs, charts, or diagrams.

WORKING WITH UNDERACHIEVERS

The results of Project DISCUS for 1967–68, which are available on request,[3] seem to indicate:

(1) That preferential treatment of educationally disadvantaged junior high school students in success-oriented science classes does improve their attitudes toward school personnel and toward the school.

(2) That without a hospitable class environment such as that provided in the DISCUS Project, the students' attitudes toward school personnel and toward the school deteriorate: the students literally "drop out" of school until they can legally "drop out."

(3) That involvement in small-group, meaningful laboratory activities in which students generate data, communicate about the data, and use the data in developing concepts does enable educationally disadvantaged underachievers to continue to develop in school.

(4) That even as late as the junior high school years it is possible to rehabilitate educationally disadvantaged underachievers who are potential drop-outs.

---

[3] DISCUS, 1011 Gilmore Street, Jacksonville, Florida 32204.

Bottle Caps, Pop Beads, and Genetics

by Mary Jane Myers

G. L. Hawkins Junior High School, Hattiesburg, Mississippi

Genetics is a logical and well-received unit of study on the eighth grade level. At this age children are eager to learn more about themselves, why they look as they do, why other people possess traits they don't have, and other phases of genetics. Discussion and questions flow endlessly once the subject of genetics is introduced.

I use the following methods in teaching Mendel's Laws of Heredity and the processes of mitosis and meiosis. Their success is corroborated by high school teachers who state that a high percentage of concise knowledge has been retained by students when the subject of genetics is expanded on in the tenth grade biology classes.

> NOTE: As a background to these methods, students should have a basic knowledge of the structure of the cell, of the nucleus as the center of activity for cell division, and of the purpose of duplicate chromosomes.

MITOSIS

Materials

All that is necessary for a visible demonstration are pop beads, Plastix, and a clean chalkboard. If Plastix is unavailable, modeling clay will serve the purpose. Pop beads may be bought at variety stores.

Procedure

1. Draw cell membranes for stage 1 (interphase) and stage 2 (prophase) on the clean board. (Plastix will not stick if chalk dust is present.)
2. Have the beads which represent genes of DNA pulled apart as single beads and placed in a box. Out of these make duplicate "chromosomes" of 2, 3, 4, or 5 beads.
3. With the Plastix, place single beads, similar in color to the groups of beads representing chromosomes in the nucleus of the cell of the stage 1 drawing. Discuss changes which take place in the interphase.
4. Remove the single beads from the stage 1 drawing.
5. Place the prearranged "chromosomes" in the nucleus of the stage 2 prophase drawing. Explain what takes place and add the matching set of "chromosomes."
6. Continue the explanation, using the same cell drawing, of metaphase (erase the nuclear membrane) as the chromosomes are lined up on a chalk-drawn spindle.
7. Continue manipulating the chromosomes as the anaphase is completed. Do not forget to amend the cell membrane to show that division has started.
8. For telephase go back to the original cell in step 1 and draw another cell touching it to show that the old cell no longer exists and that two cells have been produced. Place the single beads back in the nucleus to show the chromatin ready to start the cycle over.

Now, have the students draw and manipulate the beads. There should be enough beads so that several pairs of students can work at the same time. This exercise may be followed with a discussion of DNA and its role in holding the "master plan" for the organism's development.

MEIOSIS

To visually demonstrate meiosis, perform the following steps:

1. Show the first meiotic division using the beads to form two pairs of unlike "chromosomes" and pre-drawn cell membranes.
2. Continue with the second meiotic division, noting that there is no replication. These cells are ready to contribute half of the chromosome count to form a new organism. (Note that male gametes' sperm may be of equal size but for the egg unequal division may occur (as in humans) so that a large egg and small polar body are produced in the first meiotic division and a small polar body at the end of the second division. The first polar body may also divide in half, forming two small polar bodies—or a total of three polar bodies—all of which die.)

Again, have students manipulate the beads.

MENDEL'S LAWS OF HEREDITY

The history of Mendel's work logically follows this introduction to mitosis and meiosis. To illustrate Mendel's Laws, use drawings of tall and short peas on the poster board. The drawings of the short peas should be small enough to be hidden under the drawings of the long peas (Fig. 1). There should be at least eight drawings of each. Several sets will give students the opportunity to perform the investigation at the same time.

1. Using the Plastix, place two tall peas on top of each other and two short peas on top of each other up high on the chalkboard. These represent pure individuals.
2. Now cross the pure peas and, with the pictures, show the hybrid offspring looking like the dominant (T tall) but having the recessive trait (t short) hidden. Do this by placing the picture of a short pea behind each tall picture.
3. With the remaining pictures, show the next generation of one TT pure tall, two Tt tall hybrids with a short behind a tall, and one tt pure short.

NOTE: This presentation is the conventional one, but I have given the sets of pictures, Plastix, and an explanation of the laws to students, letting them develop their own investigation and then explain their results to the class. I prefer this method of problem solving for the student.

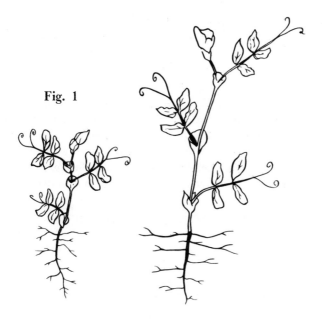

Fig. 1

A CONCLUDING ACTIVITY

As a concluding activity use bottle caps of different kinds to represent DNA or genes. Have students arrange these caps, each standing for a characteristic of their "creation." Students will describe the "individual" they have matched and, as usual, some are green-eyed dragons, others beautifully-formed models, and so on. This exercise is fun for students and provides an opportunity for you to listen for "fuzzy" concepts which need clarifying.

High School Study
of Air Pollution

by William E. Porter

Mayfield High School, Las Cruces, New Mexico

"Air: The invisible, odorless, and tasteless mixture of gases which surrounds the earth."[1] Even in 1943, Webster's definition of air was not entirely accurate. Now it is less so. For millions of people, the definition of

---

[1] *Webster's Collegiate Dictionary*, 5th ed. Springfield, Mass.: G. & C. Merriam Co., Publishers, 1943.

air might read, "The murky, stinking, brassy-tasting, gaseous sewer of industrial man." Yet in spite of the growing dangers from air pollution and the fact that atmospheric studies are easily adapted to use at the secondary school level, most high school biology and chemistry textbooks and lab manuals ignore the problem of air pollution.

FOCUS: Following are procedures for using miniature biotic communities to study various air pollutants and several methods of introducing measurable variables within these communities. Such an investigation will give students firsthand awareness of the effects of air pollution and may lead them to more active concern with this problem.

CREATING STUDY COMMUNITIES

The miniature biotic community—the terrarium—has been a classroom feature for more than 50 years. One of the easiest terraria to build consists of a pickle jar, mosses, ferns, snails, and a tight seal (Fig. 1). If all goes well, a balance should be established in the jar within several weeks. For short-term studies, a dozen or more identical terraria should be made. Half of the terraria can be used as controls, and the other half can be inoculated with pollutants. It is best to use varying amounts of a single pollutant for the study, thus demonstrating the toxicity level of the pollutant.

Studying the long-term effects of pollution is more difficult. A dozen terraria can be inoculated with identical amounts of the pollutant. Twenty-four hours after inoculation, the organisms in one of the jars should be examined for absorption of the pollutant, using such methods as visual observation, sensitivity plates, radioactive isotopes, chromatography, or, in the case of certain compounds containing phosphorus, examination under a "black lamp"—after homogenizing the organism in a blender.

Each time the jars are inoculated, another jar should be sacrificed for examination. Certain contaminates will decompose, some will be absorbed at a non-toxic level, and others will build up in plant and animal life until their death ensues.

VARIATIONS: The degree of sophistication—hence the degree of scientific accuracy—can be varied to fit the classroom situation, as further explained in the following procedures.

Students should be encouraged to make their own lists of the inaccuracies inherent in this investigation, including:

- Varying jar sizes
- Varying plant-animal balance (Any biotic community is cyclic in nature, as is any species within that biotic community)
- Varied susceptibility of plants and animals to poisons

- Inaccuracies in measuring the pollutants with the average laboratory instrumentation
- Varying potency of pollutants

The students themselves may suggest the various pollutants they will study. Some, such as DDT, lindane, chlordane, and other pesticides are, unfortunately, readily obtainable at any 5 & 10, drug, seed, or food store. Others, such as sulfur dioxide and carbon monoxide, can be manufactured in the lab.

CAUTION: In any case, all pollutants should be used with extreme care—preferably under a hood.

INVESTIGATION PROCEDURES

Either of the two following procedures can be used by students in individual or small group studies of air pollution effects. The purpose of Procedure B is to allow the introduction of pollutants while minimizing the chance of also introducing undesirable variables. Thus the pollutant can be kept "pure," and the amount of the pollutant can be more accurately measured.

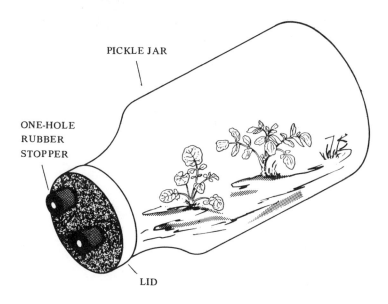

PICKLE JAR

ONE-HOLE RUBBER STOPPER

LID

Procedure A (Fig. 1)

(1) Drill two holes in the top of a pickle jar.
(2) Place soil, plants and a small animal or two in the jar.

NOTE: Small means something on the order of snails. Mice are much too large.

(3) Tightly screw on the lid, then put a stopper in each hole.

(4) Place the jar in a warm, light area.

(5) Observe the life in the jar regularly over the next four weeks. If plants and animals are thriving at the end of that time, you can safely assume that a balance has been achieved in the miniature community. *Do not open the jar lids.*

(6) Introduce pollutants by removing the stoppers and squirting the desired amounts of chemicals into one of the holes. (When a substance is sprayed in one hole, displaced air will escape through the second hole.)

(7) Replace stoppers.

(8) Await results.

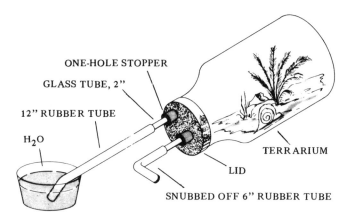

ONE-HOLE STOPPER

GLASS TUBE, 2"

12" RUBBER TUBE

H₂O

TERRARIUM

LID

SNUBBED OFF 6" RUBBER TUBE

Procedure B (Fig. 2)

(1) Drill two holes in the top of the pickle jar.

(2) Place soil, plants, and a small animal or two in the jar.

(3) Tightly screw on the lid.

(4) Assemble two one-hole rubber stoppers as follows: Slide a 2-inch glass tube into each of the stoppers. Then slide one 12-inch piece of rubber hose over one piece of glass tubing, and one 6-inch piece of hose over the other glass tubing. Snub off and clamp the 6-inch hose. Stopper the jar lid holes with the hose assemblies.

(5) Anchor the free end of the longer rubber hose in a pneumatic trough—or any other convenient body of water. Be sure that the water level remains above the end of the hose.

(6) Allow the terrarium a month to establish itself.

(7) Introduce the desired pollutant by hypodermic. Inoculate the jar directly through the snubbed off rubber hose.

NOTE: A disposable hypodermic is especially valuable for this purpose. Studies have shown that certain substances such as DDT cannot be successfully cleaned from the apparatus.

(8) Await results.

Auxiliary Problems

More able students might be assigned one of the following problems related to this investigation:

- Compute the air volume of each jar while it is still empty.
- Compute the amount of pollutant in the terrarium atmosphere. (This is often expressed in parts per million.)
- Determine the amount of pollutant that constitutes a lethal dose.
- Compare the lethal level of your pollutant with world production figures. At the present production levels, how many years would it take for pollution from the chemical to destroy life on earth? (Keep in mind that most chemicals eventually decompose and that living organisms show remarkable recuperative powers.)
- Determine the effect of multiple pollution upon a biotic community. (*Example:* Chlordane, which becomes more lethal when a small amount of pyrethrin is added.)
- Which pollutants show a cumulative effect? Which can be detected in the tissue of one plant or animal and not in another?
- Using answers to the preceding problem, does the absorption of pollutants take place over a long period of time or is it rapid? Does it vary by specie? Graph your answer.
- Using the same basic methods used in studying effects of pollution in the terrarium, study the effect of pollution on a balanced aquarium.

FOLLOW-UP ACTIVITIES

Atmospheric studies are in their infancy and few "answers" are known. Yet legislative action depends upon concrete scientific observations. Those students who do a particularly good job in this investigation of the effects of air pollution on living things should be encouraged to share their results with their legislators. Students can also report their findings in the local newspaper and discuss results with their parents.

NOTE: Above all, this investigation should demonstrate that science is not composed of vague spectral figures in a sterile lab. It should show that science is a dynamic way of life in which all should participate.

An Inductive Approach to the Compound Light Microscope

by Donald C. Orlich

Washington State University, Pullman, Washington

Biology and general science students are usually introduced to the compound microscope through a general discussion or lecture on nomenclature, microscope care, proper use of focusing knobs, lens systems, and the like. They are then given a microscope, a set of slides, cover slips, and other materials needed to complete observation exercises, and are expected to prepare suitable drawings for the teacher's examination.

> **NOTE: Students are seldom aware that the objects they view are inverted, upside down, or reversed—despite knowledge that movement of the slide causes a reverse action. Further, they are unaware that the focal area is in a plane and that by continual focusing, new planes come into view.**

This report describes an exercise used to give students a better understanding of the compound microscope than they usually acquire through traditional means of presentation. Using an inductive approach, it allows students to make "discoveries" and generalizations about the microscope for themselves. The materials involved are simple and can easily be permanently mounted for classroom use.

EXPLORING THE COMPOUND LIGHT MICROSCOPE

Objectives

The purpose of the exercise is to allow students to arrive inductively at the following three generalizations:

1. Objects appear inverted and reversed left to right.
2. The field of observation is inversely related to the power of the lens being used. As the magnifying power of the lens increases, the area of the observed field decreases.
3. Materials can be viewed as three-dimensional objects and are arranged on distinct planes.

> **USE: The exercise is presented here as it was developed and used for a class of teacher aides, however, it is readily adaptable for use with high school students.**

Part 1

For the first phase of the exercise—to help students realize the inversion of objects under the microscope and their reversal left to right—several words and other symbols were typed on sheets of cellophane paper, using carbon paper ribbon to make a dark impression. Initially, one line of typed material was mounted on a poster board slide having a quarter-inch slit to expose the typed line (Fig. 1).

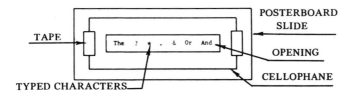

Fig. 1: Slide used to determine field area of magnification and inversion of objects.

Students were asked to observe the line of characters, especially the question mark, and to draw exactly what they observed under low power, medium power, and high power. When all students had completed their drawings, they were asked to state generalizations concerning what they had observed.

Sample results: Interestingly enough, during the period several students observed that the object being viewed was upside down. However, these students proceeded to reorient the slide on the microscope stage to give them a "corrected" image! Other students drew the figures as they appeared through the eyepiece, i.e., inverted. When asked to make generalizations regarding this phenomenon, all agreed that the objects had been reversed or upside down.

One participant who had recently completed a college biology course was astounded to realize that she had never made this observation in a full quarter of biology lab work. She stated that the slides which she had used were either stained or unstained and unprepared but that at no time had she realized inversion took place, and that no one had ever mentioned this in class—including the instructor.

Part 2

The second part of the exercise seeking generalizations relating field size to the magnifying power of the lens, was difficult for many students to comprehend immediately. However, on repeated observation, without the instructor telling them what they should observe but with leading questions, those who had difficulty were able to state that "you cannot 'see' all of the letter under the highest power that you can see under the lowest power."

Part 3

The third objective—to have students observe that the field is arranged in planes—was achieved by using overlapping pieces of cellophane with typed-on letters and other symbols. The letters on one sheet were typed with a red ribbon, those on the other with a black ribbon, so that each plane of focus would be observable even though the planes overlapped (Fig. 2).

Fig. 2: Side view of slide illustrating two viewing planes.

NOTE: While students can obviously be "told" about these phenomena, telling students is not as meaningful as helping them to make the "discoveries" themselves using an inductive method similar to that described here.

Plant Activities with Lemnaceae, or Duckweed

by Richard Allan Digon
Lincoln Junior High School, Ferndale, Michigan

Lemnaceae, or duckweeds, are ideal for use as experimental plants in activities designed to help beginning biology students discover some of the growth characteristics of a specific plant. They are seed plants which are tiny, very inexpensive, rapid in growth, and structurally simple.

Duckweed can be grown in aseptic culture, simplifying work with organic compounds. Reproduction is usually vegetative, so that genetic variability can be eliminated by using a single colony for all experiments. Controlled conditions of temperature, light, and nutrition are far easier to maintain than for most other angiosperms.

OBTAINING DUCKWEED

During the summer months, these plants can be obtained in ponds, streams, rivers, and lakes. In some lakes they form a green carpet so thick that the water beneath cannot be seen. The teacher should be able to obtain large quantities of the plants at no cost. The plants can be grown successfully in samples of water brought from the sources of the duckweed or in city tap water which has been allowed to stand for a day.

ANATOMY: Since plants are usually observed in a green mass, individual plants should be isolated for introductory study. The teacher and students should examine Lemnaceae's shape, size, color, and other physical characteristics. (Figs. 1 and 2.)

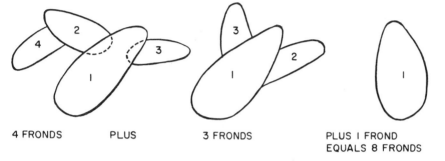

4 FRONDS   PLUS   3 FRONDS   PLUS I FROND
                                   EQUALS 8 FRONDS

Fig. 1: A Top View of Duckweed Plants. Number 1 represents a "mother" frond and numbers 2, 3, and 4 represent "daughter" fronds.

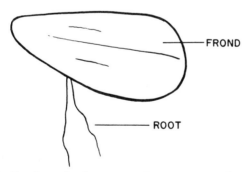

Fig. 2: Duckweed plants are flat, more or less oval in outline, and leaflike. They have a threadlike root.

CULTURING CONDITIONS

For maximum utilization of sunlight, the duckweed should be placed in windows exposed to the south and east. When the supply of sunlight is inadequate, a 75-watt light bulb can be used to provide satisfactory light. Experimentation indicates that duckweed grows best at a water temperature of 20 to 30 degrees Centigrade.

Since duckweed experimentation can be carried out in aseptic culture, some teachers may wish to use either a commercial plant food or a solution such as the following one.

Solution

10 liters redistilled water
23.3 g. KNO_3
5 g. K_2HPO_4
5 g. $MgSO_4 \cdot 7H_2O$
5 g.   NaCl
16.7 g. $CaSO_4 \cdot 2H_2O$
trace $FeCl_3$

The above solution or any other used can be diluted to fit the needs of the experimenter.

CONTAINER: It is convenient to keep the duckweed culture in a large aquarium. Duckweed from different sources can be isolated in smaller containers for studying genetic variations of different populations. Students may use any container that will hold water for individual experiments.

PLANT GROWTH EXERCISES

Following are three of the activities with *Lemnaceae* that I have used with my students. These will suggest many similar exercises to the investigative-minded teacher.

Problem #1: What does a duckweed plant look like?

Materials: To perform this exercise, students will need:

Paper and pencil
Centimeter ruler
Magnification lens (6 × 8 times)
Binocular microscope
Flat dishes or Petri dishes
Lemnaceae

Procedure: The procedure for the exercise is as follows:

1. Obtain 10 duckweed plants and some duckweed water.
2. Make a list of all of the structural characteristics that you can observe in the duckweed plant.
3. Answer these questions: (1) Can you write a general description which would apply to the duckweed plant? (2) Does a duckweed plant have roots? Stems? Leaves? Flowers?

4. After you have made all of the visual observations possible, look up *Duckweed* or *Lemna* in a botany book to help you answer the questions asked in Step 3.

Problem #2: How does the amount of light received by a plant affect its growth?

Materials: For this exercise, students will require 8 jars or beakers, paper and pencil, *Lemnaceae,* and duckweed water.

Procedure: The students should follow this procedure:

1. Place 25 duckweed plants and some duckweed water into each of the 8 jars.
2. Put 2 of the jars in a dark closet, and remove them only for observations.
3. Place 2 jars in a bright room, but not in direct sunlight.
4. Place 4 of the jars in a situation where they will receive bright sunlight most of the day.
5. Each evening, put 2 of the jars in Step 4 under a 75-watt light bulb.
6. Observe the results each day and record the number of duckweed plants in each situation.

   NOTE: For their record-keeping, students can use a simple chart, such as that shown in Fig. 3. They can also make graphs to illustrate their data.

DAYS	DIRECT SUN	DIRECT SUN & LIGHT BULB	BRIGHT ROOM	DARK CLOSET
1	25	25	25	25
3				
5				
7				

Fig. 3

Problem #3: Does *Lemnaceae* require anything other than pure water for its growth?

Materials: Students will need the following materials to conduct this exercise.

2 plastic gallon jugs with screw-on tops
Paper and pencil
Liquid No. 1 (distilled water)
Liquid No. 2, 1 gallon of distilled water, and:

$$\left\{\begin{array}{l}\text{2 tsp. baking powder, 1 containing a phosphate}\\\text{1 tsp. sodium nitrate}\\\text{1 tsp. Epsom salts}\\\text{¼ tsp. household ammonia}\end{array}\right.$$

Lemnaceae

Procedure: The procedure is as follows:

1. Prepare liquid No. 2: mix the chemicals in one gallon of distilled water. (Make certain that all of the chemicals are dissolved.) Label the container.
2. Fill one jug with liquid No. 1 (distilled water) and place 25 duckweed plants in this jug. Place the jug in the sunlight.
3. Fill the second jug with liquid No. 2 and put 25 duckweed plants in this jug. Place this jug in the sunlight, too.
4. Observe and record the results over a period of seven days. Make a graph or a chart to help organize the information that you obtain about the number of plants observed each day in each of the two situations.
5. When you have completed the exercise, answer these questions: (1) In which liquid did the duckweed grow best? *(Give evidence to support your answer.)* (2) Explain what liquid No. 1 lacked.

Additional Exercises

Students may conduct many other exercises with *Lemnaceae,* in addition to those described here. Some further problems that I have had my students investigate are:

* Does the color of light that a plant receives have an effect on its growth?
* Does duckweed give off oxygen?
* Do green plants absorb carbon dioxide in the presence of light?
* How fast does duckweed multiply under room conditions?
* Will duckweed multiply faster when the average temperature is cooler than the normal temperature?
* Will duckweed that has been placed in a freezer for varying lengths of time survive?

Observation: A Key to Outdoor Science

by Ray Deur

Western Michigan University, Kalamazoo, Michigan

Since it is the purpose of the Outdoor Science and other related courses to make one more aware of his environment, giving the student a list of suggested activities to perform or observe may prove helpful.

> **NOTE: This procedure can be used at any grade level and correlated with many other subjects besides the natural sciences.**

SELECT AN AREA

To begin the study, each student should select an area which is easily accessible—back yard, city block, vacant lot, etc. When the area has been selected, a map should be drawn showing the major features—roads, buildings, trees, streams, etc. Accurate measurements should be made so that later discoveries may be added.

After completing the preliminary surveys, one should make periodic visits throughout the school year to observe the changes that take place in each season—all the time keeping accurate records of all observations and experiments. Very often it is advisable to invite a second person who may see things previously missed.

ABIOTIC FACTORS

Since the abiotic factors have an important influence on the environment, it's important to record as many factors as possible. The temperature of the air, ground surface, subsurface, water, sidewalk, shaded area, and others should be taken on each trip, recorded, and later placed on a line graph from which some interesting observations and conclusions may be made. Other factors for study are the humidity, wind direction, wind speed, date, time of day, length of shadows, light intensity, soil type along with its acidity and moisture, and the nature of the subcell. A data worksheet for the abiotic factors, as shown in Fig. 1, may be helpful.

CLASSIFY ORGANISMS

During the early visits to the area, it is important to classify as many of the organisms as possible. Many simple keys are available for most organisms. Some specimens may be brought into the classroom for display, observation and further study. Just as changes take place in the abiotic factors, so one will find similar changes in the biotic factors. Flowers and leaves will show development; leaves will turn color and later drop; activity of ants will change with the temperature; organisms will prepare for the winter; and many other activities will take place. All of these should be accurately recorded.

Name_____

Abiotic Data Sheet

Date_____ Time_____ Place _____

Weather: Clouds_____ Sky coverage _____

Precipitation _____Pressure _____ Humidity _____

Light intensity _____Length of shadow _____

Wind speed _____Wind direction _____

Wind direction in secluded areas_____

Temperature: Moving air 1 meter from the ground in the sun_____shade _____

Still air 1 meter from the ground in the sun _____ shade _____

Air 3 inches from the ground in the sun_____ shade _____

Bare ground surface _____grassy ground surface _____ sidewalk _____

Eight inches under the ground _____snow if present_____

Water surface _____ bottom of stream or puddle _____ different

depths of river or lake if present _____ speed of flowing water _____

Soil: Type _____ Moisture _____ Acidity _____Depth of top soil _____

Type of subsoil _____ Amount of humus in the top soil _____

Erosion present_____

Land topography_____

Any other factors: _____

Fig. 1

SUGGESTED ACTIVITIES

Following is a list of suggested activities. Some are very simple while others become quite complex and may take a great deal of time. All involve some constructive activity with possible interpretation of some scientific concept or principle.

1. Observe any sign of human activity. How has it affected the area?
2. Look for special adaptations of certain organisms. How do they help the organism to survive?
3. Find an organism with a high natality rate. Count the number of young. How many survive? What ecological relationship do they have to each other?
4. Locate microhabitats in the area. List the organisms found there.

What are the abiotic factors which help it to be a small habitat? What are the limiting factors?

5. If you have different facing slopes, compare the organisms found on each.
6. Find as many ecological relationships as you can and explain each relationship.
7. Trace the energy flow through your ecosystem.
8. List the pioneer plants in the area.
9. Check the wind direction in different parts of the area. What causes these variations? How does it affect the organisms living there?
10. Draw a food web of the area.
11. Dig up some legumes. Locate the nodules and prepare a stained side of a crushed nodule.
12. Take periodic photographs of the area always from the same spot in order to show the changes taking place.
13. Make sketches of a certain area. (An art student may wish to make some colored reproductions in oil or water colors.)
14. Make a collection of as many of the organisms you may desire.
15. Make a count of different species to find the population density.
16. Cut the midrib of certain leaves and observe what happens over a period of time. Compare with normal leaf.
17. Count the leaves on a certain twig and record color changes and final shedding of the leaves. Do this on different species of trees for comparison.
18. Observe the variation in leaves on a certain twig. Make actual measurements of the petiole, width and length of leaf, number of lobes, and number of teeth per inch in the margin of the leaf.
19. Observe the rate of growth of grass in a shaded area as compared with bright sunlight.
20. Cover some grass with a board, cloth, or paper and observe what happens over a period of time. What animal life appears?
21. Try some weed killers on certain plants and keep accurate records on the results.
22. Observe the activity of ants at different temperatures.
23. Observe the number of earthworms per square foot six inches deep. Do this every six inches down to a depth of eighteen inches for a comparison.
24. Bury a fruit jar level with the surface of the soil. Record the animals caught in this trap. Check regularly.
25. Set out some food caches and observe what happens. Try different types of food such as peanut butter, jam, bread, or honey. Bury some food just underneath the surface.
26. Dig up plants and compare the length of the roots of the same species and different species.

27. Measure the speed of the flow of water in a stream at different times. Compare the temperature with that of the air and soil.

28. Remove a circular strip of bark from some undesirable sapling and observe what happens.

These are just a few of the activities. Students soon will be experimenting and observing on their own and will be pleasantly surprised by all the activities going on in the area. The world will be at their doorstep. It just takes looking.

The Dandelion—A Gold Mine for Outdoor Science

by Ray Deur

Western Michigan University, Kalamazoo, Michigan

A good subject for an ecological study is the common dandelion (*Taraxacum officinale*). Although considered by most a pestilential weed, to the outdoor science teacher, the plant may be a gold mine. By using this plant, one may illustrate many of the principles and concepts commonly taught in biology and outdoor science classes.

With a little curiosity, some initiative, and close observation, many new techniques will be discovered as the study of the plant progresses. The activity can be adapted to a number of grade levels, and can be conducted at any time of the year—even in winter.

Here are a few ideas which you can use in the study of the dandelion.

OBSERVATION

Students may be sent to the school lawn (or other designated area) to locate a dandelion plant. (At grade levels where it might be useful, special recognition can be given to students who find a plant with buds, flower, and seeds.) During an allotted period of time, each student should study the plant before removing it from the soil. He can either list all of the observations he can make, or write down a series of questions about the plant. These help develop curiosity and the power of observation.

NOTE: The questions and observations made by the students can be assimilated, compiled and organized into a laboratory worksheet which will help the student make more accurate observations. You may, if you want, help in these observations by giving the students a guidesheet such as the one shown in Fig. 1.

Guide Sheet for Observations on the Dandelion

Find a dandelion plant in some area (school lawn, home yard, vacant lot). If possible locate a plant with buds, flowers, and seeds. Describe the abiotic factors: soil .... moisture .... light .... temperature of soil .... hardness of soil .... shade .... other vegetation .... Sketch the arrangement of the leaves. Make a survey of the animals found under the leaves. Record the names and numbers. What relationship does this illustrate? How do they help each other?

Leaves: Number on plant .... Where is the longest leaf? .... Why? .... Are there any dead leaves? .... If so, why are they dead? .... How do they help the plant? .... Are there any signs of disease on the leaf? .... Pull off each leaf from the plant and arrange in order of size. Measure each leaf and record. Later transfer this information to a graph. Are any two leaves alike? .... Compare the leaves with another dandelion plant.

Stem: How long is the stem? .... What are the advantages of this type of stem? ....

Root: Dig up as much as possible. How long is it? .... Are there any secondary roots? .... If so, how many? ....

Cut the root transversely and observe the internal parts. Sketch and label. Touch it to your tongue. What is the taste? .... Are all the roots the same length? .... If not, why not? ....

Flower: Which has the longest stem—the bud, the flower, or the fruit? .... Why the difference in lengths? .... Why is the stem hollow? .... What oozes out of the stem? .... Touch it. What do you notice? .... How many flowers in one head? .... Use hand lens and look at one flower. Sketch and label. How is the flower pollinated? ....

Seeds: How many seeds in one head? .... How are they scattered? .... Sketch a single seed. Test the viability of all the seeds in one head by using a rag doll tester.

In what environments are dandelions most numerous? Use the density formula $D = \frac{N}{S}$ Explain your results. Which type of weed killer works best on the dandelion? .... Prepare some dandelion greens. Make a whistle from a dandelion stem.

Summary: List all the adaptations of the dandelion which help it survive all the punishment it takes. List as many principles as you can that are illustrated in your study of the dandelion. Does the plant grow better in a man-made community than in a natural community? ....

Fig. 1

POPULATION DENSITY STUDIES

The students may mark off an area, measuring and counting the number of dandelions in the area; density is determined by:

$$\text{density} = \frac{\text{number}}{\text{space}}$$

This experiment should be conducted in many different types of environments, such as shaded areas, vacant lots, woods, roadsides, home lawns, clay soils, and sandy soils. From the varying results, many interesting comparisons can be made and definite conclusions drawn.

PHOTOSYNTHESIS

For teaching the process of photosynthesis, the dandelion leaf demonstrates many adaptations for the maximum use of sunlight:

- The rosette arrangement of the leaves, with the longer leaves on the bottom, along with the wedged shape of each leaf, assures exposure of the light to the leaves.
- The arrangement of the leaves also helps the plant to compete with other plants and to provide a shelter for many invertebrates who in turn help to fertilize and aerate the soil near the root of the plant, thus resulting in a mutualistic relationship.
- Even when a leaf dies for lack of sunlight, the dead leaf serves the plant as a mulching agent, providing moisture and fertilizer near the plant.

NOTE: By removing the leaves from a plant, or comparing leaves of different dandelion plants, you can show the law of variation. And, too, graphical results may be obtained by measuring the length and width of each leaf and transferring the results to a chart. Plants will also vary in the number of leaves per plant.

ROOT STUDIES

The long, fleshy tap root gives the plant good anchorage, an abundant supply of stored food, and another form of reproduction. You may demonstrate the plant's adaptation to different environmental conditions through the length of the roots. Dig roots from many different areas and then attempt to explain the cause of the variation. By cutting the roots transversely and longitudinally, some studies of root structure can be made.

NOTE: An interesting experiment can be performed by cutting a root into one-inch pieces and planting each piece in a flower pot, and observing how many sections

will produce a new plant. The demonstration will help to prove that cutting a plant below the surface of the ground will not kill the plant.

REPRODUCTIVE SYSTEM

The plant's reproductive system offers many interesting observations and experiments. If you have a plant with buds, flowers, and seeds, you will observe the variation in length of each one of these reproductive parts and have the class attempt to explain the difference in length with respect to the function of each:

- The bud stem is short for protection.
- The flower stem is a little longer in order to elevate the flower so that insects will see it and help in pollination.
- The seed stem is longest, in order that the seeds will be exposed to the wind.

NOTE: The growth of the stalk from the bud stage to the seed stage may be observed by placing marks 1 mm. apart along the bud stem and by then recording at intervals the location of the growth.

Since the dandelion has a composite flower, a count of the number of ray flowers in a head and a comparison with the number of seeds in a head on the same plant may be taken. With the removal of the ray flowers, and with the use of a hand lens, the main parts of a complete flower may be identified.

By using a rag doll tester, you can discover the percentage of viability of the seeds from a single head of the dandelion. Because the percentage of germination is rather surprising, this experiment should be done by several members of the class in order to establish an average.

NOTE: You can also store the seeds for a year in order to find out whether dormancy affects the viability of the seeds.

Testing for Water Pollution

by Richard Carnes

John F. Kennedy Florence Junior High School,
Florence, Massachusetts

Perhaps the most difficult task of being a faculty advisor to a junior high school science club is finding a project which appeals to students who possess highly diversified interests and abilities. One project that our club happened upon led to such enthusiasm and excitement that it is now occupying the time of a third generation of club members. The project could easily be adapted to nearly any biology class to teach practical and meaningful testing procedures.

OBJECTIVE

The purpose of the testing project is to determine the extent of water pollution caused by our community. Investigation showed that the Massachusetts Water Resources Commission, Division of Water Pollution Control, tests the degree of pollution in the following areas: dissolved oxygen, sludge deposits, color and turbidity, coliform bacteria, taste and odor, acidity, temperature increase, chemical constituents, and radioactivity. Other states and the federal government have established similar tests for determining pollution and water usage.

RESEARCH PREPARATION

Members of the science club contacted several federal and state government departments and other organizations to familiarize themselves with the standards of water testing. The United States Department of Public Health, the Fish and Game Service, and the interstate waterway agencies were most helpful. Local sources of information included watershed councils, municipal governments, nearby colleges, and the League of Women Voters. By the time the students started their testing program, they were well versed in both the scientific and legal aspects of water standards.

Because of the club's limited funds, it was decided to limit the testing to temperature and coliform bacteria counts. However, the testing could be expanded to include more criteria where the equipment is available.

Bacterium coli: First isolated by Escherich from the feces of a patient in 1884, Bacterium coli was subsequently found as a normal inhabitant of the human intestinal tract occurring regularly in the excreta of man and many other mammals. The U.S. Department of Health recognizes the presence of this form of bacteria as an accurate indicator of the extent of sewage polluting a body of water (Fig. 1).

TESTING SITES

One large river and a smaller stream are located within our testing area. The Connecticut River forms the eastern boundary of our test city, and the smaller stream, the Mill River, runs through the center of town. The testing involved taking bacteria counts and temperature readings in both

Above   Below
Northampton   Northampton

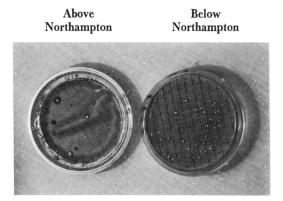

Fig. 1: The coliform bacteria colonies appear as shiny, metallic-looking circles. (Shown here are typical results from 25 ml. samples taken above and below Northampton, Massachusetts, on the Connecticut River.)

rivers where they enter the community and again at the town line where they exit. An important consideration in our particular study was that there are no other large communities situated on either river in the area where the tests were conducted.

APPARATUS

The equipment needed for testing for the coliform bacteria is relatively expensive (Fig. 2). Ours was purchased from the Millipore Filter Corporation (P.O. Box F, Bedford, Mass. 01730). A sanitarian's kit and necessary materials for six months of testing cost about $150. This equipment consists of a stainless steel syringe and graduated sampling cup, sterile sampling tubes, bacteria filters and monitors, and ampouled nutrient medium. An

Fig. 2: Pieces of Testing Equipment

incubator is also needed but is not included in the $150 price named because it was already available as part of our school's equipment, as were the thermometers and filter paper.

The membrane through which the water is filtered is 150 ± 10 microns thick and contains capillary pores .45 ± .02 microns in diameter—small enough to prevent the passage of bacterial organisms. Individual organisms trapped on the filter develop into distinctive, flat, smooth, round, and glistening colonies after the introduction of the medium and incubation at 35 C° for 18 hours. The medium is a differential type which prohibits the growth of most noncoliform bacteria. A grid on the monitors facilitates the counting of the colonies, which can be done with a 5X or 10X hand lens.

CONDUCTING THE TESTS

The U.S. Public Health Service specifies that the standard sample of water to be tested should not be less than 50 milliliters. In our testing, which started rather late in the spring, three samples of 50 ml., 100 ml., and 200 ml. were taken at each testing location. It was soon found that these samples were much too large as they resulted in confluent growths of bacteria on the monitors. Indeed, as the summer progressed we found smaller and smaller samples of water were necessary to obtain colonies few enough to be countable. During the last of August and the first weeks of September, it was necessary to test samples as small as 1 ml.

NOTE: To facilitate pumping the water through the filter, it is advisable to dilute samples less than 25 ml. with distilled water.

We also found it necessary to filter the water with standard filter paper before pumping into the monitor because silt suspended in the water would clog the syringe, block the capillary pores, and make counting nearly impossible (Fig. 3). The filter paper should be sterile to avoid contamination. It is also advisable to take different amounts of water during each test so that at least one of the samples will result in an easily counted number of colonies. In most cases some extrapolation is necessary as it is the common practice to report the results in terms of colonies per 100 ml. of water.

NOTE: More detailed instructions for this method of water testing can be found in the 11th edition of *Standard Methods for the Examination of Water and Waste-Water*, published jointly by the American Water Works Association, the American Public Health Association, and the Water Pollution Control Federation. The Millipore Corp. publication, ADM—10, "Microbiological Analysis of Water and Milk," gives detailed instructions on the use of their equipment.

Above
Northampton

Below
Northampton

Fig. 3: Shown here are 25 ml. sample results taken from the Mill River above and below Northampton. The monitor on the right shows silt which was not prefiltered out before the water sample was pumped through the monitor.

STUDENT RESPONSE

During our own testing program, three or four students were driven to the testing locations once a week on a rotation schedule so that all would become familiar with the techniques. The students were so responsive to this project that there was no difficulty involved in obtaining volunteers for the summer months.

Even during the winter months the students were actively concerned with the problem of water pollution. When the testing was discontinued because of the weather, the members of the club wrote and recorded tapes for use as public-service announcements on local radio stations. Their work was written up in the local papers and they presented a program at a P.T.A. meeting.

CONCLUSIONS

What started out as a simple science club project has become a meaningful learning experience in testing procedures, bacteriology, and practical conservation. The students are not only performing a community service, they are also directing much needed publicity concerning local water pollution. Most important, the students have become acutely aware of the extent, problems, and dangers of water pollution.

5 Physics Activities for General Science

Basic Physics Activities for
General Science Teaching   152

Ripple Tanks for Classroom
Demonstrations   154

Photographing the Pendulum   158

Student-Constructed Demonstration of
Newton's Third Law   162

The Considerate Coke Bottle   163

Making a Hydrometer   164

Attention Archimedes!   166

A Student Exercise in Molecular
Movement and Energy   167

The Problem of the Backward
Rotating Radiometer   170

A Parabolic Mirror – Real Image
Demonstration   172

Basic Physics Activities for General Science Teaching

by Betty Jo Montag
Cupertino High School, Sunnyvale, California

In teaching general science it is necessary to create some simple physics activities. Here are some that have been helpful to me, and may be to others facing the same problems.

LIGHT CONCEPTS

In the unit on light we devised a method of calculating intensity which is *not* as accurate as would be necessary in a physics class, but works well to demonstrate the concept in general science. By putting a piece of black paper between 2 paraffin discs (used for mounting tissue) and holding them in place with rubber bands, a calibrating device can be produced (Fig. 1). The student uses an ordinary candle (calibrated foot candles are too expensive) and a pen-light flashlight.

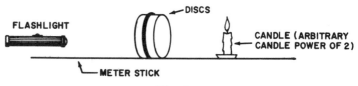

Fig. 1

NOTE: By placing the discs at the 50 cm. mark on a meter stick, the candle at the 75 cm. mark and the flashlight wherever the edges of the two discs show the same glow, it is possible to determine the centimeter candle power of the pen-light flashlight.

In dealing with the concepts of light, if you cannot afford a set of concave and convex lenses for each student, there is an excellent demonstration apparatus called the "optic disc" which shows graphically how light is

diverged or converged by the lenses. This information can be nicely correlated with the anatomy, physiology and abnormalities of the eye.

NOTE: If lenses are available, it is quite a revelation to
students to discover the focal point of a double convex lens
(and discover the image is upside down) and that the
double concave has no focal point.

HEAT CONCEPTS

In dealing with heat, it is quite dramatic to have students take thermometer readings vs. time in relation to ice melting. They get the concept
of the heat of fusion quite graphically this way—especially if they are asked
to present their data in graph form. Usually I have one side of the room
do the experiment with crushed ice at room temperature and the other
with the vial of crushed ice in a hot water bath.

NOTE: By combining results, the students see the plateau
due to the energy necessary for the phase change in both
graphs—but for a much shorter time period in the one
being supplied with additional energy (alcohol burner.)

Another simple heat experiment involves "boiling water" on a microscope
slide by holding a pea-sized piece of dry ice under a drop of water. With
this technique, injury is reduced to a minimum. Also, try heating water in
a small can (frozen orange juice) with and without asbestos bottoms. By
graphing data, students see graphically the effect of an insulator.

HOMEMADE THERMOMETERS

It is relatively easy for students to make their own thermometers. By
sealing off a 4″ piece of capillary tubing in a Bunsen burner flame, a small
closed vial can be formed. By introducing a hypodermic needle—then
another (smaller needle) attached to a hypodermic—a food-coloring liquid
can be introduced into the capillary. Since it is hard to get the fluid into
the capillary without bubbles, a fine wire can be introduced, rotated, and
the bubbles will rise to the top. The tube should not be filled more than
⅔ full. Have the students mark the colored water level at room temperature
with a glass-marking pencil. Then introduce the capillary tube into boiling
water and have students mark the level after several minutes in the boiling
water. Repeat with ice water.

NOTE: Having students make their own thermometers
stresses the fact that measuring devices are man-made—
as well as emphasizes the effects of molecular activity on a
liquid when energy is introduced or taken away.

WORK CONCEPT

One of the most difficult concepts to get across to students at the general science level is the concept of work. To teach this concept, I make use of plastic toy trucks. Use a file to even off the irregularities on the wheels, get pieces of plywood from the wood shop (for inclined planes), scraps from the metal shop (for the load), string attached to the toy trucks, and a spring scale—and you can teach the concept most effectively.

Ripple Tanks for
Classroom Demonstrations

by C. Howard Johnson
Episcopal High School, Alexandria, Virginia

As a junior high school science teacher, I have often found a need for a ripple tank to demonstrate the behavior of light and sound waves. However, it is not feasible in our school to equip students with experimental ripple tank equipment such as that used in PSSC physics. And, in any case, the PSSC type of apparatus does not work well as a demonstration since the screen is usually located beneath the ripple tank.

To meet the need for a useful, practical ripple tank for demonstrating wave behavior to large groups, I developed several designs which are presented here. Although it requires more time to make than the first, the second design is the better one for demonstration purposes.

A SIMPLE PYREX DISH APPARATUS

If time and space do not permit the construction of a larger tank, a satisfactory apparatus may be made from a rectangular Pyrex baking dish set on an overhead projector (Fig. 1). The various components for this design may be made from sheet aluminum cut to size.

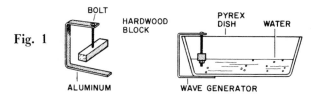

Fig. 1

- The wave generator is made from a strip of aluminum, a nut and bolt, and a hardwood block.
- Waves are generated by pushing down on the bolt in an even rhythm.
- To "bend" or refract waves, a metal prism may be constructed.

This is illustrated, with other useful devices, in Fig. 2.

The disadvantage of this Pyrex dish apparatus is that it is too small. Waves traverse its length rapidly, and space considerations make it difficult to add wave dampeners inside of the dish.

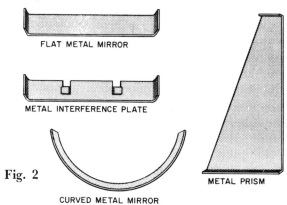

FLAT METAL MIRROR

METAL INTERFERENCE PLATE

Fig. 2

CURVED METAL MIRROR

METAL PRISM

A LARGE DEMONSTRATION APPARATUS

The second design projects the ripples onto the ceiling of the classroom, the display size depending on the height of the ceiling and the size of the tank. Completion of the entire apparatus should provide the instructor with a demonstration surface that is almost full-ceiling.

Materials

To construct the ripple tank and its base, these materials will be needed:

1 tube of Silastic bonding cement
2 sheets of cardboard 4' × 4'
1 piece of glass 30" × 30" × 1/8" (double-weight)
2 pieces of glass 30" × 3" × 1/8"
2 pieces of glass 30¼" × 3" × 1/8"
1 300-watt light bulb
1 roll of masking tape
1 3-volt miniature motor
25 3-inch nails
25 2-inch nails
1 110-volt socket

25 carpet tacks
10′ hook-up wire
1 piece of wood 2″ × 4″ × 20′
1 piece of wood 1″ × 1″ × 10′

Procedure

Following are directions for constructing the tank.

1. Using Silastic, a new rubberized plastic bonding compound, assemble the all-glass tank. (Silastic may be found in tropical fish stores.) The bottom of the tank should be square, double-weight glass. As indicated in the list of materials, two sides should be three inches high and as long as the bottom piece.

   IMPORTANT: The other two sides must be longer than the bottom piece to compensate for the overlapping of the edges.

   While they are drying, the sides may be propped up easily with books inside and out (Fig. 3).

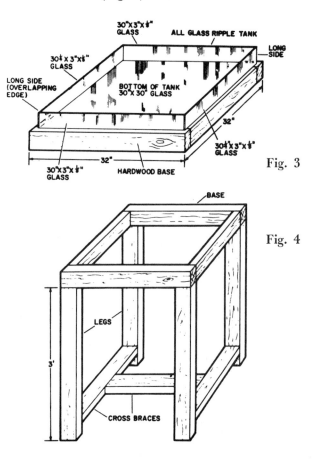

Fig. 3

Fig. 4

2. From the 20-foot piece of two- by four-inch lumber, assemble a square two inches longer on the sides than the glass tank; the extra inches will allow the tank to rest squarely on the base (Fig. 3). Add four legs, each three feet long, and cross-brace them at the bottom (Fig. 4).

NOTE: The legs make the tank accessible and help to produce an image on the ceiling of good size for class viewing.

3. Construct a reflector out of four large pieces of cardboard, cutting the pieces to size and tacking them to the frame and the bottom cross-brace. Seal the cardboard-to-cardboard seams with heavy masking tape, and line the reflector with aluminum foil, shiny side out (Fig. 5).

4. Attach a light socket inside the reflector on the cross-brace and a switch on one of the legs, and the apparatus is complete.

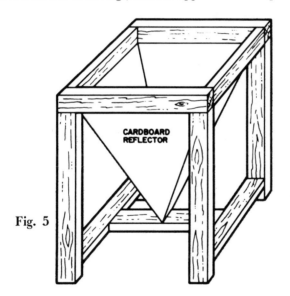

Fig. 5

Wave-Making Equipment

To be easily seen, demonstrations require a very constant and distinct wave source. I have used the PSSC physics ripple tank generator with great success and suggest it as a simple, almost flawless apparatus. For those who do not have access to this equipment, following are directions for building it.

1. Place one end of a piece of thin rubber tubing over the rotating shaft of the motor. Tie the other end of the tubing in a knot through a nut close to the shaft. This will cause unbalanced rotation, and the motor should vibrate when operating.

2. Fix the motor in the jaws of a spring clothespin. Attach the other end of the clothespin to a one- by one-inch stick running the length of one side of the tank. Float the stick on the water, using hook eyes and rubber bands hung from above (Fig. 6).

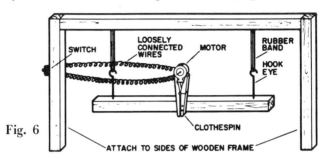

Fig. 6

3. Connect the wires loosely to a power source on the frame. The number of ripples per minute can be controlled by a variable resistor connected in series with the battery.
4. For the various reflecting surfaces necessary for demonstrations, use aluminum foil folded five or six times into inch high strips.

SUGGESTION: Let students discover for themselves the similarities between the ripple tank projections and the behavior of sound or light waves. Interesting conclusions result from the students' own comparisons.

Photographing the Pendulum

by Peter F. Steele
Fox Lane Middle School, Bedford, New York

Photographs of a pendulum's motion can be effective in teaching laws of physics that are difficult to comprehend when merely verbalized. The following rather simple photographic technique may serve to make such physical science concepts as velocity, acceleration, and deceleration more easily understood by eighth grade science students.

MATERIALS AND ASSEMBLY

The necessary apparatus for using this technique includes:

Neon stroboscope
Polaroid camera

Polaroid 3000 ASA land film
Tripod
Ring stand rod and base
20 gram mass
Double clamp
Drill and 1/16" bit
Ruler
½" diameter wooden dowel
String (10-inch piece)

A stroboscope may be borrowed from the physics lab and the Polaroid camera with 3000 ASA film may be available from the audio-visual department. Directions for the rest of the setup, which is easily rigged using odds and ends found in most general science rooms, are as follows:

1. Drill a 1/16th-inch hole through a ½-inch dowel approximately ½ inch from one end.
2. Put a 10-inch piece of string with a knot at the top end through the hole so that it hangs through by about 9 inches.
3. Tie a knot 7-7/8 inches from the underside of the wooden dowel and fasten the 20 gram mass there.
4. Fasten the dowel with a double clamp to the rod of a ring stand.
5. Place the entire apparatus in a dark room where a Polaroid camera on a tripod and a stroboscope are set up to record the pendulum's motion.

TAKING THE PHOTOS

To photograph the to and fro motion of the pendulum, first set the stroboscope as close as possible to the camera and turn on to the desired flash interval.

> **REMINDER: Don't forget to open up the camera lens to the largest f-opening and also set the shutter speed at the bulb setting.**

Have one student hold the bob. Just before he releases the bob, depress the camera shutter. As the bob reaches the other side (½ period), the shutter is released and you have recorded the swinging pendulum on film.

To obtain a variety of stop-action pictures, take several shots at different flash intervals. Since the photographs will be studied by students, it is suggested that slower flash intervals be tried so that the distances between the recorded stop-action bobs are not too close, making measurements difficult.

> **ENLARGEMENT: The photographs obtained with this technique are very small, especially for student use. Enlarged 8 x 10 photocopies are recommended. These can**

give an actual size relationship, which means that all measurements and subsequent calculations are to scale.

TEACHING APPLICATION

Once students have their copies of the same stop-action pendulum motion, the pictures may be used to help them understand several difficult concepts. Suppose, for example, that the accompanying photograph, Photo 1, were to be used. Assume that it represents the half-period of a pendulum with a full period of one second.

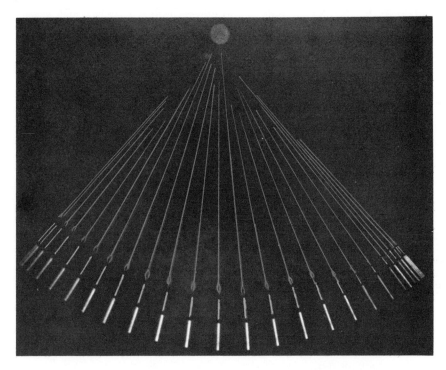

Photo 1: Stop action photograph of the half-period of a pendulum bob whose period was one second. The motion was stopped at 1/44th of a second intervals. Acceleration, velocity, kinetic energy, momentum, and other concepts can be taught using photographs similar to this one.

If the students are asked to graph this half-period showing the change in rate of velocity of the pendulum bob (acceleration and/or deceleration), they must find the two variables needed to label the independent and dependent axes. Since velocity = distance/time, these two factors must be determined.

The flash interval (time) of the stroboscope is easily accounted for by counting the number of bobs appearing in the photograph.

> COUNT: Disregard the second, fourth, and sixth bobs on the extreme right of the photo since these images represent the second half of the period (backswing). Also, disregard the first image on the extreme left as this represents the starting point.

Twenty-two images can be seen on the half-period photograph; therefore, the time between flash intervals during a period of one second must be 1/44th of a second. The distance intervals between the bob during this half-period are easily measured in millimeters. Thus, the two variables are accounted for and the graph can be constructed.

> ACCURACY: The distances measured are chords and not the actual distance traveled by the bob. At this grade level, however, the slight difference is insignificant.

USING DATA

The data recorded by the photograph, and interpreted and graphed by the students, is very meaningful information. Various questions can be asked of students to see whether they are able to utilize the data offered by these tools, the stop-action photograph, and the constructed graph.

- Which of the stop-action pendulum bobs best illustrates potential energy?
- Where in the photo is deceleration illustrated?
- The fact that the pendulum bob reaches the same height on the right side of the photo as on the left side demonstrates what law?
- How does this photo illustrate Newton's First Law of Motion?
- What is the velocity of the pendulum at $\frac{1}{4}$th of the period? (The pendulum's lowest position in its swing.)
- What is the kinetic energy at this lowest possible position? (K.E. $= \frac{1}{2}mv^2$)
- Where is the momentum of this bob at its greatest?
- What is the momentum at this point? (M = mv)
- What is the acceleration of the bob at the first three consecutive stop-action intervals? (A = change in velocity/time) Is this acceleration uniform?

Student-Constructed Demonstration of Newton's Third Law

by Paul A. Wilkinson

Manuel High School, Denver, Colorado

This device helps general science students understand Newton's Third Law: For every action there is an equal and opposite reaction.

MATERIALS

Ring stand
Thread
Bunsen burner
Screw eye bolt
Tin can, with lid (such as found on baking powder cans)

DEMONSTRATION

Solder screw eye bolt to lid of can. Dent the side of the can slightly, so that a portion of the wall is at an angle to the generally cylindrical surface. Punch a hole into indentation so that steam will come out of the hole in a path as nearly parallel to the side of the can as possible (Fig. 1).

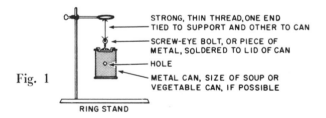

Fig. 1

STRONG, THIN THREAD, ONE END
TIED TO SUPPORT AND OTHER TO CAN

SCREW-EYE BOLT, OR PIECE OF
METAL, SOLDERED TO LID OF CAN

HOLE

METAL CAN, SIZE OF SOUP OR
VEGETABLE CAN, IF POSSIBLE

RING STAND

Fill can ¼ full of water and attach lid *tightly*. Heat bottom of can with burner. If you use a Bunsen burner, the can will start rotating within one or two minutes, depending on the size of the can, initial temperature of the water, and the amount of water in the can. After rotating, when heat is removed, the can will start rotating in the opposite direction, caused by the unwinding of the string (this latter is not part of the Third Law).

The demonstration attracts the interest of the class. The fact that it is student-performed does not answer the question "why does it spin?" but t does encourage classroom questions and discussions, guided by the teacher.

NOTE: The experiment is a modification of a steam toy made by Hero, a scientist of ancient Alexandria.

The Considerate Coke Bottle

by Michael A. Iarrapino
Crosby High School, Waterbury, Connecticut

I use this to demonstrate atmospheric pressure at the start of that particular unit. Preparation is a little tricky and requires some patience (you may break two or three bottles before getting one that works).

Drill a small hole about three quarters of the way down a Coca-Cola bottle, or any pop bottle as shown in Fig. 1 (the Coke bottle is best because the green color helps conceal the hole). Build a small "dam" of putty around the area to be drilled. Fill with paste made of carborundum powder and kerosene. Drill (slowly, to prevent buildup of heat) with an electric drill with a hardened point. Reduce the mouth of the bottle to a hole about one-

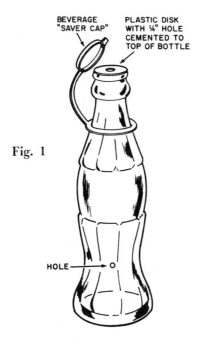

BEVERAGE "SAVER CAP"

PLASTIC DISK WITH ¼" HOLE CEMENTED TO TOP OF BOTTLE

Fig. 1

HOLE

quarter of an inch in diameter by cementing in a small plastic disk with a hole bored in the center (the bottom of an ordinary plastic vial will fit nicely).

> NOTE: A pre-prepared bottle of this type can be purchased from many magic dealers. I use the Coke bottle because it is recognized as authentic by the class. For the same reason, I avoid using bottles of metal or plastic, plus the fact that some substitutes might lack sufficient transparency for the full effect of the demonstration.

Fill the bottle with a brown liquid resembling Coca-Cola (don't use the real thing; the carbonation will spoil the effect). Fill with a funnel while blocking the hole on the side with your finger. Snap on an ordinary "saver cap" on the bottle. Atmospheric pressure and the formation of a "Torcellian vacuum" will prevent the liquid from leaking out of the hole on the side.

I present the demonstration in a humorous vein. I pick up the bottle, secretly covering the hole with my finger. I remove the saver cap, looking around for a glass to pour the Coke into. As I do this, I "accidentally" allow the bottle to tip over so that the mouth is downward. The atmospheric pressure prevents the liquid from pouring out as surface tension does not permit air to enter through the reduced opening. Acting surprised, I pick up a glass tumbler and place it under the down-turned bottle mouth and permit the Coke to be poured into it by removing my finger from the hole in the side. I can control the flow by secretly covering or uncovering the hole on the side. I find this amuses the students and they become far more eager to study atmospheric pressure to find out the reason for the mystery.

Making a Hydrometer

by Edward A. Terry

Formerly Science Teacher, Mobile County School System, Alabama

As the concluding activity in our study of density, I have each of my students make his own hydrometer which he uses in class to measure the relative density of several liquids, and then others of his own choosing at home. This learning experience gives him a working concept of relative density and an idea of its practical importance.

MATERIALS

To make his own hydrometer, each student needs the following materials:

Plastic straw
3 or more small lead shot
Small rubber band or thin thread
Metric ruler
Soft lead pencil with a sharp point
Small test tube
Water glass

NOTE: The average class requires about two packages of plastic straws, one box of BB shot, and one package of thin rubber bands.

In addition, the class as a whole will require:

1 bottle of rubbing alcohol
1 box of table salt
1 box of copper sulfate (blue stone)

NOTE: The teacher should mix the copper sulfate with water and prepare the sodium chloride solution before classes.

PROCEDURE

In presenting this exercise, I place written instructions on the blackboard, then carry out the instructions in a demonstration, having the students follow each step closely. (The directions might be written out and distributed to the students.)

1. Measure 5 cm. from one end of the straw and make a bend at the 5 cm. point.
2. Insert one small shot in this short end. Flatten this end, pushing the shot as near as possible to the bend.
3. Fold over at least 3 cm. of the short end.
4. Insert two or three small shot in the long end and work them to the bend, being careful not to crush the tube.
5. Wind the rubber band closely above the shot.

NOTE: The straw should now be watertight and the shot firmly in place. If the steps have been correctly done, the straw will float in an upright position. (Usually, poorly prepared ones can be corrected.)

6. Place the straw in the glass of water and, with the straw floating in an upright position, mark the water line with the soft pencil. Check this mark carefully.
7. Remove the straw from the water and, with the fine-pointed pencil, mark a gauge of at least two centimeters above and below the water mark using milliliters as the gauge lines.

TESTING THE HYDROMETER

Test the hydrometer first in alcohol, then, after washing it off, in the copper sulfate solution. The students will observe the fact that in neither solution does the hydrometer float near the water line. As a final test, place the hydrometer in the salt solution.

Following the instructions on the blackboard, which should list each step in the demonstration they have just observed, the students then make and test their own hydrometers. When these have been completed and tested, I encourage each student to continue his investigations at home on a suggested list of common liquids.

Attention, Archimedes!

by Terrence P. Toepker

Xavier University, Cincinnati, Ohio

I introduce buoyant force by telling the class I could float the *Queen Mary* on a few gallons of water. Students, being what they are, almost always think this is impossible. Before demonstrating my statement, I try to find out *why* they think it's impossible, just to get the thinking processes started.

I tell the story of a clever sailor who bet that he could show how to float the *Queen Mary* on a few gallons of water. A friend immediately took the bet. Much to the surprise of the friend, the clever sailor drew some pictures which explained satisfactorily how the seemingly impossible feat could be done. The pictures are Figs. 1 through 4 below.

The sailor realized that the buoyant force exerted by a liquid is equal to the weight of the liquid displaced. Most people emphasize the word *weight;* the sailor concentrated on the word *displaced.* If the liquid is displaced (as in the case of an overflow experiment), it is not necessary to retain the displaced liquid. So, the sailor drew the pictures with the following explanation:

- Fig. 1 shows a ship in fairly deep water.
- Fig. 2 shows the same ship floating in a lock. So far as the ship is concerned, it floats just as well if it has 100 feet of water under it or one foot.
- Fig. 3 shows the same ship in a special container where the walls slope in toward the middle. This reduces the amount of water needed to float the ship.
- Fig. 4 shows the clincher. If the special container is made slightly

larger than the ship, but following the contour of the ship, only a slight amount of water is necessary. Thus, it would be possible to float the *Queen Mary* on just a few gallons of water.

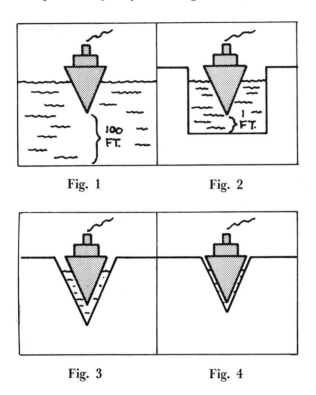

Fig. 1   Fig. 2

Fig. 3   Fig. 4

ILLUSTRATION: The principle can be easily illustrated with *two* nesting mixing bowls. One becomes the "ship," and the other the "lock" with the same contour.

A Student Exercise in Molecular Movement and Energy

by Leslie Howell

Warwick High School, Newport News, Virginia

Through close observation and the help of leading questions, the relatively slow general science student can be guided to an understanding of many important ideas and principles of science. The purpose of this exercise is to provide a fairly simple laboratory procedure utilizing a minimum of equipment that will teach the novice science student valuable concepts concerning molecular behavior and energy.

PREPARATION

Naturally, all experiments are more interesting and rewarding to the student, and to the teacher, if each student is allowed to perform the designated tasks for himself. To my knowledge, however, there are no perfectly safe laboratory operations that all students can do without incurring danger of some type.

CAUTION: Before having students conduct this exercise, the teacher should carefully instruct them in the correct techniques for safely handling hot water and glassware.

If the exercise is to be performed by the teacher, a practice run should be made to avoid any time lags during the demonstration.

OBJECTIVES

Molecules, the busy little units which hold our world together, are not often enough directly related to energy. Molecules are defined as the smallest particles of a substance that contain the properties of that substance. Energy is said to be that which produces a change in matter and has the capacity to do work. The objectives of this five-step exercise are to use water to examine molecular movement and its relationship to energy.

MATERIALS

The equipment needed for the exercise includes:

Small beaker (about 50 ml.)
Large beaker (about 500 ml.)
Glass tubing from 12″ to 18″ long
Flashlight
Concentrated dye
Grease pencil
Lead pencil
Ring stand
Rings and clamps
Ice cubes
Tap water
Bunsen burner (or portable propane burner)

PROCEDURE

The following procedure includes leading questions to guide students in making their observations and drawing appropriate conclusions.

Step 1: "Rapidly" heat the small beaker about 2/3 full of water, and look closely at the point where the bottom of the beaker touches the water.

    a. What do you see that is unusual about the behavior of the water?

    b. With the flashlight, observe closely the movement that is occurring at the bottom of the beaker. Where do you think the water gets the energy to move as it does?

Step 2: Continue to heat the water until it starts to boil, then mark the level of the water in the beaker with your grease pencil.

    a. What part of the beaker seems to be the hottest?

    b. Is water moving? In what way is the water moving more rapidly, up or down the beaker?

    c. If you hold a dry pencil over the boiling water, what collects on the pencil?

    d. How did the water get to the pencil?

    e. Do you conclude that steam and water are the same molecules and differ only in their energy?

    f. Note the level of water in the beaker. Is it the same as when we started? Where did the water go?

    g. Do you believe the water lost was destroyed or by a change in energy was able to go into the air as a gas? Why?

Step 3: Now take the burner away from the boiling water. Allow the water to stand for about five minutes, then drop one drop of dye into the water. *Do not stir the water.*

    a. Does the water become colored throughout?

    b. Do you believe hot water would color itself at a faster rate than cold water? Why?

Step 4: Set up your equipment as shown in the diagram (Fig. 1). Gently heat the water until the "perking" action begins. Be careful not to heat the water too quickly.

    a. Where do you think water gets the energy to move up the glass tube?

    b. How could we use this perking action to do work?

    c. What common household appliance works by perking?

Step 5: Fill the large beaker 2/3 full of water and place the beaker over the Bunsen burner. Drop an ice cube into the water when it is very hot, but not boiling. Closely observe the water about $1/4''$ from the bottom of the ice cube.

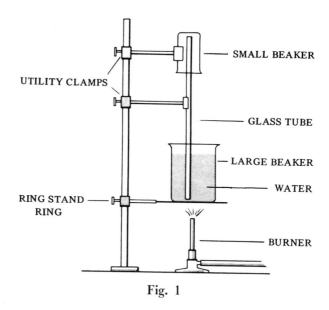

Fig. 1

a. What do you see?

b. Do you detect a movement of the water that seems to originate from the ice? Is this movement of the same type as that when we heated water?

c. Does the rate of this movement correspond to the rate the ice is melting?

d. Do you think this movement around the ice could be an indication that the crystalline ice molecules are moving into solution?

e. From what you have seen and from previous discussion, what evidence can you give that concludes that ice, water, and steam are all made up of molecules that differ only in the amount of energy they contain?

The Problem of the Backward Rotating Radiometer

by James E. Creighton

Nathan Hale Junior High School, Norwalk, Connecticut

Several years ago while I was conducting the traditional demonstration with radiometer and heat and light filters for a ninth grade general science class, one of the students made an unexpected observation: When the infrared lamp was turned off, the radiometer—after it had slowed to a stop —suddenly began to rotate in the reverse direction. Here was an observation which must be explained; a problem to solve using scientific principles.

NOTE: I found that this problem which the student had stumbled upon offered an excellent opportunity for student problem-solving and for teaching the concept of radiation and absorption of a black body.

SOLVING THE PROBLEM

Never having witnessed this phenomenon before, I had first to solve the problem myself. After pondering it for several minutes with no success, I decided that the only way to approach the problem was through basic logic. It had to be assumed at the beginning that the only way the radiometer could rotate in reverse was to be warmer at the silver vane than at the black vane. How could this happen?

The solution was immediately obvious—the black vane had cooled much faster than the silver vane.

TEACHING OPPORTUNITY

The phenomenon of the backward rotating radiometer provides a perfect example of radiation cooling by a black object. It also presents a good opportunity for student problem-solving.

Prior to showing the radiometer, in any heat unit, the class must be taught the principle of radiation and absorption of heat by a black body. This is best accomplished by a demonstration with black and silver cans filled with water and preferably set up as a laboratory exercise. Once the students are familiar with this principle, the radiometer demonstration with heat and light filters is an excellent follow-up. (See Fig. 1.)

If by the end of this demonstration no one in the class has noticed the backward rotation of the radiometer, the teacher should call it to their

Fig. 1

attention. Normally, a few students are able to come up with the correct explanation. These few may be asked to write their solution on a piece of paper and pass it in, and the class may then be led in a discussion of the problem and its eventual solution.

A Parabolic Mirror–
Real Image Demonstration

by Donna Parsons
Regional Studies Center, College of Idaho, Caldwell, Idaho

The following demonstration is a simple adaptation of a device suggested in the *PSSC Teacher's Resource Book and Guide*. It has proven very effective in my physics and general science classes and serves as an excellent introduction to the study of optics.

BACKGROUND FOR THE DEMONSTRATION

The teacher should explain to the students that although the image of ourselves we see in a mirror may seem real to us, technically, such an image is only virtual. Rays of light which form the image appear to come from *behind* the mirror while actually they are being reflected off the mirror's surface. A real image, on the other hand, is formed by the intersection of rays that really are coming from where they seem to originate.

> NOTE: Students are all familiar with the real images formed by movie and slide projector lenses on screens. But few people have had the chance to see real images formed by curved mirrors.

MATERIALS

To set up this real image demonstration, the following materials are needed: a parabolic or concave mirror, a strong light source, an object, some means of holding the preceding three items in the proper position in relation to each other.

In the blueprint of the apparatus shown in Fig. 1, the mirror is an 18-inch concave mirror with a focal length of 22 inches. The light is provided by a 200-watt bulb in a regular-sized base, and the object is an artificial bird. All parts are held together by a wooden box. Photos 1 through 5 depict the completed apparatus based upon the blueprint, removable parts of the finished apparatus, and a view of the image itself.

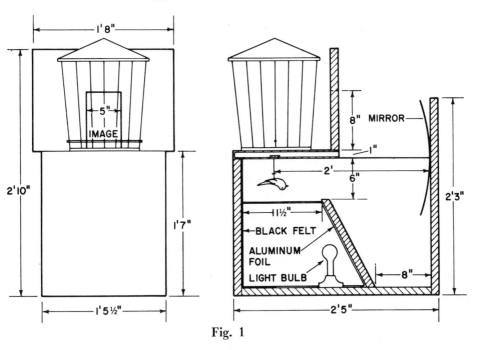

Fig. 1

APPARATUS MODIFICATIONS

The materials used in the apparatus described here were selected largely because they were readily available. A smaller mirror than that shown here can be used, though the image might not be as bright as that from a larger one. The light bulb used might be stronger or weaker than the 200-watt bulb used in this model, and the dimensions of the box can be easily made larger or smaller than those of the model.

> NOTE: It is essential, however, to be able to place the object at a distance equal to 2f, twice the focal length of the mirror, so that the image will be the same size as the object. Also, a slot or hook on which to suspend the object upside down must be provided, for real images are always inverted.

Although Fig. 1 and Photo 5 show a bird as the object, with the bird cage in front of the mirror to help the illusion, an evergreen bough can also be used effectively. Proper placing of the bough will make the image appear on a perch in the cage, or in the midst of the greenery. A flowers-vase combination or a dollar bill dangling in mid-air provide other variations.

USING THE APPARATUS

The larger the ratio of diameter of the mirror to focal length and the brighter the light, the more noticeable the image will be. Lining the lower part of the box with foil will increase the reflection. Once the box frame is finished, the major problem is adjusting the mirror in the proper position to get an undistorted image. Then, since the image can be seen only when looking directly toward the mirror (Photo 2), the observer must be in the proper place.

> NOTE: Arranging the apparatus so that students see it in operation as soon as they enter the classroom is most effective. Once they have all had a chance to notice how the image disappears with a change in their position, their interest is captured and motivation for learning is high.

The most practical use of this demonstration apparatus is in physics classes to demonstrate image formation, but it can also be profitably used in any physical science class to introduce a study of light, and in biology classes to illustrate the formation of images as related to the lenses of the eye.

Photo 1: A view of all parts of the apparatus.

Photo 2: Picture of the position one must take to see the image. (The image will appear in the bird cage.)

Photo 3: View with the bird cage removed.

Photo 4: View of the removable bird cage support.

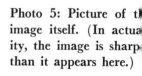

Photo 5: Picture of the image itself. (In actuality, the image is sharper than it appears here.)

6 Demonstrations in Electricity

Homemade Equipment for Static
  Electricity   176
Demonstrating Static Electricity   179
Teacher Demonstrations in
  Electricity, Electrons, and
  Gaseous Ions   180
Production of Motion from Electricity   186
Making an Electric Motor—
  A Class Exercise   190

Homemade Equipment
for Static Electricity

by J. R. Stevenson
Menlo Community School, Menlo, Iowa

Very often, when it comes time for the unit on static electricity, the teacher will find the school's supply of material to be limited to a vulcanite rod, a glass rod, a catskin and a silk pad. The result: A few teacher or student demonstrations, with the rest of the class watching.

It doesn't have to be that way. With a modest expenditure of time, some scrap items from the school shop and lab, and a dollar or two to spend for miscellaneous items, a class can be equipped to investigate the principles of static electricity in depth. Here are three devices I have made for this purpose.

NEGATIVE CHARGES

An ordinary vinyl plastic ruler, when rubbed with a wool pad, can be charged negatively. You can supply each student with two such rulers, one of them mounted on a wooden base with a nail as a pivot and a glass tube as a bearing, as shown in Fig. 1. If one end of the mounted ruler is charged, it will be repelled when a similarly charged end of another plastic rule is brought close to it.

Building the device is simple: I use a plastic ruler of the type found in many five-and-tens or stationery stores with a hole already formed in the center (along with other slots and designs); a seven penny nail fits through the hole very nicely.

> NOTE: If you cannot locate this type of ruler, a solid ruler could be used. Form the hole by heating a nail red hot and thrusting it through the mid-point of the plastic ruler.

I select a piece of glass tubing with a diameter that permits the nail to turn freely in it. I file about ¾ of an inch off the tubing and smooth each end with a file. To flare one end, I heat the piece of tube red hot, insert a tapered, round file into it as far as it will go and press it against the heated glass tube. After the glass has cooled, I insert the nail through the center hole in the ruler and through the glass bearing, and pound the nail into the wooden stand, leaving just enough of the nail sticking out to permit the ruler to rotate freely.

> NOTE: Flaring the end of the bearing is probably not necessary. Fire polishing it should be good enough to permit free rotation.

POSITIVE CHARGES

Following the same general principles, glass tubing from the chemistry lab can be used to make hollow glass rods that can be positively charged when rubbed with silk. Here is how to make and mount the rods: Select a piece of tubing that is about ½ inch (15 mm) in diameter and two or three feet long (the finished rod should be about 12 inches long).

> NOTE: I use 15 mm tubing because we have it available, and because it is the same size as commercial glass rods. If, however, you do not have this particular size, the device should work just as well with any size rod from ¼ inches (7 or 8 mm) on up.

Heat the tubing; when it gets red hot and begins to soften, pull each end rapidly apart as in the making of chemistry pipettes. After the tubes have cooled, file off the long narrow tips and reheat to seal the pointed ends. The other (or open) end can be cut to the desired 12-inch length with a file or glass cutter and smoothed by filing and fire polishing.

Mount the rods on a base similar to that used for the plastic rulers, as follows: Determine the center of gravity of the tube and heat it at that point until it becomes red hot. While still red hot, remove the tube from the burner and bring down over the pointed end of a finishing nail. This will

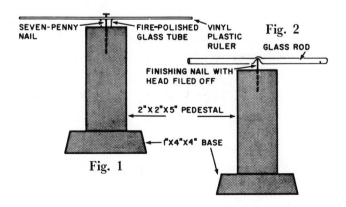

Fig. 2

Fig. 1

force the softened bottom of the wall of the tube against the upper wall; additional pressure will cause a "dimple" to be raised in the upper wall that will serve as a bearing for the mounted tube, while the nail (with the head filed off) serves as a pivot (Fig. 2).

In addition to using the glass rods to show the repulsion of like charges, you can use them in conjunction with the plastic rulers to show the attraction of unlike charges to each other.

COULOMB'S LAW: The glass rods and plastic rulers can be used in qualitative investigations of Coulomb's Law.

A SIMPLE ELECTROSCOPE

You can construct simple electroscopes in mass quantities very easily as shown in Fig. 3. Here are the steps:

• Wrap aluminum foil around a glass or beaker. Use a piece slightly bigger than the circumference of the beaker, and cellophane tape it together where it overlaps. At intervals, hold in place with cellophane tape around the top. This aluminum foil takes the place of the contact knob of the conventional electroscope.

• Bend a piece of stiff copper wire as shown in the illustration (Fig. 3) and insert between the aluminum foil and the beaker and secure with cellophane tape or masking tape.

• Cut leaves from aluminum foil and force over the hooked end of the copper wire.

In use, charged objects are presented to the electroscope via the foil wrapper around the beaker. The wrapper adds sufficient area to the electrope to act as a "reservoir" for electrons that are forced into the leaves by the approach of a negative charge, or attracted (drawn) from the leaves by the approach of a positive charge.

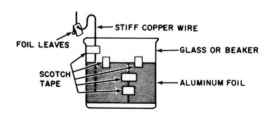

Fig. 3

Demonstrating
Static Electricity

by William J. Muha
Formerly Notre Dame High School, Niles, Illinois

Here are three simple demonstrations of static electricity which I have found useful with my physics students. The first two are effective as teacher demonstrations to rouse student interest and curiosity. The third will give students an opportunity to conduct their own demonstrations using homemade "electroscopes."

DRAMATIZING STATIC ELECTRICITY

For a dramatic display of static electricity, obtain several ordinary balloons from a local variety store and inflate the balloons with air.

- Suspend one balloon with two strings so that the strings form a "V" with the balloon at the vertex.
- Tape the second balloon to the end of a meter stick in a fixed position.
- Rub both balloons with fur, then try to bring them together.

The balloon on the string will ascend to the ceiling, or at least move away, with surprising speed and vigor. Even in a large lecture hall, this demonstration will give every student a grandstand view.

ALSO: Charge a comb by combing your hair. Then bring the teeth of the comb near a thin stream of water from a faucet. The stream will be diverted and distorted noticeably and dramatically.

DETERMINING ELECTROSCOPE VOLTAGE

When students have observed the operation of an electroscope, the teacher can ask one student to charge the instrument with his comb after he has combed his hair. This will cause the gold foil to stand at right angles to the vertical support. The teacher should ground out the electroscope with his finger in the usual way, and ask students what voltage they believe there was on the instrument to cause the effect they have observed. (Students' guesses usually range from microvolts to 10 volts.)

The teacher can then connect a penlight cell to the case and the conductor rod of the electroscope. Of course this action produces absolutely no observable effect. Next, he may connect a large (1½ volt) dry cell. (It possesses the same voltage as the penlight cell, but its size is impressive.) Then a 12-volt auto battery can be tried, with the same failing results. Finally, the teacher can bring out the variable D.C. power supply and volt meters, which at 600 volts causes the gold foil to rise to about 45°. At this point, students can be "warned" to be careful in the future about combing their hair; they may electrocute themselves!

> **NOTE: If the electroscope has calibrations, the students may be asked to plot a curve and extrapolate to determine how many volts are needed to make the foil rise to a right-angle position.**

USING HOMEMADE "ELECTROSCOPES"

After a series of teacher demonstrations of static electricity, the students may be given homemade "electroscopes" to perform their own individual demonstrations. These consist of a strip of newspaper 3 to 6 cm. in width and about 30 cm. long (60 cm. long, folded in half). There is nothing critical about either the length or width of the paper.

To use his "electroscope," the student:

- Places the double strip in a textbook with several sheets of text between the two folds, leaving the end with the fold sticking out of the book.
- Pulls the exposed end smartly.

The rubbing friction of the sheets and strips will transfer enough charges that the two strips will repel each other vigorously like an inverted "V", sometimes attaining angles up to 45°. Placing a hand between the two leaves causes them to "snap" at the hand. The leaves do not discharge too quickly.

Teacher Demonstrations in Electricity, Electrons, and Gaseous Ions

by Dudley W. Davis
Monroe Junior High School, Tampa, Florida

Here are a number of teacher demonstrations which I have found effective in creating student interest in electricity, electrons, and gaseous ions. Included also are directions for making an inexpensive Crookes tube. Each of the demonstrations can be carried out with a very small amount of science equipment using items common to most homes or available at minimal cost.

CAUTION: I have permitted students averaging 14 years of age to conduct all of these demonstrations under my supervision. However, all of the demonstrations here should first be performed by the teacher, and only then possibly conducted by selected students under the close supervision of the teacher.

DEMONSTRATING HIGH VOLTAGE ENERGY

Jacob's Ladder is our name for a demonstration apparatus which can be used to show students the energy produced by a high voltage current, such as that produced by a spark plug in engines or that present in television sets and high voltage power lines. (See Fig. 1.)

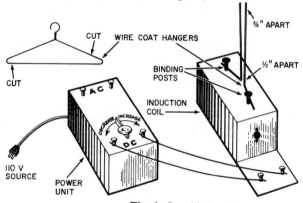

Fig. 1: Jacob's Ladder.

Materials

Materials needed for making a Jacob's Ladder are:

1 low voltage power unit (or a 6 to 12 volt automobile storage battery)
1 induction coil
2 unpainted wire coat hangers
Pair of pliers (or wire cutters)
4 pieces of insulated wire, 16 to 22 gauge, 12" to 18" long

Procedure

1. Cut each of the coat hangers at one end of the bottom to obtain the longest possible straight piece. Make the other cut on each

hanger approximately four inches (4″) around the corner at the other end. Then straighten the short end so that this piece is at an approximate right angle to the longer piece.

2. Fasten the short ends of the cut-out hanger wire to each of the high voltage binding posts of the induction coil, with the long ends of the wires in a vertical position (Fig. 1). Start with the nearest point between the wires at the bottom at about one-half inch (½″) or less, and shape the wires so that the tops are approximately three-fourths inch (¾″ apart, as indicated in the illustration.

3. Attach the low voltage power unit to the induction coil and turn it to ON or INCREASE, as appropriate. The arcs should jump between the two wires at the bottom, climb up the wires to the top ends, and make a popping sound as they jump off the tops. (Some minor adjustments of distances between the wires may have to be made to suit the output of the induction cell.)

WARNING: BE SURE TO TURN OFF OR DISCONNECT YOUR POWER UNIT BEFORE APPROACHING WITHIN TWO INCHES (2″) OF EITHER THE BINDING POST OR THE INDUCTION CELL. If 6 to 6.5 volts D.C. is used, the shock from the induction coil will not cause serious damage to a healthy person, but it is extremely uncomfortable.

DEMONSTRATING HIGH VOLTAGE PENETRATION OF INSULATORS

The following series of demonstrations shows students how high voltage current penetrates some insulators to the point that they fail to insulate. Students should be able to apply their observations to various situations in their environment.

Materials

In addition to the basic apparatus used in the preceding demonstration procedure, you will need:

2 electrodes with insulated handles (attachments which usually come with induction coils)

NOTE: If the electrodes are not available, use 2 screwdrivers which are small enough to fit the binding post of the induction cell.

1 sheet of notebook paper
1 toy balloon about 3″ long
1 common carbon lead pencil with eraser
1 used automobile condenser (capacitor)

NOTE: A capacitor can usually be obtained free for the asking from a garage.

Procedure

1. Turn off the power unit and remove the hanger wire used in the preceding demonstration from the induction coil.
2. Insert the electrodes or screwdrivers through the high voltage post binders. Hold the ends of the insulated handles and swing the metal tips toward each other to show how the arc travels from one to the other. Then arrange the electrodes so that one is at a right angle to the other and approximately one-half inch ($\frac{1}{2}''$) apart.
3. Pass the piece of paper between the electrodes and watch the arc pass through the paper. If the paper is passed quickly, it will not ignite. If it is held still, it will ignite.

WARNING: DO NOT APPROACH AS NEAR EITHER OF THE ELECTRODES AS THE ELEC- TRODES ARE APART WHEN THE CURRENT IS ON, FOR IF YOU DO THE CURRENT WILL ARC THROUGH YOU RATHER THAN TO THE OTHER ELECTRODE. (18,000 VOLTS WILL ARC APPROXI- MATELY 1'' UNDER STANDARD CONDITIONS.)

4. Turn the current off, and slip the balloon over one of the electrodes, being careful not to puncture it. (You may want to have one of the students inflate the balloon first.)
5. When the balloon is in place, turn on the current and swing the electrodes so that they are near each other where the balloon is covering the one, and the arc will penetrate the balloon in one or more places as you move the uncovered electrode back and forth.
6. Turn the current off, remove one of the electrodes, and insert the pointed end of the pencil into the high voltage post binder.
7. Turn on the current. Then with the voltage control switch on the power unit, turn the voltage down to almost off. Let one of the students who thinks that the pencil will not conduct electricity touch the eraser while you gradually turn up the voltage. The student will receive a small shock.
8. Now swing the pencil and the electrode near each other so that the point of the electrode is at a right angle with the pencil and within one-half inch ($\frac{1}{2}''$) or less. The electricity will penetrate the wood of the pencil at one or more places as you move the electrode back and forth along the pencil.
9. Turn off the current, then attach the pig tail wire of the con- denser to one of the post binders, and the body of the condenser to the other binder.

10. Turn the voltage to high and leave it on for 1 to 2 seconds.

11. Remove the condenser carefully, since it is now charged with the same amount of voltage as the induction coil puts out. It will arc the same as the electrodes. (A flashlight or automobile lamp bulb can be burnt out with the charge on the condenser.)

Interpreting Effects

The pencil, balloon, and paper demonstrations show that voltage can be increased high enough so that some things we call insulators fail to insulate. This situation can be related by the teacher to high voltage such as that in the power lines of utility companies.

NOTE: Students should be warned never to get near one of these lines or attempt to move one that is down.

The condenser (capacitor) demonstration illustrates the danger of working on a television set or other electrical appliance, unless it is known how to safely bleed off the charge on the condensers. It takes up to 24 hours for some condensers to bleed off the charge by themselves.

A CROOKES TUBE TO DEMONSTRATE ELECTRICAL DISCHARGE IN GASES AT LOW PRESSURE

Materials

If you do not have a Crookes Tube or Cathode Ray Tube available to demonstrate gaseous ions, you can easily make one that operates quite effectively. You will need these materials:

1 glass tube, approximately 9" long and ¾" in diameter
1 rubber stopper without holes to fit the glass tube
1 one-hole stopper to fit the other end of the tube
1 small glass tube, approximately 3" long to fit the one-hole stopper
2 common four to six penny nails with medium or large heads
1 electric vacuum pump

NOTE: Be certain to fire polish the glass tubing so that it will not crack under the reduced pressure.

Making the Tube

Following are directions for assembling the tube:

• Drive one of the nails through the rubber stopper (without holes), from the small end of the stopper to the large end.

• Drive the other nail through the one-hole stopper in the same manner, being careful not to damage the hole.

• Insert the small glass tube through the hole in the rubber stopper so that it extends about one-fourth inch ($\frac{1}{4}''$) through the small end of the stopper.

- Insert both stoppers tightly into the ends of the large glass tube. (A burette clamp and ring stand can be used to hold the tube. If these are unavailable, a small shoe box may be used: Stand the box on its end, cut a small hole through each side, and insert the glass tube through the holes.)
- Attach the wires from the induction coil to the points of the nails.
- Hook the vacuum pump to the small glass tube, turn on the power unit, and observe the Crookes Tube (Fig. 2).

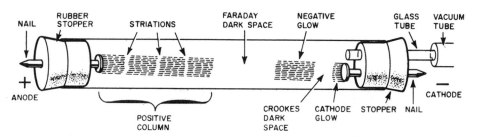

Fig. 2: Crookes Tube.

Using the Tube

When an electrical discharge occurs between the two nail heads, some beautiful and interesting effects take place as the air is pumped out of the tube. When the pressure is reduced enough, a narrow pink streamer develops between the electrodes. As the pressure is further reduced, the streamer gets larger until it almost fills the tube.

If you continue reducing the pressure (below 1 mm of Hg.), a state of discharge will be reached. The negative electrode (cathode) will develop a velvety glow known as the "cathode glow" (Fig. 2). Adjacent to his glow, toward the positive end, is an area with no streamer or glow that is known as "Crookes dark space." Next comes the area that also glows, called the "negative glow." The second dark region follows this and is known as the "Faraday dark space." Last is the largest glowing area that reaches to the positive electrode (anode). This area is known as the "positive column."

The positive column is not a solid column, but is striated across as the electrons reach their energy levels. An ion must have a chance to travel far enough to acquire energy to produce ionization by collision. This can be accomplished by reducing the pressure in the tube. If one continues to reduce the pressure, the ions may go all the way to the other electrode without having a collision. In this case, the ions may eject electrons and other ions when they strike the electrode. These are then called "secondary ions" and are instrumental in supporting the discharge.

A bar magnet may be used to demonstrate the electrical charge of the particles. If a bar magnet is placed so that the magnetic field is perpendicular to the component of motion of the charge, the stream will bend in one direction perpendicular to both the field and the original velocity of the charge. The stream will bend in the opposite direction, again perpendicular to both the original velocity and the magnetic field if the charge is opposite or if the charge is the same but the magnetic field is opposite.

> NOTE: The rays are deflected by the electrostatic field. By applying a potential difference between plates on opposite sides of the tube, the positive plate attracts and the negative plate repels the stream.

If the pressure in the tube is further reduced, the positive column shortens and Faraday dark space lengthens. This is followed by a greenish glow at the glass. If reduction of pressure continues, this greenish glow will spread over almost the entire area of the tube. It is due to the fluorescence of the glass caused by the bombardment by rays from the negative electrode of the tube. These particles are called "cathode rays."

Production of Motion from Electricity

by Ralph S. Vrana
California State Polytechnic College, San Luis Obispo, California

Here are a series of experiments which demonstrate the production of motion from electricity.

ROTATING BAR MAGNET

The principle of how an electric motor operates can be shown by placing a bar magnet on a compass stand. Two other bar magnets are held as shown in Fig. 1, to start the rotation (the hand magnets must be switched simultaneously and at the proper moment to keep the pivoted magnet rotating).

> NOTE: This is the principle of how an electric motor operates. In many motors, of course, the rotating magnet (armature) shifts its polarity by switching the direction of current in its windings. In such cases there is no need to shift the direction of the hand-held magnets (field coils).

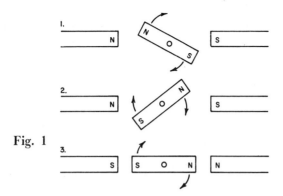

Fig. 1

DEMONSTRATION MOTOR

You can make a satisfactory demonstration motor from the armature of a small electric motor, such as is found in a vacuum clearner, auto heater, or windshield wiper. Disassemble the motor to remove the armature, which will come out in one piece, then mount the armature on a board so that the shaft is held at each end by a screw-eye and is free to rotate easily. A strong, heavy magnet is placed near the middle of the armature and wires from the power supply or storage battery are held against the commutator of the armature (Fig. 2). These wires are the "brushes" of a conventional electric motor.

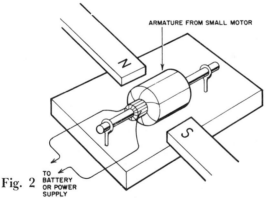

ARMATURE FROM SMALL MOTOR

Fig. 2 TO BATTERY OR POWER SUPPLY

NOTE: A little adjustment may be necessary before the armature will spin. The magnet works best when held very close to the armature, but may make contact if brought too close. Several good bar magnets placed close to each side of the armature will also get the motor going. The bar magnets on one side must have opposite polarity to those on the other.

This rejuvenation of an electric motor is a good learning experience, because the essential parts of the motor are out in the open, yet the motor runs nearly as rapidly as it did in the original, closed housing. The speed is quite responsive to the movement of the field magnets, and to pressure and position of the brushes.

MAKING AN ELECTRIC MOTOR

To make a homemade motor commutator and armature, you will need:

Shaft from coat hanger
Adhesive tape
Tin can (for strips of metal)
Two long nails
Copper wire

The device is assembled as shown in the exploded drawing at Fig. 3. In building the motor, the students should make the armature first, and hang it on bearings (Fig. 4). This much of the motor can be tested with permanent magnets and a source of direct current electricity, as also shown in Fig. 4. Then, if the motor passes the test by spinning rapidly, the students may then go on to make the field coils (electromagnets which take the place of permanent magnets). If it doesn't spin, the trouble should be found and corrected. Here are precautions to take in construction:

- Be sure the copper wire is cleaned of insulation (including enamel) wherever it is to be connected.

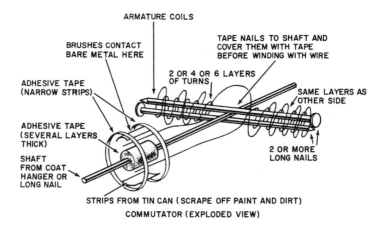

HOME-MADE MOTOR
COMMUTATOR AND ARMATURE

Fig. 3

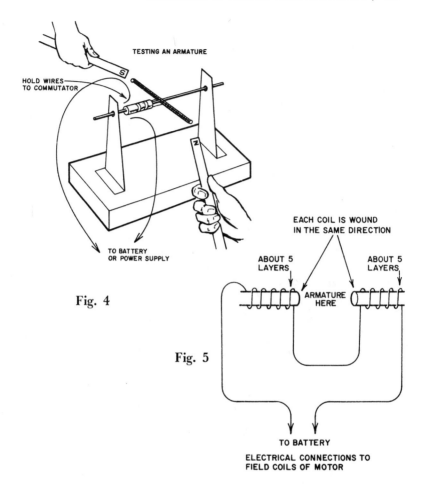

Fig. 4

Fig. 5

TESTING AN ARMATURE

HOLD WIRES TO COMMUTATOR

TO BATTERY OR POWER SUPPLY

EACH COIL IS WOUND IN THE SAME DIRECTION

ABOUT 5 LAYERS

ABOUT 5 LAYERS

ARMATURE HERE

TO BATTERY

ELECTRICAL CONNECTIONS TO FIELD COILS OF MOTOR

- Tin can material may be covered with an enameled surface of the same color as the tin. This must be scraped off with a piece of sandpaper or file wherever an electrical connection is to be made.
- When winding copper wire onto a strip of tin can, it is a good idea to cover the tin can material with one or two layers of adhesive or masking tape in order to prevent a short circuit between tin can and wire.
- If the electric motor contains more than one "field coil," these must be connected so as to produce a magnetic field which has a south pole on one side of the armature, and north pole on the other (Fig. 5).
- The commutator (contact points between the ends of the armature coil and the brushes) must be adjusted for maximum speed by twisting it on its housing.
- Brushes must touch the commutator slightly.

Making an Electric Motor—
A Class Exercise

by C. Howard Johnson

Episcopal High School, Alexandria, Virginia

The laboratory exercise described here is designed for use in a unit on electricity and magnetism in general or physical science classes. By requiring the students to actually use electricity and magnetism in building a simple motor, the exercise provides the students with the opportunity to discover more about the relationship between these two basic properties.

Though the motor to be constructed by the students is not original, it is the only motor I have ever seen that possesses *no* windings on the armature. The motor works every time, costs only about five cents to build, and is quite easy to construct and to understand. Each of my 80 students built one this year over a span of four class periods. Finally, the design allows the instructor a great deal of freedom to choose materials, depending upon what is available. Wide variations in size and design will still produce workable results.

MATERIALS

Two listings of materials needed for constructing the motors are given below. The first list should be helpful in assembling adequate materials for a class of 20 to 30 students. (Before preparing the motor parts for the class, the teacher should build a working motor himself.)

Teacher	*Student*
300 feet of hook-up wire	Sandpaper
20 feet of 6″ × 1″ planks	10 feet of insulated hook-up
Tinplate sheet, 26 gauge	wire
Galvanized steel (or aluminum) sheet, 20 gauge	4″ × 6″ × 1″ board with two nails in it
80 3″ flat-headed nails	1″ × 8″ galvanized steel
180 ½″ wood screws	(or aluminum) strip
60 1½ volt dry cells	1″ × 1″ tinplate square
60 bar magnets	3″ × 4″ tinplate rectangle
Screwdrivers	½″ wood screws (5)
Pocketknives	1½ volt dry cells (2)
Sandpaper	Bar magnets (2)
Scissors	

PREPARATION OF MATERIALS

The following preparations should be completed prior to the exercise. (Much time can be saved by having some of the parts mass-produced in the school shop.)

1. Hammer the nails into each board 2½ inches apart and 1 inch from one end, evenly centered.
2. Cut the 1″ × 1″ tinplate squares and drill holes in two opposite corners of each square. (They can be clamped and all drilled at once.) Dent the center of each square as shown in Fig. 1.
3. Cut the aluminum or galvanized metal into 1″ × 8″ strips. Drill two holes in the metal strip, one ½″ from one end and the other 1 ½″ from the same end (Fig. 2).
4. Dent the other end of the metal strip ½″ in from the end.
5. Cut 3″ × 4″ rectangles from the remaining tinplate.

PROCEDURE

Directions for building the electric motor should be mimeographed and given out to the class before materials are distributed.

CAUTION: Students should be warned that the tinplate has very sharp edges and must be handled with care.

The construction procedure is as follows:

1. Sandpaper the rough edges of the wooden block. Then strip an inch of the insulation coating off one end of the 10-foot wire. Leaving 3 inches of wire loose at the stripped end, begin winding the wire neatly up one nail. Then wind the wire back down the nail, making the wire two layers thick. (The other end of the wire should not be stripped, for there is no way of knowing how much of the wire will be used.)
2. Loop 6 inches of wire around to the other nail (Fig. 3). Make certain to wind the wire on the second nail *in the opposite direction from the windings on the first nail.* Continue winding the wire until it is two layers thick.

   (The wires are wound in different directions so that the top of one nail is an N pole and the top of the other nail is an S pole. Since the armature becomes magnetized, two N poles would prevent the motor from working. An N pole nail causes the nearest arm of the armature to become an S pole, which causes the other arm to become an N pole.)
3. Attach a battery to the two loose ends of the coils. Bring the N

pole of the bar magnet near the end of one nail. Result:____. Bring the N pole of the bar magnet near the other nail. Result:____.

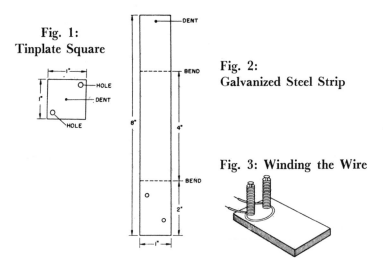

Fig. 1:
Tinplate Square

Fig. 2:
Galvanized Steel Strip

Fig. 3: Winding the Wire

NOTE: It is hoped that the student will notice that the N pole of the bar magnet is attracted to one electromagnet and repelled by the other. This *should* lead the student to believe that the direction in which the wire is wound influences the polarity of an electromagnet.

4. Screw the small tinplate square in line with the nails and directly between them. Attach one of the wire ends to one of the screws on the tinplate square.

5. Sketch an outline of the armature on the 3″ × 4″ piece of tinplate. Make sure that the rectangular arms are high enough so that when spinning the arms will not hit the nails (Fig. 4).

NOTE: Each student's armature sketch should be checked to see that the arms do indeed clear the nails. Then the students may be given scissors with which to cut out the armatures. (Small handicraft scissors will cut 26 gauge tinplate.)

6. Make a right angle bend 2 inches from the two-holed end of the aluminum or galvanized metal strip. Bend the strip away from the dented side (Fig. 2).

7. Bend the strip at the other end in the opposite direction from the first bend and 4 inches from the first bend (Fig. 2).

8. Screw down the strip so that the small dent is directly over the dent in the small square. The four-armed metal plate (armature)

should slip in easily. Make motor adjustments in the bends until the armature spins easily (Fig. 5).

9. Flick the armature with a finger and note how many seconds it spins.

NOTE: While the actual number of revolutions of the armature is unimportant, this step gives the student a feel for the force needed to sustain the motion of the armature. When the batteries are connected, the student will have an idea of how much the electromagnets aid the armature's rotation.

10. With the remaining screw, fasten a 3-inch length of wire down somewhere on the board. One end of the wire must brush against the triangular part of the armature (Fig. 6).

Fig. 4: Tinplate Armature

Fig. 5: Armature Assembly

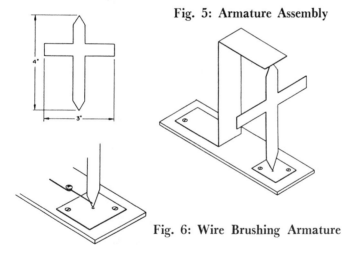

Fig. 6: Wire Brushing Armature

11. Connect the batteries in series. Attach the 3-inch piece of wire to one free battery terminal (Photo 1). Spin the armature to start the motor.

CAUTION: Students should be warned that the armature may become hot during operation and should not be touched.

12. If the motor does not work, loosen the metal strip supporting the armature. Do not be alarmed if the brush area sparks; the batteries are, in effect, shorted out for an instant with each revolution.

Photo 1: Test Model

FOLLOW-UP

When they have finished their motors, the students can complete the exercises below.

- Trace the path of the electricity from the battery through the motor and back to the battery again in writing.
- Make a circuit diagram of your motor.
- Write the symbols for an electromagnet and another of greater strength than the first.
- Explain the working of the motor and the function of the switch.
- Describe the two ways in which the motor can be made more powerful.

7 Earth Science Activities

Water Problems and Investigations   196

Demonstrating Sedimentation   203

A Model for Studying
    Topographic Maps   205

"Gonna Build a Mountain"—
    An Earth Science Project   206

Student-Centered Earth Science   209

A Useful Model to Illustrate
    Earth Phenomena   211

Earthquakes: A Long-Term
    Lab Exercise   214

The Use of Gravel Pits in
    Field Investigations   217

A Field Trip for Earth Science   221

Staking a Mining Claim   225

Creating an Economic Mineral
    Display   228

Water Problems
and Investigations

by Marjorie Elliott

Southwest High School, Kansas City, Missouri

It is not difficult to interest students in a scientific investigation if it touches their personal lives. In a recent unit on water resources and problems, I found that most of the students absorbed concepts with understanding and enthusiasm. Their scores on the test at the close of the three-week unit were excellent. Moreover, some students became so deeply interested in the subject that they pursued further investigations independently.

> NOTE: Earth science classes taking this unit are made up of students in grades 11 and 12. The classes include many slow students who have great difficulty with mathematics. The type of approach outlined here involved almost all of these students, and some potential "dropouts" took part with real interest. (The activities described might also be used with 8th or 9th grade general science students.)

To begin the unit, I read an excerpt from an article on hydrology which presents man's agelong concern about water resources and stresses the current world-wide water shortage.[1] After the reading, I asked the students two questions: "What is the source of the water used by people and industries in this great metropolitan area?" and "Why is water called the 'lifeblood' of the city?"

Discussion of these two questions stimulated the students' interest and brought out further questions which they felt merited investigation. Following are some of these problem-questions:

1. Why are our creeks and rivers so dirty?
2. How is dirty water made safe for human consumption?
3. How much water does a metropolitan area such as ours need?
4. How can anyone be certain that the water supply will be sufficient?

---

[1] "Hydrology," *Time Magazine*, Oct. 1, 1965.

5. Is water pollution a serious problem? If so, what can be done about it?

6. How can ocean water be made usable?

STUDYING WATER RESOURCES AND PROBLEMS— STUDENT INVESTIGATIONS

Students volunteered to serve on committees, each of which was to investigate a specific problem and report its findings to the class. A few wished to make individual studies on other aspects of water. This was acceptable if the topic chosen could be correlated with a general water problem.

Water Pollution

The problem that concerned the largest number of students was the pollution of our water resources. One of the first committees to report had visited a creek which winds its way from the outskirts of the city through a residential area. They reported that they had observed several examples of something that we had studied earlier—small waterfalls created where softer shale had worn away below more resistant limestone. But the waterfalls they had seen were not clear and beautiful. Pools beneath the limestone ledges which should have been ideal for fish were hidden by masses of detergent suds foaming up almost to the tops of the falls (Photos 1 and 2).

Pictures taken by this committee were passed around the class to show the present condition of the stream. From a topographic map of the area, the students pointed out the dendritic pattern of the stream and the fact that in our area all such streams eventually emptied into the Missouri River. The class noted that not only the metropolitan area but also many cities and towns downsteam must contend with the polluted water.

Several students commented that the problem of pollution is not merely local but must be national and world-wide in scope. In order to understand

Photo 1

Photo 2

how widespread pollution is and how the problem is being attacked in other areas, they read magazine articles and wrote letters to a number of foreign embassies in Washington, D.C. They then gave oral reports based on their research and illustrated with their own sketches and diagrams.

River Control

Another set of reports which evoked student controversy was centered on river control. Three of these reports were:

- A treatment of the Missouri River as a representative stream of its type, which linked the region's problems with the control of its water supply.
- A study of the meaning of control, featuring an interview with one of the engineers in the Army Corps of Engineers.
- A report on the various types of dams used for water control and the conditions for which each type is best suited (Fig. 1).

These reports started a lively discussion as to whether all the dams proposed for construction about the nation should actually be constructed. Several students had read material stating that some rivers should be left in their natural state because of their exceptional beauty and because some of them are the natural habitat for fast-disappearing species of wildlife.

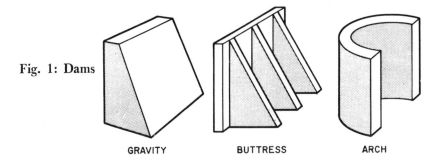

Fig. 1: Dams

GRAVITY   BUTTRESS   ARCH

Other Reports

Other topics chosen for investigation included: The Hydrologic Cycle; How the United States and Canada Are Meeting Problems of the Great Lakes; Mexico and the Colorado River; Egypt and the Nile; France and England Meet Their Water Problems; India: Floods, Drought, and Pollution; Effect of Glaciers on the World Water Supply; Untapped Water Resources of Africa.

Solutions to Water Crises

Each of the committees attempted to offer solutions to the world water crises. Among those suggested were the following:

- A gigantic effort in public education concerning the seriousness of the problem and the necessity for conservation
- Water rationing in all non-essential uses
- Finding cheaper methods of reusing water
- Draining and cultivating swampland
- Using algae in water purification
- Desalinization

LABORATORY INVESTIGATIONS OF WATER

During the three weeks of reports, one day each week was used for performing laboratory exercises related to water. The exercises were designed to help the students gain an understanding of solution, suspension, and saltation.

Investigation #1: Using pint jars about two-thirds full of cool water, the students added salt by the tablespoon, stirring the water vigorously after each addition until no more salt would dissolve (until a little salt remained in the bottom of the jar in spite of the stirring).

NOTE: Other substances that can be used are KNO_3 or even sucrose, whose solubilities increase markedly with temperature. According to the "Handbook of Chemistry and Physics,"[2] the solubility of NaCl in 100 grams of cold water is 35.7 grams, while in an equal amount of hot water it is 39.8 grams. Similar figures for KNO_3 are 13.3 g and 246 g respectively.

The students then heated the jars in pans of water over Bunsen burners, adding more salt until it would no longer dissolve. A thermometer was left in each jar during the entire time of the exercise. Each student plotted the number of tablespoonfuls of salt dissolved against temperature on a graph (Table 1).

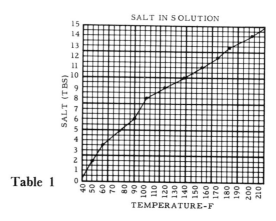

Table 1

Conclusions: Some substances will dissolve in water and may be carried in solution as part of liquid. The dissolved material is only a small fraction of the total load (Fig. 2). As the water becomes warmer, greater amounts of these substances will dissolve before saturation is reached.

Investigation #2: On the following week, the students filled several quart jars about three-fourths full of water (Fig. 3), then added a handful of soil to the water. After screwing lids on the jars, they shook the jars for several minutes. They observed that the water cleared very slowly, with larger particles settling out first and remaining in suspension only as long as the water was agitated. The students also noted that some of the finest particles did not settle out during the class period, but that all sediments appeared at the bottoms of the jars by the next day. Finally, they observed that the particles were stratified.

---

[2] R. C. Weast, *Handbook of Chemistry and Physics* (Cleveland, Ohio 44128: Chemical Rubber Co.).

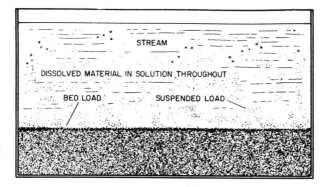

Fig. 2

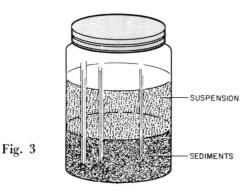

Fig. 3

Conclusion: Large particles require greater water energy than smaller particles to keep them from settling out.

Investigation #3: During the last week of the unit, the students constructed a trough using a piece of wide guttering about 10 feet long, 2 pails, a section of old garden hose about 4 feet long, wire for supports, boxes, and blocks of wood (Fig. 4).

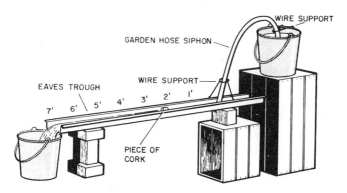

Fig. 4

With this apparatus, they performed two exercises, one to test the effect of slope on stream velocity, the other to test the effect of volume on stream velocity. In the first exercise, small pieces of cork were sent down the trough, which was adjusted at the end opposite the source to angles of 5°, 10°, and 15°. (The angles were measured by protractor and level and raised or lowered by means of small wooden blocks.) A stopwatch was used to time the cork's speed. The speed at each angle was tested three times and the results were recorded and averaged in a table (Table 2).

SLOPE AND STREAM VELOCITY

SLOPE ANGLE 5°			REPEAT TABLE FOR SLOPE ANGLES OF 10° AND 15°
DISTANCE TRAVELED	TIME	RATE (D/T)	
TRIAL 1 10'	4. 3 sec	2. 3 ft/sec	
TRIAL 2 10'	4. 8 sec	2.1 ft/sec	
TRIAL 3 10'	4. 6 sec	2. 2 ft/sec	COMPARE VELOCITIES
AVERAGE RATE 2. 2 ft/sec			

Table 2

NOTE: It is necessary to keep the distance from the water level in the pail to the lower end of the siphon (hose) constant.

To test the effect of changing the quantity of water, the students set the trough at an angle of 10°, and fed water into it from first one siphon, then two, then three. Their results were recorded in another table (Table 3).

Conclusions: (1) As the slope increases, the velocity of the water also increases. (2) As the volume of the water increases, the stream's velocity increases.

WATER VOLUME AND STREAM VELOCITY

USING ONE SIPHON	DISTANCE TRAVELED	TIME	RATE (D/T)	REPEAT TABLE FOR TWO SIPHONS AND THREE SIPHONS
TRIAL 1	10 FT	5.0 sec	2.0 ft/sec	
TRIAL 2	10 FT	5.5 sec	1.8 ft/sec	
TRIAL 3	10 FT	5. 3 sec	1. 9 ft/sec	
AVERAGE RATE 1. 9 FT/SEC				

Table 3

Demonstrating Sedimentation

by George R. Wells

Joliet Township High School, Joliet, Illinois

The laboratory exercise presented below has aroused much interest among students. It is used in an Earth Science unit dealing with the work of water and has many applications—with rivers, flood plains, deltas, alluvial fans, lake deposits, and geologic history as it can be read in different kinds of sedimentary rock.

> **NOTE: A simple demonstration and hypothetical case will convince students that there is more to the explanation of sedimentation than simply saying that gravel is heaviest and so sinks fastest. To help students understand surface exposed to resistance per unit of mass, have them hold a sheet of notebook paper horizontally and allow it to float down. Then ask them to crumple up the paper and drop it from the same height. They will observe that although the weight of the paper is the same in both cases, the rate of fall is far faster in the latter case.**

The phenomena of sedimentation and its active principles can be demonstrated as follows:

MATERIALS

1000cc. glass cylinder jar
250cc. glass beaker
Bunsen burner
gravel
coarse sand
fine sand
powdered clay (silt)
water

PROCEDURE

Part I

- Place a small handful of the solids in the glass cylinder jar, and then fill it about three-fourths full of water.
- Put a hand tightly over the top of the jar and shake it vigorously until the contents are thoroughly mixed.

- Bring the jar quickly to an upright position and allow its contents to stand until fully settled.
- Observe the order of the sedimentation (size of the materials). Are the materials well sorted and stratified?

The sorting is not clear-cut in the lower layer of the cylinder jar where a great deal of fine material will be mixed with the larger gravel. This is largely because much fine material was at the bottom when shaking stopped. Students will also see that large particles cannot pack closely together but leave many spaces through which finer particles can settle.

Part II

- Allow the cylinder jar and its contents to stand overnight. (Not all of the colloidal silt will settle for many hours. Explain to the students that colloids also exist in gases. An example with which they are all familiar is smoke.)

  NOTE: To be scientifically correct, distilled water should be used in order to show what has actually gone into solution from the sediments. However, if tap water is used, one may point out what exists in most potable water supplies.

- After settling is complete, pour off a small amount of the remaining clear water, and boil it away over the Bunsen burner.
- Observe what remains in the beaker. What does this material represent? Why was it not visible in the water? Does such material exist in ocean and river waters?

OBSERVATIONS

The questions included in the outline of procedure and those following may be used in having students write up their observations for the demonstration.

1. How did the water appear after shaking?
2. In what order did the solid materials settle?
3. Was there any sand and silt mixed with the coarse gravel at the bottom of the cylinder jar? Account for this.
4. Was there any evidence to show that sorting or grading occurred within the silt? (Stir the water gently in a whirling motion and observe the results.)
5. The finest material of all, on top, is called colloidal silt. What is a colloid?

A Model for Studying Topographic Maps

by William T. Jackson

Lockport East High School, Lockport, Illinois

Topographic maps—especially the U.S.G.S. Quadrangles—are widely used in the study of land forms in earth science courses, and they are often difficult for students to comprehend. I have found that an effective way of preparing students for study of these maps is having them create a simple model.

MATERIALS

To build the model, the class will need the following materials:

Flat-bottomed container, such as a small aquarium, at least 12″ in diameter
1 quart of glazing compound or putty
Dissecting needle (from the biology department) or a sharp pencil
Ruler
Means of adding water to the tank

NOTE: As many models can be built and used in class as available materials permit.

PROCEDURE

Have the students fashion a model of an island with the glazing compound (Fig. 1), encouraging them to use their imaginations to produce the best model possible. Minimum characteristics for the model should be:

1. Steeper on one side than on the other
2. 4 to 6 inches high
3. A valley
4. A ridge

When the model has been completed, place it in the tank and add water to a depth of 1 centimeter. Then make a mark with the needle (or draw a line with the pencil) at the water line. Follow this by adding another centimeter of water and drawing another line.

Explain to the students that these lines are actually contour lines. Continue to add water and to draw or mark the lines until the water covers the model. (If more contour lines are desired, the depth interval used may be ¼ inch instead of 1 centimeter.)

> **NOTE: If the model is kept covered with water until it is no longer needed, the glazing compound can be returned to an airtight container and be used for several years.**

While the students are examining the finished model, instruct them to look at it from directly above to get the proper perspective of model and contour lines (Fig. 2). They should be told to pay particular attention to how the contour lines show the various features of the model. These observations should be followed by a study of a U.S.G.S. Quadrangle, with students looking for the same features on the map.

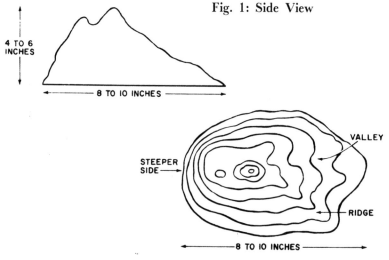

Fig. 1: Side View

Fig. 2: View from Above

"Gonna Build a Mountain"— An Earth Science Project

by Ole C. Davis
Buckroe Junior High School, Hampton, Virginia

"Gonna build a mountain; gonna build it high; Don' know how I'm gonna build it; only know I'm gonna try." This might be the theme song for our earth science students while studying the forces that shape or sculpture the earth's surface, for in our locality—Southeast Virginia—the only major landform immediately available for study is the Atlantic Coastal Plain. The nearest mountains are 200 miles to the west, too far for a class field trip. Thus the study of mountains and underlying rock formations is accomplished using student-built models.

> NOTE: Even if the teacher has ample funds to purchase landform models, student construction of the models assists in the learning process. For those with limited budgets, this type of project can be completed at little or no expense.

PREPARATION

In preparation for model-building, students must become familiar with the subject through use of the text, references, and audio-visual aids. It is also helpful if they have completed the study of minerals and rocks.

After reading the literature and viewing films, students should have a good idea of what they will represent with their models. The teacher can then assign various landform projects. By allowing each student team to make a model of a different landform, the subject area can be covered more rapidly and, in my opinion, more effectively than by having 15 teams make models of the same landform. As each model is assigned, its origin, steps in weathering and erosion, and the final product may be explained.

MATERIALS AND CONSTRUCTION

The next step, which may be carried out during the reading phase, is the collection of materials to be used in making the models.

Obtaining a Base

The first acquisition should be a piece of wood or plywood that is strong enough to serve as a base for the landform to be built. Small scraps of plywood from the shop, wooden boxes, old desk tops, and strong cardboard boxes can be used for this purpose.

In modeling faults, cardboard boxes are desirable for they allow painting of the rock layers on the box. Different colors may be used to represent different rock formations. The box can then be cut and uplifted on one side to form the fault. The resulting space can be filled with cardboard, taped into place and painted the appropriate colors.

Outlining the Landform

With bases on hand, students can proceed to build a rough outline of their landform using smaller, wooden or cardboard boxes and chicken wire or hardware screen. The outlines can be rounded to approximate the final shape with flour/water paste and newspaper or mud.

> NOTE: Papier-mâché or mud may be used to build the entire model, though adequate drying time must be allowed between applications of layers. If the paste or mud is given the right consistency, a layer will dry between class periods.

When using the flour/water paste, it is best not to mix too large a batch at a time. The paste can be used after standing overnight, but the longer it stands, the thicker it gets. The teacher should keep on hand a good supply of newspapers for desk coverings. This speeds cleanup, though ample cleanup time must always be allowed at the end of the period.

Finishing the Model

The final stages in construction are shaping and decorating the landforms. Smaller strips of paper and careful molding of the mud can result in shaping that is in every detail what the student wants.

> VARIATIONS: Models may also be finished with plaster of Paris or modeling clay. The latter allows representation of different rock layers with different colors.

Students can color their landforms using water colors or another medium. Though a few will indiscriminately use pinks and purples to represent different rock formations, most students will probably attempt to match colors with the objects they are representing.

> REPORTS: With the completion of the model and as time for reporting approaches, some students will probably be unprepared. The teacher may allow another period or two for the finalization of reports.

A Class Project

While the preceding presents only the barest of details of our model-building project, each teacher will think of variations and improvements. A little work, collecting of materials, some supervision, and the class can develop a series of landforms that illustrate many of the items studied in the unit on shaping and sculpturing the landscape.

If a stream table is available, this may be the best aid for showing sculpturing. If not, old paper and paste can be used again and again to show various steps in building and tearing down the face of the earth. Why not build a model of the earth in change, constant change?

Student-Centered
Earth Science

by Merrick A. Owen

Edinboro State College, Edinboro, Pennsylvania

It is misleading to spend Monday, Wednesday, and Friday in the class-room and Tuesday and Thursday in the laboratory. To be realistic, science should be consistently taught as a student-centered, investigatory, problem-solving subject. Throughout the course, the student must work as a scientist using the methods necessary to help him solve a problem. Each problem he investigates should lead to fresh problems and investigations.

> NOTE: The investigatory approach to earth science described here is part of the New York State Experimental Regents Earth Science Course. I am currently using this approach with two ninth grade classes without extra laboratory periods.

In my two earth science classes, 80 percent of our class time—five periods of 52 minutes per week—is devoted to investigations of a laboratory nature. The remaining 20 percent of our time is used for pre-labs, short lectures and discussions of problems, and post-labs. Each new investigation is begun with a statement of its behavioral objectives and ended with an evaluation of the student's success in meeting these objectives.

"PUDDLE PUZZLE"[1]

Pre-Lab

A student investigation might start with the topic, "Puddle Puzzle." To begin, the behavioral objectives are defined for the student. In this case the objectives are: "To be able to distinguish an Observation from an Inference, and, from a list, separate the Inference from the Observations, explaining your choices." These objectives are discussed, then the procedures to be followed in the investigation are defined.

> NOTE: This lab can be conducted on any nearby construction site where students can explore and list their observations of the existing mud puddles.

During the pre-lab, students are also given a list of the tools they will need for the activity in the field—knives, corkborers, and rulers.

---

[1] "Puddle Puzzle," Student Investigation, *New York State Experimental Earth Science Syllabus.*

Observations

Several observations made by one team of students follow:
- The dried puddle had dents in it.
- We cut a section out of the puddle and it had three layers.
- There were small gullies at both ends of the puddle.
- There were tracks in the mud.

Post-Lab

The post-lab time is used for discussion of students' lists of observations and the compilation of one class list using the overhead projector. Each item is also discussed and classified as an Observation or Inference. The teams are then given a list of questions to answer with an Inference, for example: How deep was the puddle? Why was the puddle no deeper? Has deposition taken place in the puddle?

Samples of the puddle area may be collected and exhibited, accompanied with appropriate questions that can be answered from observation.

Lab-Evaluation

To evaluate the lab, a test is constructed to see how well the behavioral objectives have been met. The evaluation might include a group of statements for the student to categorize as either Observations or Inferences.

FOLLOW-UP: Many times in science classes the evaluation ends the topic. Not so with this approach. The theme of "Energy and Change" and the student's ability to make inferences from observations is reinforced by another activity—"Observing the Sun's Motion."

"OBSERVING THE SUN'S MOTION"[2]

Procedures

In this follow-up investigation, the student draws a five-inch radius circle on a flat outdoor surface in direct sunlight.

Using the compass, he marks off the directional points and secures a ten-inch stick upright in the center with a piece of clay. The student then marks the shadow of the stick on the circle and repeats the marking procedure every hour. When this has been done three or four times, he measures the angle between each shadow mark.

---

[2] This is a variation on "Sun Watch," an investigation in *Investigating the Earth,* Earth Science Curriculum Project (Boston: Houghton Mifflin Company, 1967), p. 27. (Teacher's Guide, Part 1, p. 57.)

From the data the student collects and observes, he is asked to make inferences: Did the sun change position in the sky? Was the movement of the shadow caused by the apparent change in the sun's position? How many degrees did the sun appear to move each hour?

Post-Lab

In the post-lab, the student discusses the relationship between the sun's motion and earth rotation, the calculation of the apparent hourly shift, and the measurement and motion of the shadow he observed.

> **NOTE: Placing the initiative and responsibility for learning directly on the student, this type of science teaching puts the student—not the teacher—in the center of the learning process. Well-planned activities and laboratory situations can be open-ended to allow the gifted and motivated student to go beyond the activity in his search for answers.**

A Useful Model to Illustrate Earth Phenomena

by Donald F. Brandewie

Swanson Junior High School, Arlington, Virginia

Many companies specialize in the creation of teaching tools and visual aids designed to supplement and enhance the science teacher's instructional program. Detailed, realistic, and accurate models help transform abstract concepts into shapes and materials the student can see, touch, study, and investigate at first hand. Teachers agree that the use of such materials makes textbook readings and study plans far more meaningful.

However, with the continuing rise in the cost of education, many teachers find it increasingly difficult to obtain the money required to purchase educational tools. More and more teachers find it necessary to improvise to supplement their instructional program with visual aids. Interestingly enough, they often discover that actual experience in building and using their own simple models can give students an even better understanding of the subject under study than mere use of a commercially built model.

> **EXAMPLE: While earth science teachers can purchase models depicting such things as various types of shorelines, structural mapping, map contouring, and stream develop-**

ment, they can easily build an ordinary sand box to help them accomplish many of the same objectives.

MAKING A SIMPLE MODEL

A piece of three-quarter inch plywood cut 4′ × 4′ and sided with 4′ × 6″ strips can be placed on a table in the middle of the classroom. (Painting the top surface blue to simulate water will give a more realistic effect to some of the suggestions offered here.) Several bucketfuls of sand are then placed on the middle of the board. Wetting the sand will allow the teacher or students to mold it into any desired shape.

This simple setup can be used to depict coastlines of submergence and emergence by shaping the sand to show the characteristics of each type of shoreline. Or, for better understanding of dip and strike of rock strata and its application to structural mapping, the sand can be molded to represent any surface topography. Sheets of cardboard can then be inserted in the sand in different positions and at different angles to represent rock strata. By assigning directions to the sides of the plywood board, students can determine strike direction and angle of dip.

Studying Topographic Mapping

The sand box has many applications in the study of topographic mapping. Again, the sand can be molded to represent an island or continental margin with any desired surface features, such as hills, depressions, and river valleys. White cord string may be used to represent contour lines. To insure that the string is at the same elevation at all points on the sand, a thin steel rod with measured markings can be inserted in the sand to determine a number of points of equal elevation.

By use of this technique, the following general rules concerning contour lines can be demonstrated:

- Steep slopes have contour lines close together; on gentle slopes the lines are farther apart.
- Where contour lines cross a stream valley they must bend upstream to remain at the same elevation.
- All points enclosed by an ordinary contour line are higher in elevation than that line.
- If a hill is cone-shaped, with a smooth surface, the contours are a series of concentric circles, successively smaller toward the top of the hill.
- Contour lines never split.
- Every contour line closes on itself either within or beyond the limits of the map.

PROBLEMS: In addition to its use in illustrating these general rules, the model can be employed with problems involving the determination of direction, location, and map scaling.

USING A WATERPROOFED MODEL

Substituting a sheet of glass for one of the plywood sides (Fig. 1) and making the box watertight with aquarium cement and putty will allow further activities. When the sand box is waterproofed:

1. Completely cover the bottom with several inches of sand.
2. Create a stream valley in the sand.
3. Cut a cardboard tube in half longitudinally and insert it in the sand with the cut edge facing the glass front. (This will represent an ordinary well.)
4. Now pour water in the sand so that the upper level of the water is higher than both the bottom of the stream valley and the lower portion of the simulated well.

This will enable students to see the zones of saturation and aeration separated by the water table. They will observe how the ground water maintains the stream and the well and, after days of slow evaporation, watch the well and stream gradually dry up as the water table falls.

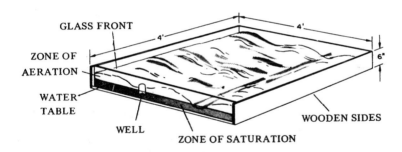

Fig. 1: Construction of the Waterproof Sandbox

Simulating Other Formations

Two more uses for the waterproofed model are in the study of artesian formation and rock strata. Inserting thin layers of modeling clay to represent impermeable rock layers will enable construction of an artesian formation with an accompanying artesian well. To present problems in the correlating of rock strata, the teacher can separate the sand into two mounds using one-fourth inch and one-half inch Styrofoam sheets cut to size (Fig. 2). The Styrofoam sheets should be painted in different colors on their edges to simulate different types of sedimentary rocks.

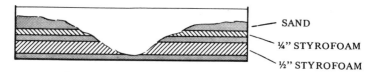

Fig. 2: Correlating Rock Strata

Earthquakes: A Long-Term Lab Exercise

by Nicholas K. Yost
Keithley Junior High School, Tacoma, Washington

This lab exercise, for junior high or high school students in the area of geology or earth science, is in line with modern efforts to get student involvement in science teaching. An earthquake cannot very well be duplicated in a laboratory; these rapid destructive forces are but a minute portion of the time and force in the warping and buckling of the crust of the earth into mountains and folds.

Recent theories explain the formation of island arcs and trenches as the beginnings of new coastal mountains being formed along coastal regions (see Fig. 1). The lab exercise described here lets students investigate this formerly sophisticated theory for themselves.

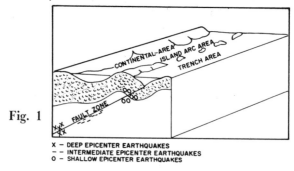

Fig. 1

X — DEEP EPICENTER EARTHQUAKES
– – INTERMEDIATE EPICENTER EARTHQUAKES
0 – SHALLOW EPICENTER EARTHQUAKES

OBJECTIVES

The lab has four purposes, each aimed at a desired objective in science teaching:

1. To furnish the student with the idea of long-term experimentation. In most demonstrations and experiments this is lacking; the students never are

led to the actual time element involved in the collecting of data in a true scientific investigation. Most labs require less than two hours. In this investigation, collection of data requires a few minutes a day, but for three or four months, and the data becomes more and more reliable with the length of time over which it is collected.

2. To allow students to obtain their own data to support or disprove recent theories. Most lab exercises allow students to prove theories which have been accepted for many, perhaps hundreds, of years. This investigation allows students to support (or perhaps tend to disprove) a recent theory which is not necessarily accepted by all scientists working in the area.

3. To show frequency of crustal movement or disturbance (earthquakes). Most students consider such things as earthquakes, hurricanes, volcano eruptions, and so on, as rare. This exercise attempts to show the frequency of earthquakes over the earth and at the same time allows students to plot an analysis by depth and magnitude.

4. To show the relationship of island arcs to earth movements. The shape of the continents, island groups, and ocean bottom all relate to one another, and have been studied for years. Recent theories have attempted to relate these even closer and support their relationships by seismic data. In this exercise, students collect data which may add to this relationship.

MATERIALS

- Map of Japan and near island groups (Cartocraft Outline Map), obtainable from: Denoyer and Geppert, 5235 Ravenswood Ave., Chicago, Ill.

  NOTE: It is not necessary that you select this particular location; a good map of any island arc group will do. However, the Japanese and Aleutian arcs seem to work best.
- Map tacks: 100 blue, 100 red, 100 green.
- *Earthquake Report* (Selected List of World Wide Epicenter), obtainable from U.S. Department of Commerce, Coast & Geodetic Survey, Washington, D.C., 20235.
- Preliminary Determination of Epicenters Cards, obtainable from U.S. Department of Commerce, Coast and Geodetic Survey, Washington Service Center, Rockville, Maryland, 20852.

  IMPORTANT: Be sure to send for these cards at least 30 days before you wish to start the lab.

PROCEDURE

On your outline map of an island arc group (preferably one with a longitude and latitude scale of 2° or 5° lines), draw in as accurately as you can the longitude and latitude lines to the nearest degree. From this make a transparency for the overhead projector, and project it on 2 foot by 3 foot tagboard, cardboard, construction paper or heavy white paper. With a fine felt tip pen, draw the enlarged projection on the paper. Use different colors for land boundaries, longitude, and latitude. Put the enlarged drawing on a bulletin board that will accept tacks. (Fig. 2.)

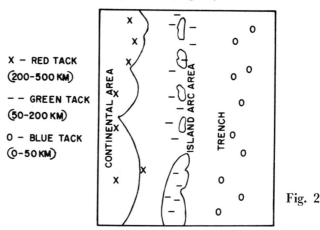

X – RED TACK
(200-500 KM)

– – GREEN TACK
(50-200 KM)

O – BLUE TACK
(0-50 KM)

Fig. 2

NOTE: It is important that students know how to plot a point on a map using longitude and latitude. Thus, the first part of the investigation should include an opportunity to plot on a map. You can use outline maps of the type used for the enlargement to permit students to plot a few earthquakes on their own individual maps. Students can be given a copy of the *Earthquake Report* referred to. The epicenters are listed by area and are easily selected for the area you want to plot.

Actual plotting of earthquakes is from the "Preliminary Determination of Epicenters" cards, which list recent earthquakes as they occur. The date, region, latitude, longitude, depth and magnitude of each are given on the card. About 400 earthquakes are listed as they occur each month, and each card has from 20 to 100 epicenters listed. You will receive three or four cards a week.

Depending on the island arc you select, the investigation should take from three to four months to complete. Naturally, the longer the data are plotted, the more reliable they become. This point itself is a concept well worth stressing to all science students.

NOTE: Since with the more points you plot the better the results, you can if you wish plot additional points from the *Earthquake Report* already referred to.

The mechanics are simple. Students will place a blue tack at the latitude and longitude location where earthquake depths are less than 50 kilometers, a green tack where they are between 50 and 200 kilometers, and a red tack where the depth is greater than 200 kilometers. The number of earthquakes to be plotted each week will vary from six to sometimes thirty. A different student should be assigned to plot each earthquake right from the cards; it takes only a few minutes a day and can be done before or after class time.

After about six weeks, a pattern similar to that shown in Fig. 2 should be evident. The continental region will show most of the deep focus earthquakes, the geosynclinal area between the island arc and continent the intermediate depth earthquakes, and the trench area the shallow focus earthquakes. Referring back to Fig. 1, the pattern thus formed would give support to this theory of island arc development.

The Use of Gravel Pits in Field Investigations

by Jerry W. Vincent

Stephen F. Austin State University, Nacogdoches, Texas

To teach geology and earth science effectively as sciences, the teacher must involve the students in what geologists really do, that is, making and recording observations, sampling, collecting and interpreting data, and arriving at conclusions based on data. This approach invariably necessitates a field trip to some locality that illustrates the concepts covered in the classroom.

The use of sand and gravel pits for such field investigations is particularly suitable to demonstrate sedimentary processes and principles of stratigraphy in areas of igneous and metamorphic rock. Due to the demand for road-building materials, gravel pits are fairly common over most of the nation. Also they are often close to populated areas, thus are easily accessible.

CHARACTERISTICS OF DEPOSITS

Most sand and gravel deposits are the result of fluvial or glaciofluvial deposition and, as such, should contain the characteristics of deposition in these environments. Fluvial deposits in the form of stream terraces associated with mature streams would probably be the most common sites for pits outside of the unglaciated parts of the country. Outwash plains, glacial deltas, eskers, kames, or kame terraces are the most common sites for sand and gravel deposits in glaciated regions.

NOTE: In either case, water-deposited sediments of different types are exposed, and this is the primary requisite. Variation of the basic concepts can be explored, depending upon the type of deposit exposed. The exposed sedimentary beds can be measured, sampled, and examined in detail.

FIELD TRIP PREPARATION

Once a gravel pit has been located within reasonable distance of the school, the teacher should make several visits to the pit to familiarize himself completely with what is there. If assistance is needed, geology departments of nearby colleges, or state geological surveys are usually most cooperative.

An excellent reference for planning and preparing for the field trip is the *Geology and Earth Science Sourcebook* (National Academy of Sciences, New York: Holt, Rinehart & Winston, 1967). This is one of the best available general references dealing with methods of teaching the earth sciences, and should definitely be consulted if the teacher lacks field experience.

FIELD TRIP PROCEDURE

Following is a sequence of suggested procedures to be used in connection with those offered in the *Sourcebook*, but with particular stress on gravel pit investigation. Some of the steps can be modified or omitted by the teacher, depending upon the problem to be investigated and the amount of time available in which to complete it.

Step 1: After the topics of stratigraphy and sedimentation have been covered in the classroom, the problem to be investigated should be outlined in detail. The students must have a good idea of what they are investigating. (A good problem might be to determine the environments of deposition reflected in the sediments of the deposit in which the pit is located.)

Step 2: The regional geologic setting of the deposit should then be developed.

READING: This is a good place for outside reading assignments on the geology of the area and, ideally, on the deposit itself, or others similar to it. From this reading, the students can get ideas as to how others have described and interpreted the deposit.

Laboratory preparation should include the use of aerial photographs and topographic and/or geologic maps of the area. With these tools, the student will gain some insight into such things as the geometry of the deposit and its relation to the surrounding area.

In this step, the students should be working toward the development of a reasonable hypothesis on what they might expect to find as a result of their research.

Step 3: Immediately prior to the trip, instruction should be given in the use of the compass, pacing to measure distance, note-taking, sampling, and safety so that these things will be fresh in the students' minds. And the students should be instructed to equip themselves with good field shoes or boots, a shovel or trowel, a notebook, sample sacks of some type, and marking pens.

Step 4: The teacher should then explain the methods the students are to employ in dealing with the problem. A suggested procedure is as follows:

a. Prepare a sketch map of the pit drawn to scale (Fig. 1).

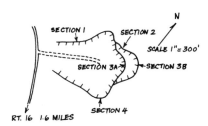

Fig. 1: Sample Sketch Map

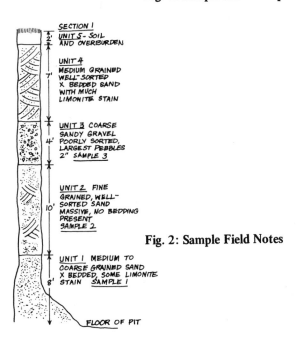

Fig. 2: Sample Field Notes

b. Select five or six equally well-spaced sites along the entire circumference of the pit, and locate them on your sketch map using the
compass and pace method and some landmark in the pit as a cross-
reference. (Spots with a maximum amount of pit face exposure
should be selected.)

c. Consider each site a "section" and measure it as follows. Beginning
at the base of the section, for each bed:

• Measure its thickness.

• Take a two or three pound sample, properly labeled with reference to section and bed.

• Record the thickness and sample number in your notebook
(Fig. 2).

• Describe in your notebook the lithology of the bed, taking
particular note of any sedimentary structures, such as cross
bedding, laminations, and ripple marks.

• Make notes of or sample anything else of possible importance,
such as fossils.

d. After measuring the sections, walk over or "cruise" the area around
the pit to see how it compares with the maps and photos. Make
note of any changes so that maps and photos can be corrected.

Step 5: All samples and field notes should be brought to the lab for
further examination. For each sample, students may be asked to:

• Determine the gross minerology

• Estimate the grain size and degree of sorting

• Record this data in an appropriate place in the field notes

Step 6: Now that the data has been collected, it must be interpreted.
The students can prepare a graphic representation of each measured section
using standard symbols and descriptions. With their sketch maps and
measured sections, they can then create a fence diagram. This will serve as a
three-dimensional model of the pit.

**NOTE: In order to prepare this diagram properly, beds
must be correlated across the pit, and such factors as
changes in thickness and facies must be taken into consideration.**

Step 7: Students should now be required to draw some conclusions of
their own based upon the evidence they have collected in the form of a
final report. In addition to conclusions about sedimentary environments, the
report might also include a sequence of events demonstrated by the deposit
and a comparison of conclusions with those of previous investigators.

Step 8: When the work has been completed, the results should be reviewed
and dissected by the entire class. Students should have the opportunity to
present and defend their interpretations supported by their evidence. Thus
weaknesses and/or strengths in their interpretations may pointed out by

fellow students as well as the teacher. From a discussion of this type should come a fairly good understanding of what was "going on" in the area at the time the sediments were being developed. Another aspect to be considered is that students will have to see that in geology and other sciences as well there may not be *one* correct answer and that lacking more definitive evidence, different interpretations have equal validity.

> NOTE: When students have had the experience of their first field trip, it would be a good idea to let them devise their own approach the next time out.

A Field Trip for Earth Science

by Harry F. Pomeroy, Jr.
Yucca Junior High School, Clovis, New Mexico

Regardless of his location, the earth science teacher should be able to design a field trip to "bring to life" the material learned in the classroom. Even the most "geologically sterile" area offers many opportunities for helping students to relate and apply learning to their environment. And students' work in the field may provide the best measure of the value of the earth science course.

> NOTE: The field trip described here is confined to a school ground on the High Plains which lacks outcrops. Requiring only one 50-minute period to complete, the procedures involved can be easily adapted to any area of the country.

The trip was designed to summarize our study of the earth in ninth-grade earth science and followed completion of the first three units of *Investigating the Earth* (ESCP, Boston: Houghton Mifflin Company, 1967).

OBJECTIVES

In planning the field trip, we set these objectives:

- To tie together the variables affecting change on the earth and on man's handiwork—buildings, streets, and landscaping.
- To use a topographic map of a small area, the local school grounds.
- To get students to think about what is below the soil.

- To familiarize students with their local terrain.
- To show practical applications of earth science knowledge.

Each objective was considered in light of our particular limitations. The trip had to be conducted within the city since the school system does not provide for extensive travel. Also, students could not miss other classes, so the observations to be made around the school had to be completed within a 50-minute period.

Further limitations were posed by the fact that Clovis is on the High Staked Plains, an area of low relief. There are no outcrops within a 40-mile radius of the city, and the only ones to be seen are pebbles in the soil or exposed in concrete. (Earth scientists call the area "geologically sterile.") Finally, since Yucca Junior High School is a new building, there is little change observable in man's work other than patches in the adjacent streets and cracks in the school building.

PREPARATION

After setting objectives for the field trip, I developed a series of items for the students to look for. These were based on my own observations during the six months the school had been in use and a tour of the school grounds. To ensure that students made the observations, each observation included questions designed to tie in what students had learned in class with what was present on the school property.

Next, I assembled materials for the trip: maps of the area, sacks to collect soil or rock specimens (we used Baggies), magnifying glasses to examine specimens, and lists of the observations and questions to direct the field activities.

MAP: We were fortunate to have access to the architect's site and grading plan, which we scaled down and duplicated for students (Fig. 1). Other teachers might make a map from a topographic map or have students draw approximate maps of the school grounds.

To make certain that students would complete their observations in one class period, I took a dry run of the trip and grouped the observation questions so there would be no need for backtracking. I also preceded each question with directions for finding the appropriate location to make observations. (On the day of the field trip, I accompanied each class, and if students took too much time at a stop, they were asked to speed up their work.)

OBSERVATIONS AND QUESTIONS

Following are the observations and questions included in the field trip.
Observation 1: After every rain, students track mud on the school's light-

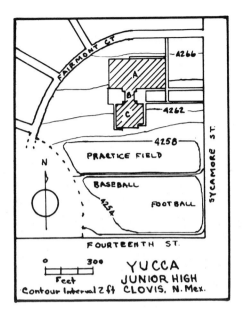

Fig. 1: A. Academic Wing
B. Music Wing
C. Physical Education Wing

colored floors and leave mud and sand under the tables. Very heavy rains flood the athletic and playing fields (Photo 1) and force the physical

Photo 1: View from the school's roof looking toward City Park. Note water on the playing fields.

education classes to remain indoors. *Questions:* Mark the following on your map of the school grounds: (a) the drainage pattern around the building, (b) areas where water might stand after a rain (Photo 2), (c)

Photo 2: Baseball field on the morning of April 24, 1969, after a rain of 0.73 inches.

areas that become flooded after a rain. Write out your recommendations for paving of paths, driveways, or parking areas.

Observation 2: An underground telephone cable is located 150 yards from the school. About 3 feet below the ground is a layer of caliche which was overturned and exposed along the telephone line. *Question:* Describe the material below the soil layer. (This was included to see whether students could visualize the earth in the third dimension.)

ADAPTATION: If there is a road cut or outcrop in the school area, students might be asked to describe the type of rock and the strike and dip of the beds.

Observation 3: There are no outcrops in our area. *Question:* Describe the soil material around the school—composition, size of particles, and distribution.

Observation 4: The athletic and playing fields are flat, but they have terraces around them. *Questions:* Where are the areas of: (a) erosion, (b) deposition? Which terrace shows the most erosion, and how might the erosion be slowed down?

Observation 5: On windy days following a dry period, sand is blown into the halls when the doors are opened. Sand also accumulates in sheltered areas and around vegetation. *Question:* Describe the materials that are carried by water and wind and explain how you can tell which agent carried them.

Observation 6: The careful observer can see settling cracks in the school building and places in the street where erosion, freezing, water, or wear has made cracks or holes. *Question:* Describe any changes in the school building and in the surrounding area.

The day after the field trip, which took place during our normally dry spring, we discussed the results of the trip. We were fortunate indeed, for overnight 0.73 inches of rain had fallen. The fields we had visited only the before were now flooded and muddy, and students were thus able to check the accuracy of their answers.

Having just completed a field trip on the subject, the students were too interested in the effects of the rain to be upset by the mud and water they had to skirt. The rain brought home the value of their earth science knowledge. I hope our rain dance works the next time we carry out this study.

Staking a Mining Claim

by C. E. Riddell and W. G. Casper, Jr.
West Junior High School, Rapid City, South Dakota

This outdoor exercise serves as a supplementary unit in our required ninth-grade earth science course. It is conducted on the school grounds and takes about three 45-minute periods to complete. We have found that periodic use of this and other outdoor science units does much to increase student interest and participation in the course.

> NOTE: The exercise acquaints students with the legal methods involved in staking a mining claim. Each student works as a member of a crew, helping to stake a legal claim across a predetermined lode line.

BEHAVIORAL OBJECTIVES

When students have completed their claim stakes, they should be able to perform these tasks:

- Given a set of corner posts, read bearings on each of them.
- Given a description of a recorded claim, accurately locate the claim.
- Write a brief paragraph describing the procedures for staking a claim. (Included should be references to the section corner inter-

section, bearings and distances to the various corner posts, and the reason for legally staking a claim.)

PREPARATION AND MATERIALS

Before he can adapt the exercise, the teacher must become familiar with the mining laws of his state. Information about these laws is available from the state Bureau of Mines. Using this knowledge, he can then prepare a scale diagram of a legal-sized mining claim in the state similar to that shown in Fig. 1. Brief instructions for the exercise may also be included with the diagram, and copies should be mimeographed for the students.

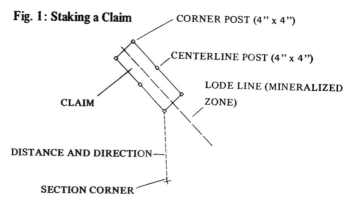

Fig. 1: Staking a Claim

CORNER POST (4" x 4")

CENTERLINE POST (4" x 4")

LODE LINE (MINERALIZED ZONE)

CLAIM

DISTANCE AND DIRECTION—

SECTION CORNER

Name claim and record description with the recording office. The recorder will note time. Your claim description will be checked for accuracy by the mineral surveyor and he will inform the recorder as to the validity of your claim.

Claim size: 20' x 60'

Number corner posts: #1, #2, #3, #4,

Note centerline posts.

Describe location of one corner post by direction and distance from the section corner. Then describe the next corner post by direction and distance from the first, and so on.

The first accurately recorded claim wins the LODE BONUS.

To organize the class for claim staking, select one student as a claim recorder and two students as claim surveyors. Divide the rest of the class into teams of four, with one member of each team as crew chief.

MATERIALS: Each crew will need a yardstick, compass, 10 feet of cord, six medium-sized rocks, and six 4-inch squares of paper (to be used as corner posts).

Next, a lode line must be determined for students to use in their staking. The line marking can be almost anything, such as the corner of the school building, a tree, telephone pole, or goal post. Draw a section corner intersection on a sidewalk somewhere fairly close to the lode line (50 to 200 feet). This will be used as the legal reference point to describe the first claim post.

On the day before the exercise, it is a good idea to advise students to wear some sort of outdoor working clothes the next day. If there is a school dress code, you may have to check with the school administration on this.

PRELIMINARY INSTRUCTION

To introduce students to the exercise, briefly discuss the state requirements for staking a legal-sized mining claim, referring them to their diagrams and explaining that their claims will be made to scale. In our case, students were told that:

1. The size of the claim should be 20 feet by 60 feet.
2. The sidelines of the claim must be parallel.
3. Each team must establish four corner posts and two sideline posts 30 feet from the corner posts. (By law, these posts must be $4'' \times 4'' \times 3'$ high.)
4. The posts (pieces of paper) should be weighed down with rocks and each of the posts must be numbered, #1 through #4 for the corner posts, #5 and #6 for the centerline posts. Post #1 should also be dated.

Students were instructed that for a legal description of the #1 post, the crews must take a bearing reading on it from the previously drawn section line intersection and also measure the distance from the section corner to the corner post. This corner post is then legally described and may be used as a legal reference point for locating the next corner post.

Bearings and distances must be recorded from post #1 to #2, #2 to #3, #3 to #4, #4 to #5, and #5 to #6. (Corner posts #5 and #6 will be the centerline posts.)

READINGS: At this point, students may require some instruction on taking bearing readings with a compass.

STAKING CLAIMS

Students should now be ready to begin work on their own, though they will have many questions to ask the teacher. Each team should record all of their information on paper, including the name of their claim, the names of the crew members, and all bearing readings and distances.

When a crew feels that it has its claim properly staked and described, they will turn over their description to the claim recorder who will record the time, name of claim, and the names of crew members. The recorder should then give the description to the surveyors who will recheck the crew's figures. If all figures are correct and the claim has been legally described, the crew wins a *lode bonus*.

FOLLOW-UP

Stress the need for accuracy in claim staking. Years ago when a company had several claim crews in its employ, it often awarded lode bonuses to the crew which could accurately record the greatest number of claims. Often the bonus was a barrel of whiskey or some home brew. We use ice cream bars or some similar treat as a lode bonus.

Creating an Economic Mineral Display

by Harry F. Pomeroy, Jr.
Yucca Junior High School, Clovis, New Mexico

Two goals in teaching earth science students about minerals are to develop students' awareness of minerals' uses and of the location of economic deposits. While students learn how to identify minerals by their physical properties, they have some difficulty learning their uses since they possess only a limited knowledge of what many substances such as metals, look like. Often students associate dissimilar substances.

> **EXAMPLE: For instance, students frequently confuse the metal lead, obtained from the mineral galena, with "lead" used in pencils. (The lead in pencils is actually obtained from the mineral graphite.)**

To clarify the uses of minerals, samples can be passed around for the students to study. However, it is not always possible to obtain actual examples of the minerals' uses. In overcoming this problem, we first circulated pictures of various mineral products which would be meaningful to the students. Then we decided to build the permanent display of the economic use of minerals described here. This display has proven effective in use and can easily be adapted to other locations.

PLANNING THE DISPLAY

Since New Mexico is a mining state and has a large area whose geography is not known to all students, we sought to combine a map showing the state's past and present mining areas with illustrations of the minerals being studied and their uses. In those cases where minerals included on the display are not mined in the state, we typed in their mining localities for students' reference.

ADAPTATIONS: For those living in non-mining states, a map of the United States might be used to show locations of mineral deposits. (Two mineral deposits common to all states are sand and gravel.)

BUILDING THE DISPLAY

To mount the minerals, we used a piece of plywood $\frac{1}{4}'' \times 37'' \times 27''$, though any convenient or available size may be utilized. Holes were drilled at the top for hanging the display on the wall.

The top of the board was labeled "Economic Minerals," and a state map ($3\frac{1}{2}''$ square) was mounted with glue in the center of the display. Colored construction paper was cut in various geometric shapes (circles, squares, hexagons, etc.) or in irregular shapes and pasted to the board to provide contrast between the plywood and light-colored minerals. The minerals were then fixed to the paper with glue or cement.

NOTE: Either Elmer's glue or Duco cement will hold the minerals to the board, but the board must be placed in a horizontal position until the glue sets.

Minerals included on the display board were hand-specimen size, the largest being $2'' \times 2'' \times 1''$. Smaller sizes are recommended for minerals with high specific gravities for it may be difficult to get them to adhere to the board.

After mounting the minerals, either samples of the metals or pictures showing the metals' uses or both were pasted to the board in the vicinity of the samples. Labels naming the minerals, metals, and their uses were typed, cut out, and pasted beside each item. A label indicating mining localities was placed beneath each mineral and a line was drawn from the mineral to the mining area on the map.

Selecting Material

The mineral samples used in the display were mostly those which the students were identifying in their laboratory work. A few samples were included of other minerals mined in the state not part of the lab activity (Table 1). Some of these samples were supplied by mining companies in the state.

MINERAL USES: Examples of mineral uses were obtained from stock material, i.e., zinc, iron, lead, and

Minerals and Their Uses

Mineral	Use
Quartz	Glass*, radio crystal (two-way radio**), Semi-precious gems (amethyst*)
Talc	Talcum powder**
Coffinite	Uranium
Galena	Lead*
Graphite	Pencil* (for pencil "lead"), lubricants
Sphalerite	Zinc*
Native copper Cuprite Malachite Chalcopyrite	Copper*
Turquoise	Gem stone
Halite	Salt**, sodium, chlorine
Potash ore	Potash, fertilizers**, detergents**, ceramics** (picture of cups), dyes**, and chemicals
Muscovite	Electric appliances (toaster**, irons**)
Gypsum	Plaster of Paris
Hematite Magnetite	Iron* and steel (nails*, wire*)
Calcite (limestone)	Cement** (cement mixer**)
Serpentine (asbestos)	Fireproofing, insulation
Orthoclase feldspar	Glaze for china (dinner-ware**)
Zircon	Gems, high temperature crucibles**

*Indicates actual example of mineral's use mounted

**Indicates picture of use mounted on board

(If not starred, no example or picture used.)

copper. In cases where materials were unavailable or too large to mount, pictures were used, taken from scientific or mail order catalogs or from magazine advertisements.

To give students an idea of the monetary value of the various minerals, a summary of the minerals mined in New Mexico was typed out and pasted at the bottom of the board. Many of the students were surprised to learn that New Mexico was first (as of 1962) among the 50 states in the production of uranium and potash, third in copper, sixth in oil and gas (technically not minerals), ninth in silver, and twelfth in gold. (In making such a display for the United States, either the mineral rank of the entire country to the rest of the world or the rank of certain states might be used.)

REFERENCES

The following references should be of help to teachers in locating mining areas and defining mineral uses. (The ESCP Reference Series provides lists of pertinent magazine articles and addresses of the individual state's bureau of mines.)

Earth Science Curriculum Project, *Reference Series, RS-1, Sources of Earth Science Information* and *RS-9, Selected Guides for Geologic Field Study* (Englewood Cliffs, New Jersey: Prentice-Hall, Inc. 1965).

Hurlbut, Cornelius S., Jr., ed., *Dana's Manual of Mineralogy* (New York: John Wiley & Sons, 1952).

Northrop, Stuart A., *Minerals of New Mexico* (Albuquerque, New Mexico: University of New Mexico Press, 1959).

United States Geological Survey, *Mineral and Water Resources of New Mexico*, Bulletin 87 (Socorro, New Mexico: State Bureau of Mines and Mineral Resources, 1965).

8 Meteorology

Barometers for Determining
    Atmospheric Highs and Lows   234
A Simple Weather Indicator   237
Cloud Study and Weather Forecasting   238

Barometers for Determining Atmospheric Highs and Lows

by Raymond F. Gray

Kecoughtan High School, Hampton, Virginia

The easily made, inexpensive barometer described here can be used by students to maintain daily barometric readings over a period of several months. Making barometers, using them daily to collect data, and graphing and interpreting their results, all help to give students a working knowledge of how instruments and graphing help us in understanding and forecasting weather.

MATERIALS

For creating each barometer you will need:

36" length of glass tubing
One-hole rubber stopper
Test tube clamp
Eye dropper
Crucible or small container
Ring stand
Bunsen burner, gas supply
Triangular file
Liquid mercury (1 to 2 lbs.)
Long, thin wire
Piece of cardboard

PROCEDURE

Directions for making the barometer are as follows:

1. Heat the glass tubing 3 inches from either end over a Bunsen burner, until the two parts separate (Fig. 1). Close the heated end of the long tube.

2. Measuring from the closed end of the tube, measure exactly 32

inches and file a groove across the tube with a triangular file (Fig. 2). Turn the tube around and apply pressure with your thumbs directly behind the groove while pulling the tube in the opposite direction with your fingers.

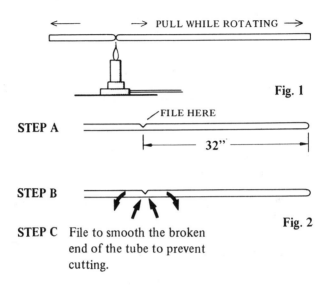

PULL WHILE ROTATING

Fig. 1

FILE HERE

STEP A

32"

STEP B

Fig. 2

STEP C   File to smooth the broken
end of the tube to prevent
cutting.

3. Wet the rubber stopper and slide it halfway up the glass tube.
4. Invert the tube to a vertical position and with an eye dropper, fill the tube completely full with liquid mercury. Remove air bubbles with a long, thin wire.

CAUTION: Mercury is volatile—giving off vapors. Work in a well-ventilated room and avoid direct inhalation.

5. Now place your finger tightly over the open end of the tube and submerge finger and tube into the mercury remaining in the crucible or small container. Then remove your finger. (The mercury in the tube will fall 1 ½" to 2 ½", thus leaving a vacuum in the top of the tube.)

CAUTION: If mercury spills, scoop up the scattered beads of mercury on a sheet of paper. The beads have a strong affinity for each other. If it is still clean, the mercury may be used.

6. Place a test tube clamp on a ring stand around the rubber stopper and secure the clamp (Fig. 3). (It may be beneficial to have two clamps and stoppers.)
7. Measure off 1-inch intervals on a piece of cardboard as shown in the segment depicted in Fig. 3.

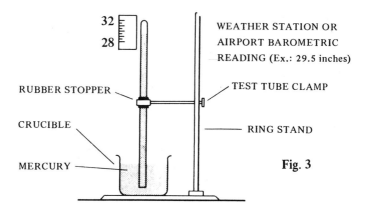

RUBBER STOPPER

CRUCIBLE

MERCURY

32
28

WEATHER STATION OR
AIRPORT BAROMETRIC
READING (Ex.: 29.5 inches)

TEST TUBE CLAMP

RING STAND

Fig. 3

8. Call the local weather station or airport and ask for a correct barometric reading.
9. Locate the reading given on your cardboard and correspond this reading to the top of the mercury in the tube. Tape or otherwise attach the card to the tube at the point where the height of the mercury (Hg) matches the barometric reading.

EXPLANATION

The weight of the mercury in the tube corresponds to the weight of a column of air (the diameter of the tube) from the barometer location to the top of the atmosphere. Whenever the air pressure increases, the pressure on the exposed mercury in the container pushes the mercury upward in the tube. There is no resistance in the tube because a vacuum exists in the top of the tube. High readings usually indicate clear and cooler weather; low readings, warmer and cloudy or rainy weather.

SUGGESTION: When students have finished their barometers, have them take and graph barometric readings over a given period. Each day weather conditions should be written on the graph near the barometric reading for that day (i.e., clear, cloud type, visibility, fog, rain, snow, etc.). To supplement this activity, students may also be asked to make and graph a temperature reading at a given hour each day.

A Simple Weather Indicator

by Edward A. Terry

Mobile County Training School, Mobile, Alabama

A white paper napkin soaked in a solution of cobalt chloride is an effective device for indicating weather, showing increasing and decreasing humidity, and stressing the hygroscopic qualities of materials. This simple device works well in an open classroom or under shelter outdoors, and has proven very satisfactory as a means of rousing student interest in weather and humidity.

PROCEDURE

To make the indicator, put 5 grams of cobalt chloride in enough water to saturate a white paper napkin, then place the napkin in the solution and allow it to absorb the solution. When the napkin is thoroughly saturated, suspend it and let it drip; *do not squeeze*. Fold the damp napkin to a convenient size and tack it to the bulletin board.

RESULTS: In dry weather the napkin will turn a brilliant blue. On humid days it will often feel damp as well as show changing color. Untouched, the napkin should serve as a weather indicator for many months.

For junior high school students, make up a solution of 1 liter (10 grams of $CoCl_2$ in 1 liter of H_2O) and, using very small napkins, prepare an indicator for each student in the class. Students can wrap their napkins in paper towels and take them home for further observation. This practice has proven most effective in keeping students' interest in the weather and moisture content of the air at a high point.

NOTE: If a hygrometer is available, a definite relationship can be established between the color of the napkin and the percentage of moisture in the air. This will activate many amateur forecasters, particularly on a spring day.

Cloud Study and Weather Forecasting

by Alice Weschgel

Oakleigh Middle School, Grand Rapids, Michigan

Making cloud observations and correlating them with wind direction and air pressure can give students a fresh awareness of natural phenomena and a concrete understanding of clouds as harbingers of weather. In the following activity, as students learn to associate certain cloud types and wind direction with various kinds of weather happenings, a pattern emerges. They discover that clouds and wind direction are essential parts of weather and actually set the stage for weather's performance.

This investigation is based on the statement that clouds are like "smoke signals" giving us messages about tomorrow's weather. Specifically, students are presented with the problem of how to learn to recognize basic cloud types and relate them to weather which will occur.

> MATERIALS: To conduct their study of clouds, students will need a Polaroid camera and film, a barometer, and a tag board. (To cut glare, a Polaroid cloud filter can be used.)

PROCEDURE

The student procedure is as follows:

1. Each day at about the same time, go out-of-doors and photograph the dominant cloud type(s).
2. Observe the wind direction and the stability of the barometer.
3. Develop the photo and place the data on the back of the print when dry.
4. Write out the data on a separate card, and place this card and the photo on the tag board. (See Photos 1 through 4.)
5. On the following day, record the weather that occurred.
6. After a fair sampling, interpret the accumulated data, and start making your own weather forecasts.

ANALYZING DATA

These questions may be used to guide students in interpreting their results: Which cloud types correlated with wind direction predicted stormy weather? Fair weather? Overcast skies? Warmer weather? Colder weather?

Photo 1:
Wind: North to northeast.
Barometer: Unsteady.
Following Day: Sky overcast.

Photo 2:
Wind: West.
Barometer: Steady.
Following Day: Fair weather.

Photo 3:
Wind: South to southwest.
Barometer: Falling.
Following Day: Storm during the early evening the day the photo was made. This was followed by fair and cooler weather. The wind shifted to the west to northwest.

Photo 4: (Squall Line Storm)
Wind: East.
Barometer: Falling rapidly.
Following Day: Clear weather. Cooler.

Students can also be asked to try to predict the stability of the barometer by observing the clouds and/or wind direction.

ADDITIONAL IDEAS

Other activities which the teacher might use with this study are:

- Have students listen to a local weather forecast and predict the basic cloud types that should occur the next day.
- Observe a weather map in the newspaper and predict the clouds and wind direction that should accompany the incoming weather.
- Use a radiometer to test the intensity of radiation that occurs during the time when the sky is overcast. Compare results with those recorded when the sky is clear. (How does the intensity of radiation change as clouds move across the sun?)
- Look up some weather lore based on clouds and see whether it may have any relationship to this study, e.g., "A mackerel sky, not twenty-four hours dry."

9 Astronomy and Space Science Exercises

The Coriolis Effect—
An Inductive Approach   244

Build a "Stellorama"   253

Some Astronomical Calculations
Made Easy   259

Observations of the Moon   263

Lunar Mirrors—One Dollar Each   265

The Planetarium as a Laboratory   271

A Celestial Sphere for Teaching
Astronomy Concepts   274

The Coriolis Effect—
An Inductive Approach

by Harrie E. Caldwell
Wilkes College, Wilkes-Barre, Pennsylvania

The universe and earth's relationship to celestial bodies have always attracted men. However, in this era of rocketry and space travel, astronomy is more than simply fascinating; it is relevant to our lives. A combination of relevance and fascination makes astronomy or earth-space science an interesting and enjoyable study for many students.

> **NOTE: One topic often taught in physics and earth-space science classes is the Coriolis Effect. In presenting this subject to sixth and ninth grade students, we have found the following transparency-based lesson particularly effective.**

BACKGROUND MATERIALS

Named after Gaspar G. Coriolis (1792–1843), who first analyzed the apparent deflection of objects moving from one point on the earth to another,[1] the Coriolis Effect can be explained as follows: The earth rotates 360° every 24 hours. Each point not on the earth's axis moves in a circular point around the axis. Due to differences in distance from the axis, all points on the earth's surface do not move at the same linear speed or velocity. Points on the equator move at about 1040 miles per hour while points at other latitudes move at lower velocities.[2]

Objects moving from one point on the earth to another thus have a velocity component due to the rotational motion of the point they leave. For example, when a projectile is aimed due north (or south) and fired, it will not land due north (or south) of the location from which it was

---

[1] Earth Science Curriculum Project, *Investigating the Earth*. American Geological Institute, pp. 3–4.

[2] One may approximate the linear velocity V_L of the surface at any latitude using the formula: $V_L V_O \cos L$ (V_O is the linear velocity of a point on the equator and L is the latitude measured in degrees).

fired because of the velocity due to rotation.[3] If the latitude to which it is fired is moving eastwardly at a faster rate than the latitude from which it left, the projectile will land west of the point at which it was aimed. If the latitude to which it is fired is moving slower than its point of origin, the projectile will land east of the point to which it was fired.

> **ILLUSTRATION: Fig. 1 shows paths of projectiles moving north or south above the earth. The projectiles were originally aimed due north (or due south). As illustrated, projectiles do not move in straight lines relative to the earth.**

This non-linear motion of objects relative to a rotating coordinate system is often attributed to an imaginary force called "Coriolis Force." Since no real force is acting on objects, it is more appropriate to use the phrase "Coriolis Effect."

Examples

Following are several examples of the Coriolis Effect which are observable in our real world:

- Projectiles moving in a direction other than due east or due west appear to be deflected; those moving away from the equator seem to be deflected eastward and those moving toward the equator seem to be deflected westward.
- Prevailing winds (Fig. 2) in various sectors occur because the earth's surface is heated unevenly. At the equator, warmed air rises and flows toward the poles. This air, cooled at higher altitudes, settles eastward near latitude 30° and flows north and south over the earth's surface. However, these air masses do not flow due north or due south.

  Those masses moving toward the equator appear to come from an easterly direction (they are deflected to the west) and are called "easterlies" or "trades." Those moving away from the equator appear to come from a westerly direction (they are deflected to the east) and are called "westerlies." Also, cold polar air masses moving toward the equator appear to be deflected westward and are called "easterlies."
- Cyclonic winds (around low pressure areas) move counterclockwise in the northern hemisphere and clockwise in the southern hemisphere. Anti-cyclonic winds (around high pressure areas) move in the opposite direction.

---

[3] Unless it lands in a corresponding latitude in the other hemisphere. (A projectile aimed due north and fired from X^0S latitude to X^0N latitude will land on the same meridian it left.)

NOTE: Another expression of the Coriolis Effect, some-times called Ferrel's Law, is: Projectiles or winds are deflected to the right in the northern hemisphere and to the left in the southern hemisphere.

LESSON: THE CORIOLIS EFFECT

This lesson is centered around a set of nine simple transparencies for use on an overhead projector. Following is a description of each transparency and suggestions for its effective use.

Transparency 1 (Fig. 1): Showing of Transparency 1, which illustrates the paths of projectiles moving north or south above the earth, may be accompanied by two statements:

1. The sun moves across the sky every day.
2. A pendulum is set in motion. Although gravity is the only force to act on the pendulum, the plane of the pendulum's swing is observed to turn relative to the earth.

These two statements provide data from which students may infer rotation of the earth.

The teacher may wish to have students discuss implications of the two statements immediately. Or he may want to give students the opportunity to relate this data to the problems presented in later transparencies before any discussion is held. The latter approach seems appropriate for average or above average students, while the former approach might be better for slower students.

Transparency 2 (Fig. 2): Transparency 2 shows the direction of prevailing winds in various sectors of the earth. The direction of prevailing winds is explained by the Coriolis Effect. This diagram should be shown again later when students have generalized the concept of the Coriolis Effect to give them an opportunity to apply their generalization. It should not be discussed before students have generalized the concept.

Transparencies 3-9 (Figs. 3-9): Each of the remaining transparencies actually consists of two transparencies connected so that one side (side B) can be placed on top of the other (side A). Side A in each case poses a problem. It contains a diagram of the earth, a rocket, and three points labeled A, B, and C. The rocket is aimed due east, due north, etc., and fired. Point B is always in line with the direction the rocket is aimed; points A and C are located on either side of point B. A caption reads: "1. A rocket is aimed due...., and fired. 2. Will the rocket land at point A, B, or C?"

When side B is placed on top of side A, students are provided with the correct answer. Side B contains a black spot to cover the rocket on side A and diagram of a rocket which makes it appear that the rocket's nose is

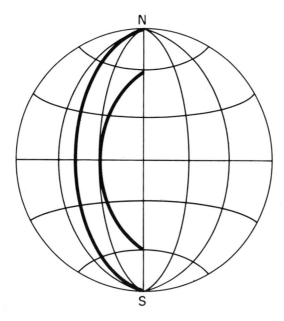

Fig. 1: The heavy lines represent paths, relative to the earth, the projectiles aimed due north (or south) and fired would follow.

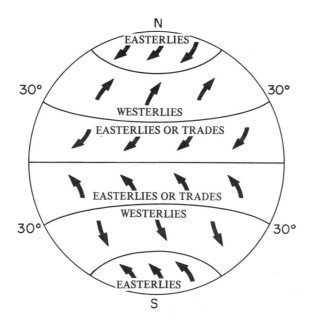

Fig. 2: Prevailing winds in various parts of the earth.

SIDE A   SIDE B

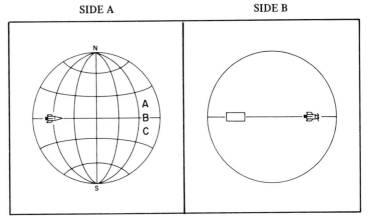

a. The rocket is aimed due east and fired.

b. Will the rocket land at A, B, or C?

Fig. 3: (*Transparency 3*) The rocket is located on the equator and aimed due east. Points A, B, and C are located in the east. The rocket will land at point B, which is due east relative to the point from which the rocket was fired.

SIDE A   SIDE B

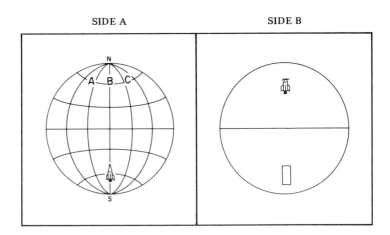

a. The rocket is aimed due north and fired.

b. Will the rocket land at A, B, or C?

Fig. 4: (*Transparency 4*) The rocket is located near the South Pole and aimed due north. Points A, B, and C are located near the North Pole. The rocket will land at point B because the eastward velocity (due to rotation) of points A, B, and C is the same as the eastward velocity (due to rotation) of the rocket.

SIDE A   SIDE B

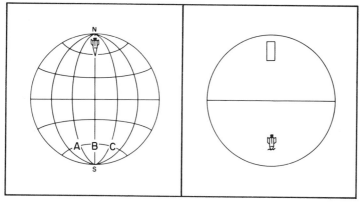

a. The rocket is aimed due south and fired.

b. Will the rocket land at point A, B, or C?

Fig. 5: (*Transparency 5*) The rocket is located near
the North Pole and aimed due south. Points A, B, and
C are located near the South Pole. The rocket will
land at point B because the eastward velocity (due to
rotation) of points A, B, and C and the eastward
velocity (due to rotation) of the rocket are equal.

SIDE A   SIDE B

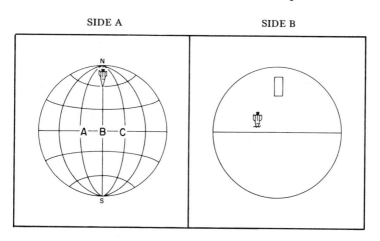

a. The rocket is aimed due south and fired.

b. Will the rocket land at A, B, or C?

Fig. 6: (*Transparency 6*) The rocket is located near
the North Pole and aimed due south. Points A, B, and
C are located on the equator. The rocket will land at
point A because the eastward velocity of points A, B,
and C is greater than the eastward velocity of the
rocket.

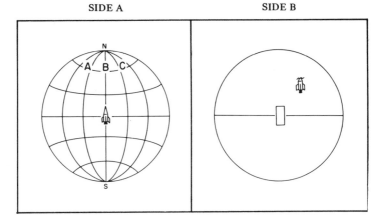

a. The rocket is aimed due north and fired.

b. Will the rocket land at A, B, or C?

Fig. 7: (*Transparency 7*) The rocket is located near the equator and aimed due north. Points A, B, and C are located near the North Pole. The rocket will land at point C because the eastward velocity of points A, B, and C is less than the eastward velocity of the rocket.

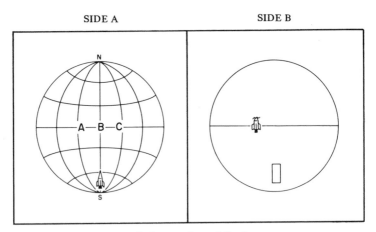

a. The rocket is aimed due north and fired.

b. Will the rocket land at A, B, or C?

Fig. 8: (*Transparency 8*) The rocket is located near the South Pole and aimed due north. Points A, B, and C are located on the equator. The rocket will land at point A because the eastward velocity of points A, B, and C is greater than the eastward velocity of the rocket.

SIDE A   SIDE B

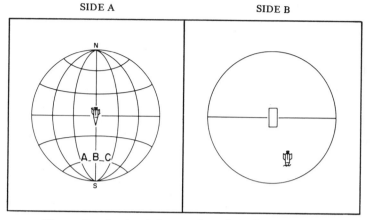

a. The rocket is aimed due south and fired.

b. Will the rocket land at A, B, or C?

Fig. 9: (*Transparency 9*) The rocket is located near the equator and aimed due south. Points A, B, and C are located near the South Pole. The rocket will land at point C because the eastward velocity of points A, B, and C is less than the eastward velocity of the rocket.

buried in the ground. The rocket on side B is positioned to coincide with the correct solution (A, B, or C) on side A.

The first time Transparencies 3-9 are shown, students should not discuss them. Show the transparencies. When students have had sufficient opportunity to react to the solution (side B) on one transparency, show the problem (side A) with the next transparency. Continue this procedure until students have reacted to all of the problems and observed all of the solutions. Then let them choose transparencies they wish to see again.

> NOTE: Teachers should be careful not to allow one student to solve a problem aloud before other students have had an opportunity to solve it for themselves.

USING THE INDUCTIVE APPROACH

Learning

It is not suggested that each student will be able to verbalize the Coriolis Effect from these transparencies. However, when a student is able to predict answers consistently, he probably has an internalized concept, at least at a sub-verbal level. When this student then hears a verbal statement of the Coriolis Effect, he should be able to associate the verbal statement with his sub-verbal concept.

It would be easy to find out which students are able to verbalize statements of the concept. Before discussing data, have students write a statement(s) explaining how they solved the problems or how they would explain the answers to someone else.

DISCUSSION: The final step is to discuss the problems and conclusions with the class. This will probably entail going back over the transparencies and discussing each transparency individually and, also, relating each transparency to the others.

Variations

If an overhead projector is unavailable, the diagrams might be reproduced on cards or papers, perhaps in booklet form. Students could work individually at their own rates, or in small groups with other students of similar ability. (They might also take materials home and attempt to teach their parents the concept. Teaching the concept may help them to learn it.)

To get students to think about this phenomenon, the transparencies might be shown without discussion several days prior to a lesson on the Coriolis Effect. For example, the lesson could be scheduled for a Monday. The overlays could be shown during the last 10 minutes of the period on the preceding Friday. Some students will undoubtedly forget about the phenomenon as soon as the bell rings, but others may be intrigued. The latter may even work on the puzzle over the weekend.

Build a "Stellorama"

by Donald B. Peck
Scotch Plains-Fanwood Public Schools, Scotch Plains, N. J.

Descriptive astronomy is best taught at night and out of doors, where the student can observe, enjoy, and become familiar with the stellar panorama. Most schools, however, will find that the restrictions of the school day and transportation problems make this very difficult, if not impossible. Furthermore, few have convenient access to a planetarium.

In an effort to combat these obstacles, I have developed a small, homemade celestial hemisphere (I call it a Stellorama) which includes many instructive features. Its design is based on my own conviction that an introduction to astronomy should be at the "eyeball" level, since this is the only instrument used by most observers.

I will outline here the purpose, construction and use of the Stellorama.

PURPOSE

Here are the principal purposes of the Stellorama:

- To provide a mechanical means of transferring a daytime, in-school study of astronomy to a nighttime, at-home study.
- To provide each student with his own spherical map of the stars which will: (a) Reduce the difficulties which beginners encounter in using flat charts, particularly the Mercator projections. (b) Rectify the problem of reversal encountered in using a standard celestial globe.
- To provide a means to an understanding of, and familiarity with, celestial coordinates as a means of locating stars, planets, and so on.
- To provide a visual aid which will lead to an understanding of the sidereal motion of the stars and of sidereal time.
- To provide, most importantly, an aid through the use of which a student can develop a small degree of familiarity with the workings of the universe.

NOTE: I use the Stellorama with eighth and ninth grade general science classes; it has worked well with the astronomy portion of the course. It would, of course, be most useful if you have an astronomy club. As to time: I use one day plotting constellations with the students, completing this phase as homework; one day in construction; and a part of another day in learning how to use it.

CONSTRUCTION

The components of the Stellorama are:

- Four curved panels on thin cardboard which form a hemisphere.
- A semicircular cardboard panel used to eliminate the south polar region.
- Thin coat hanger wire for a frame.
- Masking or cellophane tape.

NOTE: The directions given here will give you a device with a diameter of 20 cm. You can scale it up, if you wish.

Template

First, prepare a template for the panels on thin cardboard, such as oaktag, laying it out diagonally so it will fit on a 8½ × 11 sheet. Rule a vertical line 31.5 cm long, bisecting it perpendicularly at mid-point (Fig. 1). The bisecting line should extend at least 4 cm to either side of the vertical axis. It represents the celestial equator. Moving both north and south, rule in a series of perpendicular lines at intervals of 1.75 cm. They represent declination circles at 10° intervals. There are nine such intervals in each direction.

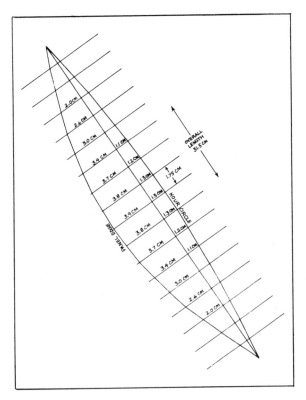

Fig. 1

Refer to column A in Table 1. Using the dimensions given, lay out the correct distances on the right-hand side of the axis. When these lines have been connected, you have produced the edge of the panel. Next refer to column B of Table 1. Using the dimensions given, construct an hour curve on the left side of the axis. Cut out the template carefully.

Next, subtract the latitude of the community in which you live from 90° and cut off one end of the template at the indicated declination. For example, if you live at latitude 40°, cut off one end at 50° (90° − 40° = 50°). This represents the declination at the southern horizon and thus the limit of visibility.

Table 1: Dimensions for Templates

Declination	A half width of panel	B half width for hour circle	C Radius of declination circle
0° Equator	3.9 cm.	1.3 cm.	10.0 cm.
10°	3.8 cm.	1.3 cm.	9.85 cm.
20°	3.7 cm.	1.2 cm.	9.4 cm.
30°	3.4 cm.	1.1 cm.	8.65 cm.
40°	3.0 cm.	1.0 cm.	7.65 cm.
50°	2.6 cm.	0.9 cm.	6.45 cm.
60°	2.0 cm.	0.7 cm.	5.0 cm.
70°	1.2 cm.	0.4 cm.	3.45 cm.
80°	0.7 cm.	0.2 cm.	1.75 cm.
90° Poles	0.0 cm.	0.0 cm.	0.0 cm.

Panels

You then prepare duplicate panels for student use on a duplicating machine. Lay the template on the master and trace around it. Mark the extremities of all lines. Flip the template over, and make sure the main axis and ends properly register. Trace around the template again. Rule in the declination lines, *but not the main axis*. Since the master is big enough for two panels, repeat the process.

> NOTE: The master would look like Fig. 2, but without the written data filled in. Each edge of the panel, and each curved longitudinal line, represents an hour circle of right ascension.

On another master sheet, trace a semicircular panel, with a radius taken from column C of Table 1. Following through on the illustration, if you cut the template at 50°, the radius would be 6.45 cm.

> NOTE: In all probability, the radius which relates to your exact longitude is not available. The formula to compute your radius is: $r = 10 \text{ cm} \times \cos o$. ($r$ is radius; o is declination.)

Run off the copies on thin cardboard or oaktag. For making the Stellorama, each student will need four panels and one semicircular panel.

Data Sheet

Determine the right ascension (r.a.) of the celestial meridian on the date you expect the students to have completed the Stellorama for use, and round

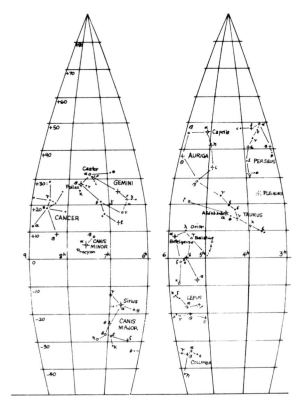

Fig. 2

the figure *up* to a whole number hour (i.e., 9:00 P.M.). This will be the r.a. of the junction between the two center panels of the device when completed. Then, using any good star chart (such as a Mercator projection) prepare a data sheet, as shown in Table 2, for each constellation up to 6^h r.a. on each side of the meridian.

> NOTE: Depending on your preference, this sheet *may* include such information as magnitudes and the Greek letter designations of the stars. It *should* include the r.a. and declination of each major star in the constellation and a sketch of the pattern. The number of constellations to include is up to you.

Student Plotting

When you are sure your students know the meaning of right ascension and declination, have them mark the appropriate values along the celestial equator and central meridian (see Fig. 2).

Star	Maq.	r.a.	dec.	Sketch
α	✧ Sirius	$6^h 40^m$	$-17°$	
β	o	$6^h 20^m$	$-19°$	
γ	+	$7^h 00^m$	$-13°$	
δ	o	$7^h 05^m$	$-27°$	
ε	o	$6^h 50^m$	$-28°$	
ζ	+	$6^h 25^m$	$-29°$	
η	o	$7^h 20^m$	$-29°$	
θ	+	$6^h 55^m$	$-23°$	
ι	•	$6^h 50^m$	$-17°$	
κ	•	$6^h 45^m$	$-31°$	

Approximate Magnitudes
✧ o + •
1 2 3 4

Greek Letters
α alpha   ζ zeta
β beta   η eta
γ gamma   θ theta
δ delta   ι iota
ε epsilon κ Kappa

Table 2: Data Sheet for Canis Major

Then, have the students cut out the panels (leaving in the edge lines) and plot the stars from the data sheets. If the connecting lines between the stars cross from one panel to another, the panels should be tangent at the point of crossing when the line is drawn.

Construction

The students then can complete the mechanical construction, following these steps:

- Using *short* lengths of masking or cellophane tape, fasten the panels together, taping from the equator to the poles. The printed and written side, of course, will be on the *inside,* or concave side, of the completed device. Also using tape, fasten in the semicircular panel or base.
- Using coat hanger wire, bend two semicircles to a 10 cm radius. Tape one of these along the outside at the equator, and the other over the top of the front edge. Then, cut a third piece 26 cm long, and bend a 3 cm section at each end, 90° in the same direction. Tape this across the open front so that it joints the two ends of the equator. This is the horizon line.
- Paint a small dot of white paint at the midpoint of the horizon wire. This represents the position of the observer.

See Fig. 3.

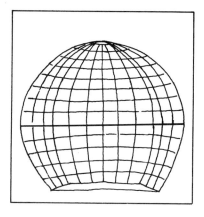

Fig. 3

USE

On the first clear night following the date set (the panels used in this illustration were designed for use on March 21 at 9:00 P.M.) take the Stellorama outside with a small flashlight. Face due south. Hold the hemisphere with the top resting on the forehead and the white dot in line with the apex of the semicircular base. Light up the inside with the flashlight and pick out a constellation to look at (at the start, begin in the center region). Keep the eyes fixed in the same direction, and remove the Stellorama. You should be looking at the same pattern in the sky.

Sidereal Motion and Time

Within a few days of original sighting the stars will have shifted their original positions noticeably. This leads to sidereal motion and sidereal time. For "eyeball" observations, the following simple method of computing time is quite satisfactory:

- Multiply the number of calendar months since the date of sighting by two hours per month, and add four minutes per day since the last occurring day of the month on which the original sighting was made. This will give the approximate sidereal time at noon standard time on any given day of the year.
- To this add the number of clock hours and minutes between noon and the time of observation. If the result is greater than 24 hours, substract 24 hours from the total.

EXAMPLE: Using the original sighting at 9:00 P.M. on March 21, compute as of 9:30 P.M. on the following March 1:

11 mo. × 2 h/mo =	22 h	
8 days × 4 m/day =		32 m
9 hr 30 min. since noon =	9 h	30 m
Total	32 h	02 m
—	24 h	00 m
Approximate sidereal time:	8 h	02 m

Thus, daily and annual motion can be studied with the aid of the Stellorama by rolling it 15° each hour or every two weeks respectively.

Some Astronomical Calculations Made Easy[1]

by William R. Minardi

Mark Hopkins Campus Laboratory School, North Adams, Mass.

In teaching astronomy in junior high school (or perhaps high school for that matter) you will find the students asking questions like these: How can we determine the circumference of the earth? How can we find the distance to the moon? How can we compute the distance to the stars? These are questions that concern scientists as well.

How much value is there, for example, in merely telling students of this age that a certain star is 10 light years away and then have them look up the distances of other stars? To me, this kind of information is superficial and temporary. I believe it is much better to supply them with facts and guidance and let them solve questions like these themselves.

Some illustrations are given below. Obviously, the figures are not thoroughly accurate, but the important point is that the students are piecing together information they know or can learn to form a logical conclusion.

CIRCUMFERENCE OF THE EARTH

One of the problems facing the ancient Greeks was the value of the circumference of the earth. The story of how Eratosthenes solved this by

---

[1] Some of the ideas presented herein were gained from The Elementary School Science Project of the University of Illinois, 1964.

determining the number of degrees between two points in Egypt (Aswan and Alexandria) and how he knew the distance in miles is known to science teachers and makes an interesting presentation to the students. It is also a prime example of how we can permit students to be faced with the same problem, be armed with the same set of facts, and let them arrive at the same result.

Without going into too great detail, you can show that when the distance of a segment of the earth's circumference is known in miles and in degrees, the whole circumference can be found (Fig. 1).

7° AND 490 MILES

7° =	490 miles	
1° =	70 miles	(These figures are rounded off
360° =	25,200 miles	and are only approximate.)

Fig. 1

The important fact is that the students learn not just *what* the earth's circumference is but how it was determined with a reasonable degree of accuracy over two thousand years ago.

> NOTE: This could lead to interesting and deeper research resulting from questions such as: "How is the circumference determined today?" "What is the precise circumference?" "Why does it differ around the poles and at the equator?"

HEIGHT OF A SATELLITE ABOVE THE EARTH

As soon as students know how to use a protractor, they can be taught to make scale drawings easily. It then becomes relatively easy for them, through the use of a scale drawing, to find the height of a satellite above the earth. Here is a typical problem:

> What is the height of a satellite which is sighted 48° south of the zenith of a city which is at 42° B latitude, and 64° north of the zenith of a city at 25° N latitude? Scale: $\frac{1}{2}'' = 1,000$ miles.

The solution of the problem is not difficult, using the procedure given in Fig. 2.

> NOTE: It thus becomes one application of their new knowledge to find the distance to the satellite we call our moon by using exactly the same method.

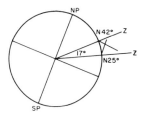

Fig. 2: Preliminary Diagram

DIAMETER OF THE MOON

Armed with this knowledge, and already having learned the circum-ference of the earth (and thus its radius) some bright students will be able to find the diameter of the moon without further stimulus from the teacher; if some is needed, this method can be suggested:

If we place a pencil, whose diameter is $\frac{1}{4}''$ at a distance of $30''$ from the eye, and it covers the disc of the moon, we can represent this in a diagram as shown in Fig. 3.

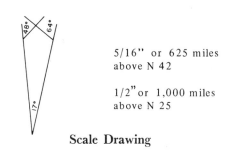

5/16" or 625 miles
above N 42

1/2" or 1,000 miles
above N 25

Scale Drawing

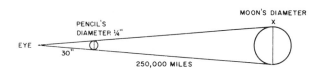

Fig. 3

It then becomes obvious to even an average student that this is a simple matter of finding a single unknown. They see two triangles in the diagram with values listed that enable them to solve for X:

$$\frac{.25''}{30''} = \frac{X}{250,000 \text{ miles}}$$

This calculation comes to 2,083 miles which is certainly accurate enough to satisfy anyone.

HOW FAR ARE THE STARS?

At this age, students consistently and persistently will ask: "If stars are so very distant, how do we know how far they really are?" It is probably true that no scientist is completely satisfied that we know star distances as precisely as we would wish; we can, for students, show one method of determining the distance to some of the relatively close stars without involving them in any complicated mathematics. Fig. 4 will help explain the method.

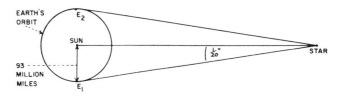

Fig. 4

If a star is sighted while the earth is at position E_1 and six months later when the earth is at position E_2, the angle at the star can be determined. One half of that angle is called its parallax. Let it be $1/20''$ of arc. The distance from the earth to the sun is known (or it can be discovered by the students using the methods already described). It can be assumed, therefore, that the distance from the sun to the star is the radius of a large circle with the star at the center so that if we find the value of the whole circumference, we can find the value of the radius. The same technique can be applied as was applied in determining the circumference of the earth.

They know the value of a small portion of the circumference ($1/20'' = $ 93,000,000 miles). They can determine the value of the large, imaginary circle with the star at the center. They should, therefore, be able to find the distance from the sun to the star since $r = C/2\pi$.

ACCELERATION OF THE MOON

Even the problem of the acceleration of the moon, or the rate at which it is "falling" toward the earth, can be solved by students at this level. They can easily find the speed of the moon in its orbit in feet per second, and the number of degrees travelled per day. The solution of the problem of acceleration may well be worked out by some students independently; others may need varying degrees of help.

The speed of the moon in orbit is approximately 3,400 feet per second, and it travels about 13.3° per day. On a scale of $1'' = 1,000$ ft./sec., we could represent this by the diagram in Fig. 5.

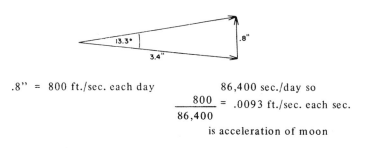

.8" = 800 ft./sec. each day

$$\frac{800}{86,400} = .0093 \text{ ft./sec. each sec.}$$

86,400 sec./day so

is acceleration of moon

Fig. 5

Observations of the Moon

by Verne A. Troxel

Miami University, Miami, Ohio

In view of the difficulty beginning earth science students have making astronomical observations, the following investigation has been unusually successful. In this exercise, the students record, organize, and analyze quantitative observations of the motion and shape of the moon. Their observations lead them to discover a model of the relationship of the moon and earth and to use the model as a basis for making generalizations about the moon's motion.

PROCEDURE

The procedure for the investigation is as follows:

1. Devise an instrument for measuring the angle of elevation (altitude) of the moon and the angle (azimuth) of the moon clockwise from true north (Fig. 1).
2. Have students make three observations one hour apart each night for at least a week. Observations should be made the same time each

day; e.g., 8:00, 9:00, and 10:00. (A cloud cover obstructing the observation of the moon is regarded as an observation.)

3. Record each observation as accurately as possible.

INTERPRETING DATA

From their observations of the moon's motion, students soon discover:

- Changes in the shape of the moon.
- There is a regular pattern of change.
- The daily eastward drift of the moon–about 13 degrees per day–on successive nights of observations measured at the same time.
- The pattern of change in the azimuth of the moon for successive nights and for the same night.
- Changes in altitude for successive nights at the same time and for different times on the same evening.

NOTE: Based on these observations and his data, the student can easily develop a physical model of the earth-moon system as shown in Fig. 1.

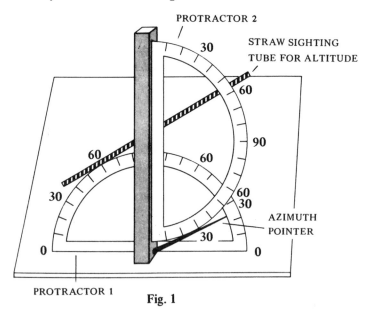

Fig. 1

NECESSARY MATERIALS

To build the model, in addition to his data tables and the information he has gained in previous interpretation of data, the student will need two protractors, thumbtacks, a straw, a 5″ × 8″ board, a 1″ × 1″ × 6″ stick, and a toothpick.

Lunar Mirrors—
One Dollar Each

by Robert E. Kyrlach

Sandia High School, Albuquerque, New Mexico

That mirror-making is an art only for perfectionists is a myth. The average amateur telescope maker today would probably be horrified by the figure, flexures, and images of some of Herschel's reflectors, but he is credited with the discovery of Uranus, two satellites each of Uranus and Saturn, and many nebulas and clusters. It is also a myth that mirror-making requires great expense and months of labor.

Here is a way to have your students grind quite serviceable mirrors for less than a dollar each, and in only a few hours.

There are three secrets in breaking the mirror grinding complexity and cost:

- The first is to buy glass furniture leg cups, three inches in diameter and packaged four for 60 cents in a local five and dime store.
- Second, no testing of the mirrors is necessary if one does not attempt a full polish. The reason for this is that the grinding process automatically gives a "perfect" surface, while polishing is carried only far enough to obliterate most of the pits created in grinding. The images formed are relatively unaffected by the remaining pits.
- Third, the mirror does not have to be silvered or aluminumized for excellent views of the moon.

MAKING YOUR OWN MIRRORS

Materials

Ten mirrors will cost about $9.00 to make, and each should take no more than four or five hours' work to complete. To save time during construction, obtain the following materials before beginning:

20 castor cups 3″ in diameter
grinding abrasives:[1]
    12 oz. coarse carborundum # 120 ($1.60)
    4 oz. medium coarse carborundum # 220 ($ .80)
    3 oz. medium carborundum # 320 ($ .80)
    3 oz. medium fine carborundum # 400 ($ .80)
    2 oz. fine carborundum # 600 ($ .60)

---

[1] Grinding abrasives are available in some hardware stores, and can always be obtained from A. Jaegers, 691 Merrick Road, Lynbrook, New York.

NOTE: Except for the coarse grade, each of these grades should be divided ten ways, and completely used up by each mirror-maker. The coarse need not be, for it is only used to grind the mirror to curvature and no further.

4 oz. cerium oxide polishing powder ($1.50)
½ can ordinary roofing tar
several pieces of scrap lumber
newspapers
30 small nails

Procedure

Fasten each tool—one castor cup—to a more or less squarish board in such a way that it will not slide off, but can be lifted for cleaning. This is easily accomplished by placing three nails in the board in a circle into which the tool can be snugly placed, bottom up. The nails should be driven deeply enough so that their heads are below the flat surface of the tool.

Next, place a few drops of water and a pinch of coarse carborundum from the tip of a knife blade on the tool, and place the second castor cup—the mirror—on top with its flat side down so that the two surfaces can be ground together (Photo 1).

Photo 1: Grinding Setup

To obtain radial symmetry, grind "by the clock," as follows:

1. Imagine the tool is a clock-face with twelve numbers around the edge.

2. Push the mirror, top glass, back and forth across the top of the tool once, in line with the twelve.
3. Then push it back and forth once toward one. Repeat toward the two, three, etc.

With gentle pressure on the top glass and about a two-inch long stroke, an audible grinding noise will occur.

NOTE: It is also necessary to rotate the mirror, top glass, slightly with each stroke.

The motions are such that, as the mirror is developing a concavity and the tool is becoming convex, only two spherical surfaces can result. However, the first noticeable thing is not, of course, the shape of the surfaces, but the need for more water for lubrication and another pinch of "carbo" to keep the grinding sound going (Photo 2). About an hour of steady work will yield the necessary curvature.

Photo 2: Grinding

Check the curvature at the end of this time with a straight edge. This can be done by cutting the thinnest straight pin available into several pieces, placing one of the pieces in the middle of the mirror, and laying the straight edge across a diameter to see whether it rocks on the pin. It should just touch it. If this is the case, it is time to begin using the medium coarse carborundum.

NOTE: If the straight edge clears the piece of pin by too much, the mirror will have too short a focal length for very much magnification. It is better to have it rock or teeter slightly than to clear it with a slight gap.

Proceed to use up all the finer carborundum grades one at a time, taking scrupulous pains to wash the tool, mirror, board, nails, table etc., between each grade. For the finer grades use a shorter grinding stroke, one inch instead of the two used for roughing. After about another hour of grinding, averaging 15 minutes with each grade, the finest grade should be finished. Now, the mirror is ready to be polished.

Employ the same stroke for polishing as for grinding, using rouge—cerium oxide—on a pitch lap. The pitch lap is made right on the tool used for grinding by melting the pitch and pouring it onto the tool, covering it to a depth of at least 1/8 inch. Make a paper collar around the tool before pouring the melted pitch so that it does not run off. The collar can be peeled off before the pitch cools much so that the mirror can be pressed down on top for shaping. To keep the mirror from sticking, slosh on soapy water. And it helps to trim the edge of the lap with a knife to get a smooth mirror fit.

> **CONTACT: Sometimes when the pitch is stiff, contact with the mirror may take an hour or more of heavy pressure on the mirror with a big stack of books or some similar weight.**

After the pitch "fits" the mirror, cut grooves in it with a pocket knife. These should be V-shaped, as deep as practical, and arranged to form a checkerboard pattern of small squares, at least five or six each way (Photo 3).

Photo 3: Lap and Mirror Before Polishing

A few minutes of "cold pressing" is desirable at this point, since the cutting of the grooves usually hurts the mirror fit. For this, use an old medicine dropper bottle as a good rouge applicator. Shake a thimbleful of rouge to an ounce of water. Apply a few drops of this slurry, then polish "by the clock" using relatively short strokes and considerable pressure (Photo 4).

Photo 4:
Left: Fine grind before polishing
Right: After polishing

Photo 5: Seven Student's Mirrors

With five minutes of polishing, the frosty surface of the mirror begins to take on shine. A very good image of the sun about 30 inches from the mirror can now be obtained. This gives the focal length. An hour or two of polishing brightens up images enough so that a good moon image can be formed (Photo 5).

MAKING A SIMPLE TELESCOPE

For very little more money, a simple telescope can be constructed using a 30-inch cardboard rug tube with a wood plug at one end. Stick the mirror onto the wood plug with masking tape or glue, and secure the plug in the tube with three thumbtacks. Then, readjust the thumbtacks and plug one at a time while looking in the other end of the tube, until the mirror is collimated with the tube.

A small mirror (for instance, #40,283 sold by Edmund Scientific Company, Barrington, N.J. 08007, for 35 cents) can be mounted at an angle of 45° in the center of the open end of the cardboard tube, with a hole opposite it in the tube for an eyepiece. Edmund's Ramsden pair #5194 (Edmund Scientific Company, 65 cents) can be mounted in cardboard with masking tape, making an excellent lunar telescope (Photo 6). And with a piece of exposed color film in the eyepiece, it also makes a fine solar telescope.

Photo 6: An Inexpensive Telescope

The Planetarium as a Laboratory

by Merrick A. Owen

Edinboro State College, Edinboro, Pennsylvania

Many school districts now have a planetarium available to their science classes. Often, however, students see a visit to the planetarium as simply entertainment. The visit should also be interesting, educational, and relevant to what they are doing in the classroom.

One way to involve students in a planetarium experience is to use the inquiry approach, as in the exercise described here. This exercise leads students through Tycho Brahe's investigation of the changing angle of the sun at noon during one year. It is appropriate for grades six through college.

> **MATERIALS: Have students bring pencils, a note pad, and graph paper.**

PREPARATION

Before beginning the exercise, provide students with a brief biographical sketch of Tycho Brahe. Next, give them a simple description of the investigation: Using the planetarium, we are going to record the angle of the sun at noon, once a month for one year.

SETTING THE INSTRUMENT

To begin the exercise, set the sun at noon on the dome. (In the United States, the sun is directly south at noon.) Put the ecliptic on the dome. Put the meridian on the dome. Then:

- Have students record the angle of the sun and the month.
- Move the sun one month and have students again record the month and the sun's angle (sun on meridian, noon).
- Continue moving the sun a month at a time, having the students record the data for each month. They should compile a list of data like the following.

Sample Data

Sept.	45°	Feb.	37°	June	68°
Oct.	38	Mar.	45	July	60
Nov.	30	Apr.	52	Aug.	52
Dec.	22	May	60		
Jan.	29				

NOTE: Explain how long it would take to collect this data using the real sun. Bring out the patience and forbearance needed to be a good observer and data collector.

GRAPHING THE DATA

Direct students in graphing their data as follows:

- On the vertical axis, mark off degrees from 0 to 90.
- On the horizontal axis, mark off the twelve months.
- Graph the results, as shown in Fig. 1.

INTERPRETING THE DATA

Here are guidelines for leading students to interpret their data:

1. What does the graph show? (the apparent motion of the sun for one year; the angle of the sun above the horizon at noon each month)
2. Draw a line across the graph at 45 degrees. This is the celestial equator.
   a. When is the sun above the celestial equator? (months)
   b. What months is the sun on the celestial equator?
   c. What months is the sun below the celestial equator?
3. This graph (Fig. 1) can indicate the beginning of each season at 45 degrees N. Label the winter solstice, vernal equinox, summer solstice, and autumnal equinox.
4. When is the sun highest and what is the number of degrees above the horizon? What season is this?
5. When is the sun lowest and how many degrees is this above the horizon? What season is this?
6. After question 4 and 5 have been answered, explain why winter is colder and summer is warmer.

FOLLOW-UP: Students showing greater interest in this study and astronomy can go further in the investigation by reading about the annalema[1] and calculating their latitude from the sun's position any time during the year.

---

[1] Annalema gives the sun's position, in degrees north or south of the equator, for any day of the year.

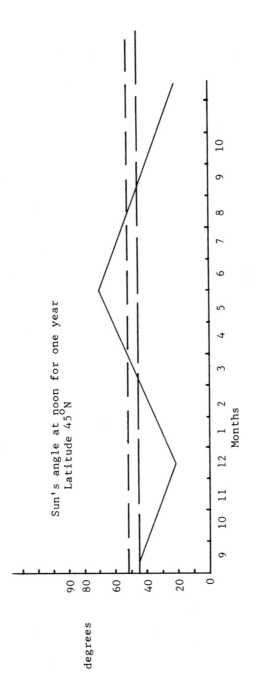

Fig. 1

NO PLANETARIUM AVAILABLE?

If you do not have access to a planetarium, you can still conduct this investigation by supplying the following data for the angle of the sun at noon, for each month of the year:

Sample Data: Latitude 45°N.

March	45°	Sept.	45°	March	45°
April	52	Oct.	38		
May	61	Nov.	31		
June	$68\frac{1}{2}$	Dec.	$21\frac{1}{2}$		
July	61	Jan.	31		
Aug.	52	Feb.	38		

A Celestial Sphere for Teaching Astronomy Concepts

by William R. Minardi

Mark Hopkins Campus Laboratory School, North Adams, Massachusetts

One of the most frequent complaints of teachers of astronomy at the high school level is a lack of inexpensive, usable equipment, particularly aids for illustrating difficult concepts. While commercial products such as planetariums and telescopes are available, most are expensive and beyond the means of small school systems.

> NOTE: In our case, a limited budget led us to develop a Celestial Sphere. This model, which can be made for practically no cost, has proven effective in teaching many difficult and abstract ideas.

The sphere is easily adapted to illustrate each of the following concepts:

Celestial Sphere	Zenith
Celestial Poles	Nadir
Celestial Equator	Westward and eastward motions among
Ecliptic	the stars
Plane	Apparent daily rotation of stars
Equinoxes	Apparent annual revolution of the
Horizon	sun

MATERIALS AND CONSTRUCTION

The Celestial Sphere consists primarily of wires of appropriate lengths shaped to form a large globe-like structure. To facilitate easy use and storage, a size three feet or less in diameter is recommended. Construction procedures are simple:

- Shape four wires in complete lengths—about 9 ½ feet if the diameter is 3 feet—to form the celestial equator, the ecliptic, and two polar circumferences at right angles to each other.
- Use as many more wires as desired for additional declination lines (equivalent to latitude lines) and right ascension lines (equivalent to longitude lines).

SIMPLICITY: For simplicity of construction and clarity in understanding, keep the wires few in number.

- Weld the ends of the wires for sturdiness. Place two metal rings at the poles for welding the right ascension wires. (The rings will also ensure that the apparatus will not roll when put down.)

The completed apparatus in its simplest form should look similar to the diagram in Fig. 1. Following are directions for adapting this basic sphere in teaching some of the key concepts of astronomy.

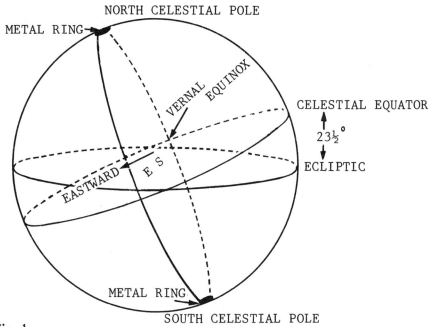

Fig. 1

USING THE CELESTIAL SPHERE

Placing the Earth

To show the earth's location near the center of the celestial sphere, fix a small earth-globe perhaps three inches in diameter on a firm, straight wire and fasten the wire at the top of the sphere. Allow part of the wire to extend beyond the top of the sphere so that it can be grasped. Fasten the wire in such a way that the earth can be revolved around the center of the celestial sphere—which would be the approximate position of the sun.

> NOTE: To show the location of the vernal equinox, simply allow the sun to be seen in the direction of that point, as illustrated in Fig. 1.

Establishing Coordinates

Allowing the wire which goes from the north celestial pole to be a kind of "prime meridian," mark off several other "meridian lines" either mentally or by actually putting in more wires. This establishes one of the coordinates for locating stars—right ascension.

> IMPORTANT: It must be pointed out, however, that right ascension lines are numbered consecutively eastward along the celestial equator 0° through 360° rather than 180° westward and 180° eastward.

If a small globe has been used for the earth near the center, it is easy to show that directions in space are exactly opposite terrestrial directions. Most students have been taught that as we face north on most maps of the world, east is to our right and west to our left. This is true, of course, but if we "put our backs" to the earth and look into space, west is then to our right and east to our left.

Use wires parallel to the celestial equator numbered 0° for the celestial equator through 90° for the celestial poles to show the other coordinate, declination, which is the equivalent of latitude. Given both coordinates, right ascension and declination, any junior high school student should be able to locate a star on the celestial sphere.

To make the apparatus more effective, paint certain common and useful constellations on a transparent substance, such as Saran Wrap, and put them around the celestial sphere in the appropriate places. The constellations of the zodiac should be put in close to the ecliptic with Aries near the celestial equator. (Students should be able to tell which constellations are prominent at various seasons of the year and where the sun is located during those seasons.)

> NOTE: At this point, the sphere may be used to show the Ptolemaic concept of the daily revolution of the stars

about the earth and why this appeared to be reality to the ancients. It could show a stationary earth and the daily rising and setting of stars which, to the ancients, "proved" the motion of the stars around the earth.

If more wires are included—one at 30° and one at 60° for both the northern and southern hemispheres—and other right ascension wires are used, the apparatus can be useful for teaching terrestrial longitude and latitude as well as for locating stars by the altitude-azimuth method.

Making a Terrestrial Globe

For adapting the apparatus to use as a terrestrial globe and to show the horizon in the altitude-azimuth system, attach a small (6 inches in diameter), circular disc of light wood to the outside of the wires at a desired position. Place a common pin at the center of the disc to represent an observer.

It should be stressed to students that the apparatus now represents the earth; the pin, an observer with the bottom of his feet pointing toward the center of the earth—and eventually to his nadir—and his head toward its zenith. It can then be shown what is meant by the altitude of a star, the angular distance from the astronomical horizon measured along a vertical circle, and by its azimuth, the angle at the zenith between the vertical circle through the south point and the vertical circle through the star measured from south through west. The room in which this is being taught could represent the celestial sphere, and the apparatus might appear as in Fig. 2.

SUGGESTION: Fix the wooden disc which represents the horizon so that it attaches and detaches easily from the wires. The disc can then be moved to various positions to show that different observers have different zenith and nadir points and different horizons.

Many additional uses of the apparatus as a terrestrial globe are possible. For example, a wire with a sliding yellow bead on it to represent the sun may be used to show how high or low the sun appears above the horizon at different times of the year and at various hours of the day, as in Fig. 3. Since the horizon, the wooden disc, is easily moved, the model can be used to illustrate the sun's position for the hour of the day and the time of the year for any latitude.

NOTE: Assembly of materials, construction of the apparatus, and research on the concepts to be learned and the many uses of the Celestial Sphere make for increased interest of the students participating. They enjoy this activity, learn much from it, and usually make many excellent suggestions for further uses and innovations.

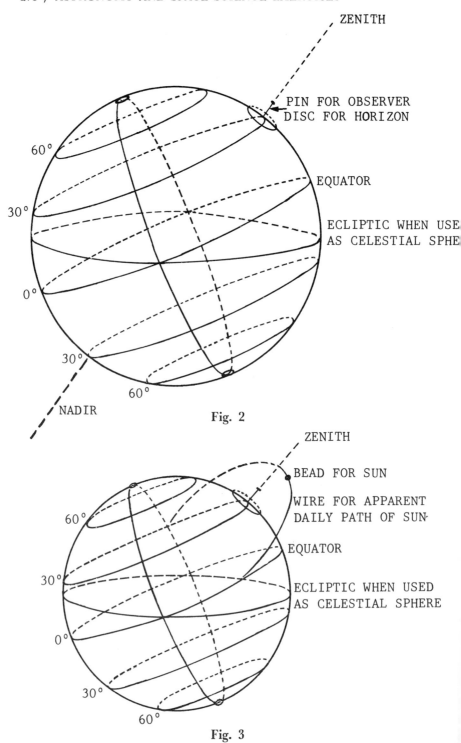

Fig. 2

Fig. 3

Index

A

Abramowitz, Jack, 38
Abscissa, 45
Aeration, 213
Air pollution:
    air, definition, 127
    carbon monoxide, potential effects on
        humans, 99–100
    controlling vehicle emissions, 99–100
    elements of engine exhaust, 94–96
        carbon monoxide, 94–95
        unburned hydrocarbons and oxides
            of nitrogen, 95–96
    follow-up activities, 131
    high school study, 127–131
        creating study communities, 128–129
        investigation procedures, 129–131
    measuring exhaust emissions, 96–99
        demonstration procedure, 98–99
        necessary apparatus, 96–98
Altizer, John R., 19
Anode, 185
Appearance, 64, 65
Aquaria:
    cracking glass, 105–106
    dulling sharp edge, 106–107
    glass cutter, 105
    heat to crack glass, 104
    lung demonstrator, 107
    no Pyrex, 104
    one-gallon glass jugs, 104
    Petri dishes, 107
    scoring the glass, 105
    taping with adhesive, 107
    trays for photographic chemicals, 107
Area, measuring, 54–55
Areas, irregular, 61
Aronstein, Laurence W., 33
Artesian formation, 213
Astronomy:
    acceleration of moon, 262–263
    calculations, 259–263
    Celestial Sphere, 274–277 (see also

Astronomy (cont.)
    Celestial Sphere)
    circumference of earth, 259–260
    Coriolis Effect, 244–252 (see also
        Coriolis Effect)
    diameter of moon, 261–262
    height of satellite above earth, 260
    introduction at "eyeball" level, 252
    lunar mirrors, 265–270 (see also
        Mirrors, lunar)
    moon, 263–264
    planetarium as laboratory, 271–274
        (see also Planetarium)
    star distances, 262
    Stellorama, 252–259 (see also
        Stellorama)
    telescope, making, 270
Atmospheric highs and lows, 234–236
Atmospheric pressure, 163–164
Automobiles, air pollution from, 94–100
    (see also Air pollution)

B

Bacterium coli, 146
Balancing equations, 18–19
Ball in ring demonstration, 34–36
Bar magnet, rotating, 186
Barometers:
    caution, 235
    explanation, 236
    graphing readings, 236
    materials, 234
    mercury, 235
    procedure, 234–236
Binocular vision, 109
Biotic community, miniature, 128
Bireline, Irene, 17
Black box, 32–33
Blind spot, 110
Blots, ink, 108–109
Borax bead test, 76
Budget, "micro" chemistry, 78–80

Buoyancy of liquids, 73–74
Buoyant force, 166–167
Burning:
  seed, 77
  sugar, 76–77

C

Calcium, quantitative isolation:
  obtaining representative samples,
    80–81
    foods and leaves, 81
    solids, 80–81
    water, 81
  sample analysis, 81–84
    calculations, 82–83
    further investigations, 83–84
    procedure, 81–82
Caldwell, Harrie E., 244
Candles, experiments with, 77
Capacitor, 182, 183, 184
Carbon monoxide (see Air pollution)
Carnes, Richard, 145
Cathode, 185
"Cathode glow," 185
Cathode Ray Tube, 184–186
Celestial Sphere:
  establishing coordinates, 276
  placing earth, 276
  terrestrial globe, 277
  using, 276–277
  materials and construction, 275
  simplicity, 275
Cell division, 125
Celsius thermometer, 57
Charades, 31
Charcoal and wood distillation, 69–70
Chemical properties:
  compounds, 67–68
  heating a substance, 67
  radicals, 68
Chemicals, 64
Chemistry investigations:
  air pollution from autos, 94–100
    (see also Air pollution)
  calcium, quantitative isolation, 80–84
    (see also Calcium, quantitative
    isolation)
  changes by heating, 75–77 (see also
    Heating)
  Eclectic Science Teaching Program,

Chemistry investigations (cont.)
  84–91 (see also Eclectic Science
    Teaching Program)
  interest student, 71–75
    buoyancy of liquids, 73–74
    making soap, 72–73
    production of rayon, 74–75
  junior high school, 69–71
    charcoal and wood distillation, 69–70
    coating metals, 70–71
    quick cloud chamber, 71
  limited budget, 78–80
    elements, 78–79
    heat source, 78
    ringstand, 78
    simple experiments, 79–80
    weighing scales, 79
  oxidation-reduction, 91–94 (see also
    Oxidation-reduction)
  techniques, 64–68
    chemical properties, 67–68 (see also
    Chemical properties)
    materials, 64
    physical properties of substances,
    65–66 (see also Physical
    properties)
Chlorella, 117, 119
Choroid layer, 112
Chromosomes, 125–126
Cilia, 116–117
Claim, mining, 225–231 (see also Earth
  science)
Clark, George, C., 112
Clark, Julian C., 64
Classification, organisms, 139–140
Cloud chamber, quick, 71
Cloud study, 238–241
Coastlines, 212
Cold-blooded animals, 121–124
Coliform bacteria, 147
Compound:
  identification, 65, 67–68
  molecular, 85
Compound light microscope:
  exploring, 132–134
  field arranged in planes, 132, 134
  field size related to power of lens, 132,
    133–134
  inversion of objects, 132, 133
  objectives, 132
  reversal left to right, 132, 133
Concept identification, 31–32
Condenser, 182, 183, 184

Coriolis Effect:
  background materials, 244–245
  examples, 245
  explained, 244
  illustration, 245
  inductive approach, 251–252
    discussion, 252
    learning, 251–252
    variations, 252
  lesson, 246, 251
Cornea, 111–112
Corrie, Mary-China, 47
Cote, Francis E., 84
Coulomb's Law, 178
Cow eyeball, 107–112 (see also Sight)
Creighton, James E., 170
Cronin, C. R., 120
"Crookes dark space," 185
Crookes tube, 184–186
Curiosity, rousing, 19–20
Cutter, styrofoam, 21

D

Dandelion:
  observation, 142
  photosynthesis, 144
  population density studies, 144
  reproductive system, 145
  root studies, 144–145
Davis, Dudley W., 180
Debates, team, 31
Demonstration:
  ball in ring, 34–36
  live, 34
Density, 18, 64, 66
Dependent variable, 45
Depth, 19
Desalinization, 199
Description, 22–24
Deur, Ray, 142–145
DeWitt, Vernon, 22
Discovery method, 12
DISCUS, 120–121
Distance judgement, 109
Distances, measuring, 52–54
Dixon, Robert F., 24
DNA, 126, 127
Duckweed:
  amount of light, 137
  anatomy, 135
  container, 136

Duckweed (cont.)
  culturing conditions, 135–136
  "daughter" fronds, 135, 137
  eliminating genetic variability, 134
  exercises, additional, 138
  "mother" frond, 135
  obtaining, 134–135
  plant growth exercises, 136–138
  rapid in growth, 134
  reproduction usually vegetative, 134
  requirements other than pure water,
    137–138
  seed plants, 134
  solution, 136
  structurally simple, 134
  threadlike root, 135
  very inexpensive, 134
  what it looks like, 136–137
Dunning, Ernest A., 69, 71

E

Earth science:
  earthquakes, 214–217 (see also
    Earthquakes)
  field investigations, 217–221
    characteristics of deposits, 217–218
    preparation, 218
    procedure, 218–221
  field trip, 221–225
    follow-up, 225
    objectives, 221–222
    observations and questions, 222–225
    preparation, 222
  gravel pits, 217–221
  mineral display, 228–231 (see also
    Mineral display)
  models, 211–214
    aeration, 213
    artesian formation, 213
    coastlines, 212
    cost, 211
    making, 212–213
    rock strata, 212, 213
    saturation, 213
    waterproofed, 213–214
  mountains, 207–208 (see also
    Mountains)
  puddles, 209–210
  sedimentation, 203–204
  staking mining claim, 225–228

Earth Science (*cont.*)
  staking mining claim (*cont.*)
    behavioral objectives, 225–226
    claim recorder, 227–228
    follow-up, 228
    lode bonus, 228
    preliminary instruction, 227
    preparation and materials, 226–227
  student-centered, 209–211
  sun's motion, 210–211
  topographic maps, 205–206, 212–213
  water problems, 196–202 (*see also*
    Water problems)
Earthquakes:
  Earthquake Report, 216
  epicenters, 216
  latitude and longitude, 216
  materials, 215
  objectives, 214–215
  procedure, 215–217
Eclectic Science Teaching Program:
  example, 85–91
  nature of particles in solution, 85–91
    discussion, 85–86
    materials and equipment, 86–87
    objectives, 85
    procedure and observations
      (student), 87–89
    procedure (teacher) 90–91
    "stepping stone to scientific
      exploration," 91
Electricity:
  anode, 185
  cathode, 185
  "cathode glow," 185
  Coulomb's Law, 178
  "Crookes dark space," 185
  Crookes Tube or Cathode Ray Tube,
    184–186
  discharge in gases at low pressure,
    184–186
    making tube, 184–185
    materials, 184
    using the tube, 185–186
  electricity, electrons, gaseous ions,
    180–186
  "Faraday dark space," 185
  high voltage energy, 181–182
    materials, 181
    procedure, 181–182
  high voltage penetration of insulators,
    182–184
    interpreting effects, 184
    materials, 182–183

Electricity (*cont.*)
  high voltage penetration (*cont.*)
    procedure, 183–184
  motion, production, 186–189
    demonstration motor, 187–188
    electric motor making, 188–194 (*see
      also* Motor, electric)
    rotating bar magnet, 186
    negative electrode, 185
    "negative glow," 185
    "positive column," 185
    positive electrode, 185
    "secondary ions," 185
  static, 176–180 (*see also* Static
    electricity)
  warnings, 181, 182, 183, 191, 193
Electrons, 180
Electroscope:
  calibrations, 180
  homemade, using, 180
  simple, 178
  voltage, 179–180
Elements, 78–79
Energy:
  high voltage, 181–184 (*see also*
    Electricity)
  molecular movement and, 167–170
    (*see also* Molecular movement and
    energy)
Engine exhaust, 94–96
Enlargement, 159
Equations, balancing, 18–19
Escherich, 146
E.S.T.P., 84–91 (*see also* Eclectic Science
  Teaching Program)
Evaporation, 24–30
Exhaust emissions, measuring, 96–99
Exhaust, engine, 94–96
Experimental purpose, 25
Experiments, open-ended, 14–17
Eye (*see* Sight)

F

Fahrenheit thermometer, 57
"Faraday dark space," 185
Field investigation, gravel pits, 217–221
Field trip, earth science, 221–225
Foods, calcium, 81

G

Gas exchanger, photosynthetic, 117–119

Gaseous ions, 180
Gasoline engine emissions, 96
Genes, 127
Genetics:
  meiosis, 126
  Mendel's Laws of Heredity, 125, 126
  mitosis, 125–126
Glass, scoring and cracking, 105–106
Glasses, safety, 72
Glassware, 64
Goehring, Harvey J., 38
Graphing, 27–28, 45, 236, 272
Gravel pits, 217–221
Gray, Raymond F., 234
Griddles, mica, 75–76

H

Heat:
  concepts, 153
  source, 78
Heating:
  borax bead tests, 76
  burning of seed, 77
  candles, 77
  complete burning of sugar, 76–77
  mica griddles, 75–76
  substance, 64, 67
Heredity, Mendel's Laws, 126
Highs and lows, atmospheric, 234–236
Hoffman, Banesh, 38
Horner, Charles E., 84
Howell, Leslie, 167
Hutto, Thomas A., 38
Hydrocarbons, unburned, 95
Hydrology, 196
Hydrometer, making:
  materials, 164–165
  procedure, 165
  testing, 166
Hygrometer, 237

I

Iarrapino, 163
Identification, concept, 31–32
Illusions, optical, 109
Independent variable, 45
Ink blots, 108–109
Instruments, 64
Insulators, high voltage penetration,
  182–184

Ionic solution, 85
Ions, gaseous, 180
Iris, 111, 112
Iris light reflex, 109–110
Irregular areas, measurement, 61

J

Jacob's Ladder, 181
Johnson, C. Howard, 154, 190

K

Kutliroff, David, 58
Kyrlach, Robert E., 265

L

Lab procedures, simplicity, 24–30
Latitude, 216, 217
Law of levers, 12–14
Leaves, calcium, 81
Lemnaceae, 134–138 (see also
  Duckweed)
Lens, 111, 112
Levers, law of, 12–14
Life science:
  air polution, 127–131 (see also Air
    pollution)
  compound light microscope, 132–134
    (see also Compound light
    microscope)
  dandelion, 142–145 (see also Dandelion)
  free aquaria, 104–107 (see also
    Aquaria)
  frog on moon, 117–119
  genetics, 124–127 (see also Genetics)
  lemnaceae or duckweed, 134–138 (see
    also Duckweed)
  observation, 139–142 (see also
    Observation)
  photosynthetic gas exchanger, 117–119
  respiration, 112–117 (see also
    Respiration)
  seventh grade units, 102–104
  sight, teaching sense of 107–112 (see
    also Sight)
  underachiever, 120–124
    "concrete objects," 121
    conditioned to failure, 120
    controlled situations, 121

Life science (cont.)
    underachiever (cont.)
        measured difficulty, 121
        problem of attitude, 120
        Project DISCUS, 120
        selecting suitable activities, 120-121
        small groups, 120
        students' common experience, 121
        temperature changes and cold
            blooded animals, 121-124
        working with, 124
        water pollution, 145-149 (see also
            Water pollution)
Light concepts, 152-153
Link, Frances R., 38
Liquid:
    buoyancy, 73-74
    measuring volume, 56-57
Lisonbee, Lorenzo, 38
Live lab demonstrations, 34
Longitude, 216, 217
Lows, atmospheric highs and, 234-236

M

Magnet, rotating bar, 186
Mapping, topographic, 205-206, 212-213
Mass, 55-56, 64, 65
Mathematics:
    metric system, 47-50
    number pairing, 43-46 (see also
        Number pairing)
    role in science, 40-43
        deriving formula, 42-43
        materials and preparation, 40-41
        problem, 41-42
Measurement unit:
    area, 54-55
    devices, 50
    distances, 52-54
    interrelationships of units, 50
    liquid volumes, 56-57
    objectives, 50-51
    organization, 51
    summary, 57
    systems, 50
    use, 50
    volume, 55
    weight or mass, 55-56
Measurements, physics lab:
    irregular areas, 61
    triangulations, 58-61
Meiosis, 126

Mendel's Laws, 126
Mercury, 235, 236
Metal oxide, 92-93
Metals, coating, 70-71
Meteorology:
    barometers, 234-236 (see also
        Barometers)
    cloud study and weather forecasting,
        238-241
    analyzing data, 238-241
    materials, 238
    predicting cloud types, 241
    predicting wind direction and
        clouds, 241
    procedure, 238
    radiation intensity, 241
    simple weather indicator, 237
Mica griddles, 75-76
"Micro" chemistry, 78-80
Microscope, compound light, 132-134
    (see also Compound light
    microscope)
Minardi, William R., 259, 274
Mineral display:
    adaptions, 229
    building, 229
    planning, 228-229
    references, 231
    selecting material, 229
    uses of minerals, 229, 231
Mining claim, staking, 225-231 (see also
    Earth science)
Mirrors lunar:
    after polishing, 269
    contact, 268
    fine grind, 269
    grinding, 267-268
    grinding setup, 266-267
    lap and mirror before polishing, 248
    making, 265-270
    materials, 265-266
    procedure, 266-270
Mitosis, 125-126
Models:
    earth science, 211-214 (see also Earth
        science)
    motivation, 19-22
Modiolus demissus plicatulus, 116
Molecular compound, 85
Molecular movement and energy:
    materials, 168
    objectives, 168
    preparation, 168
    procedure, 169-170

Molecular solution, 85
Montag, Betty Jo, 78, 152
Moon:
  interpreting data, 264
  necessary materials, 264
  procedure, 263–264
Motivation, models and, 19–22
Motor, electric:
  armature assembly, 193
  caution, 191, 193
  follow-up, 194
  galvanized steel strip, 192
  materials, 188, 190, 191
  precautions, 188–189, 191
  preparation of materials, 191
  procedure, 191–194
  test model, 194
  tinplate armature, 193
  tinplate square, 192
  winding the wire, 192
  wire brushing armature, 193
Mountains:
  class project, 208
  materials and construction, 207–208
    finishing the model, 208
    obtaining base, 207
    outlining landform, 207–208
  preparation, 207
  reports, 208
  variations, 208
Mud puddles, 209-210
Muha, William J., 179
Multiple-guess objective question, 34
Mussel, Ribbed, 116
Myers, Mary Jane, 124

N

Negative charges, 176–177
Negative electrode, 185
"Negative glow," 185
Neon stroboscope, 158
Newton's Third Law, 162–163
Nicotine, 116–117
Nitrogen, oxides of, 95–96
Norman, Nelle B., 80
Norton, Jerry I., 38
Nucleus, 125
Number pairing:
  further development, 45–46
  introduction, 43–44
  presenting problem, 44–45
    calculating values, 45

Number pairing (cont.)
  presenting problem (cont.)
    finding rule, 44–45
    graphing relations, 45

O

Observation:
  abiotic factors, 139
  any grade level, 139
  classify organisms, 139–140
  correlated with other subjects, 139
  select an area, 139
  suggested activities, 140–142
Ohaus Cent-o-gram balance, 81
Open-ended experiments, 14–17
Optic nerve, 111
Optical illusions, 109
Ordinate, 45
Organisms, classify, 139–140
Orlich, Donald C., 132
Owen, Merrick A., 271
Oxidation, 91
Oxidation-reduction:
  demonstration techniques, 92–94
    further demonstrations, 93–94
    reducing metal oxide, 92–93
    removing stains, 93
  materials, 92
  rules, 91
Oxides of nitrogen, 95–96

P

Parabolic mirror, 172–174
Parsons, Donna, 172
Particles in solution, 85–91
Paulk, L. J., 120
Pearce, Robert, 91
Peck, Donald B., 252
Pedagogical purposes, 25
Pendulum, photographing:
  accuracy, 161
  count, 161
  enlargement, 159–160
  materials and assembly, 158–159
  taking photos, 159–160
  teaching application, 160–161
  using data, 161
Photos, 159–160
Photosynthesis, 144
Photosynthetic gas exchanger, 117–119

Physical properties:
 appearance, 65
 density, 66
 mass, 65
 solubility, 66
 volume, 65–66
Physics:
 atmospheric pressure, 163–164
 buoyant force, 166–167
 heat, 153
 homemade thermometers, 153
 hydrometer, making: 164–166 (see
  also Hydrometer, making)
 light, 152–153
 molecular movement and energy,
  167–170 (see also Molecular
  movement and energy)
 Newton's Third Law, 162–163
 pendulum, photographing, 158–161
  (see also Pendulum, photographing)
 radiometer, backward rotating, 170–172
  solving problem, 171
  teaching opportunity, 171–172
 real image demonstration, 172–174
  apparatus modifications, 173
  background, 172
  materials, 172
  using apparatus, 173–174
 ripple tanks, 154–158 (see also Ripple
  tanks)
 work concept, 154
Pitluga, George E., 14
Planetarium:
 graphing data, 272
 interpreting data, 272
 materials, 271
 none available, 274
 preparation, 271
 setting the instrument, 271
Pollution:
 air, 94–100, 127–131 (see also Air
  pollution)
 water, 145–149, 197–198 (see also
  Water pollution)
Population density studies, 144
Porter, David D., 24
Porter, William E., 127
Positive charges, 177–178
"Positive column," 185
Positive electrode, 185
Project DISCUS, 120, 121
Puddles, 209–210

Q

Quantitative isolation, calcium, 80–84

R

Radiation, intensity, 241
Radicals, identification, 68
Radiometer, 170–172
Rayon, production, 74–75
Ratzlaff, 117
Real image demonstration, 172–174
Reduction, 91
Respiration:
 cilia, effect of nicotine on, 116–117
 smoking machine, 116
 spirometer, 112–115 (see also
  Spirometer)
Retina, 112
Ribbed Mussel, 116
Ringstand, 78
Ripple, tanks:
 large demonstration apparatus,
  155–158
  materials, 155–156
  procedure, 156–157
  wave-making equipment, 157–158
 Pyrex dish apparatus, 154–155
River control, 198
Roberts, Charles L., 12
Rock strata, 212, 213, 214
Romig, Ronald F., 102
Root studies, 144–145
Rorschach test, 108
Rotating bar magnet, 186

S

Salt particles, nature, 88
Salt solution, 88
Saltation, 199
Sanders, Merrill, 43
Saturation, 200, 213
Scales, weighing, 79
Science charades, 31
Science teaching (see Eclectic Science
 Teaching Program)
Sclerotic coat, 112
"Secondary ions," 185
Sedimentation:
 materials, 203

Sedimentation (*cont.*)
  observations, 204
  procedure, 203–204
Seed, burning, 76–77
Sight:
  blind spot, 110
  dissecting cow's eyeball, 110–112
    background, 110
    choroid layer, 112
    cornea, 111, 112
    goggles, 111
    iris, 111, 112
    lens, 111
    optic nerve, 111, 112
    preparation of materials, 110–111
    procedure, 111–112
    razor blade, 111
    retina, 112
    sclerotic coat, 112
    shape of cow's pupil, 112
    substance in vitreous humor
      chamber, 112
    use of formaldehyde, 111
    vitreous humor, 111
    vitreous humor jelly, 111
  eye traits, 109–110
    binocular vision, 109
    distance judgment, 109
    two eyes better than one, 109
  ink blots, 108–109
    depict figures and forms, 109
    discussion, 108
    intense dislikes, 109
    interests or likes, 109
    number, 108
    phobias, 109
    recording what seen, 108
    Rorschach test, 108
    what we see, 109
  iris light reflex, 109–110
  lab work, 107
  light and dark, adjustment, 109–110
  motivational devices, 108
  opaque projector, 108
  optical illusions, 109
  overhead projector, 108
  transparencies, 108
Slow learners, junior high, 30–33
Smoking machine, 116
Soap, making, 72
Solids, calcium, 80–81
Solubility, 64, 66
Solute particles, 89

Solution:
  ionic, 85
  laboratory investigations of water,
    199, 200
  molecular, 85
  particles in, 85–91
  salt, 88
  sugar, 88–89
Space science (*see* Astronomy)
Spirometer:
  blowing into, 115
  building, 114–115
    construction procedure, 114–115
    materials, 114
    preparing mouthpieces, 115
  economy, 112–113
  use, 113
Stains, removing, 93
Staking mining claim, 225–231 (*see also*
  Earth science)
Starkman, Ernest, 36, 38, 94
Static electricity:
  demonstration, 179–180
  determining electroscope voltage,
    179–180
  dramatizing, 179
  homemade equipment, 176–178
  negative charges, 176–177
  positive charges, 177–178
  simple electroscope, 178
  using homemade "electroscopes," 180
Steele, Peter F., 158
Stellorama:
  astronomy club, 253
  celestial coordinates, 253
  celestial hemisphere, 252
  construction, 253–258
  data sheet, 255–256
  panels, 255
  purpose, 253
  rectify reversal problem, 253
  sidereal motion and time, 253,
    258–259
  spherical map of stars, 253
  student plotting, 256–257
  template, 253–255
  time, 253
Stevenson, J. R., 176
Stroboscope, neon, 158
Stundick, Bernadette Beres, 107
Styrofoam cutter, 21
Sugar:
  burning, 76–77

Sugar *(cont.)*
   nature of particles, 88
   solution, 88–89
Sun, motion, 210–211
Suspension, 199–200
Swampland, 199

T

Taraxacum officinale, 142 *(see also*
   Dandelion)
Team debates, 31
Techniques:
   demonstrations, 17–19
   discovering laws of science, 12–14
   laboratory exercise in description,
      22–24
   models and motivation, 19–22
   open-ended experiments, 14–17
   simplicity in lab procedures, 24–30
   slow learners, 30–33
   visual-auditory testing, 33–38
Telescope, making, 270
Temperature changes, 121–124
Temperatures, 57
Terrarium, 128
Terry, Edward A., 164, 237
Testing:
   inadequacies, 34
   visual-auditory, 33–38
Thermometers, homemade, 153
Toepker, Terrence, P., 166
Tomer, D. W., 40
Topographic maps, 205–206, 212–213
Topography, 19
Triangulations, 58–61
Troxel, Verne A., 263

U

Underachiever, life science, 120–124
   (see also Life science)
Upchurch, Richard L., 30

V

Variables, 45
Visual-auditory testing:

Visual-auditory testing *(cont.)*
   advantages, 36, 38
   introduction, 33–34
   using, 34, 36
Vitreous humor, 111
Vitreous humor chamber, 112
Vitreous humor jelly, 111
Voltage *(see* Electricity)
Volume, 55, 64, 65–66
Vrana, Ralph S., 75, 186

W

Water particles, nature, 88
Water pollution:
   apparatus for testing, 147
   bacterium coli, 146
   coliform bacteria colonies, 147
   conclusions, 149
   conducting tests, 148–149
   objective, 146
   problem, 197–198
   research preparation, 146
   student response, 149
   testing for, 145–149
   testing sites, 146–147
Water problems:
   laboratory investigations, 199–202
   pollution, 197–198 *(see also* Water
      pollution)
   river control, 198
   saltation, 199
   saturation, 200
   slope and stream velocity, 202
   solutions, 199, 200
   studying, 197–199
   suspension, 199, 200–201
   volume and stream velocity, 202
Wave-making equipment, 157
Weather:
   forecasting, 238–241 *(see also*
      Meteorology)
   indicator, 237
Weight, 55–56, 79
Weschgel, Alice, 238
Wilkinson, Paul A., 162
Wind direction, 241
Wood distillation, charcoal and, 69–70